Climate, God and Uncertainty

Climate, God and Uncertainty

A transcendental naturalistic approach beyond Bruno Latour

Arthur C. Petersen

UCL PRESS

First published in 2023 by
UCL Press
University College London
Gower Street
London WC1E 6BT

Available to download free: www.uclpress.co.uk

A CIP catalogue record for this book is available from The British Library.

ISBN: 978-1-80008-596-1 (Hbk)
ISBN: 978-1-80008-595-4 (Pbk)
ISBN: 978-1-80008-594-7 (PDF)
ISBN: 978-1-80008-597-8 (epub)
DOI: https://doi.org/10.14324/111.9781800085947

Contents

List of figures and tables

Figure

Tables

Preface

My first attempt at writing about God and uncertainty dates from a decade ago. It was published in 2014 as 'Uncertainty and God: A Jamesian pragmatist approach to uncertainty and ignorance in science and religion', in *Zygon: Journal of Religion and Science*. Crucial elements of the argument of the present book did not yet feature in that sketchy article: the impact of climate change on philosophy, the importance of transcendental philosophy and the value of the two other philosophers who are central to this book, Rickert and Latour. Still, the reflections on wonder in that article have found their way into Chapter 2 of this book.

The last section of Chapter 7 derives largely from a commentary that I gave on a lecture in 2016. That was published in 2021 as a chapter 'Values and accountability in science advice: The case of the IPCC', in *Science, Values, and Democracy: The 2016 Descartes Lectures by Heather Douglas*, edited by Ted Richards, 97–108, Tempe, AZ: Consortium for Science, Policy & Outcomes, Arizona State University.

It was the work of Heinrich Rickert (1863–1936) that helped me to go beyond William James (1842–1910) and Bruno Latour (1947–2022). In the early 1990s I had first delved into Latour's work. Reading James in the early 2010s rekindled my long-standing interest in science-and-religion and led to the article mentioned above. From 2015 to 2021, after I had started as Professor of Science, Technology and Public Policy at UCL (University College London), I worked on the present book, advised by Alister McGrath as my supervisor in the part-time doctoral programme in theology at the University of Oxford.

The outline of the book/doctoral thesis that I produced in the autumn of 2016 set out the work that still had to be done in the subsequent five years, with central roles for Rickert and Latour. After a brief encounter in 2001 through the book/doctoral thesis of Christian Krijnen, I had rediscovered Rickert in 2016. Also in 2016 I had first got to grips with Latour's *We Have Never Been Modern* ([1991] 1993) and *An Inquiry into Modes of Existence: An anthropology of the Moderns* ([2012] 2013). Later, after I had read *Facing Gaia: Eight lectures on the new climatic regime* ([2015] 2017), I gradually engaged more and more with Latour – he consequently made it to the subtitle. After I had completed the work I sent Latour the doctoral thesis, to which he responded on 6 June 2022:

> Dear colleague, many thanks for this. I know nothing of Rickert so I will be glad to learn more about his philosophy and I am intrigued by transcendental naturalism. I am old and weakened so it could take time, but if you come to France it would be a nice way to interact even more. … Thanks for sending the book, Bruno.

Unfortunately we never got to meet; on 9 October 2022 Latour died of the illness that had weakened him for years.

Since the book presents a systematic argument, involving multiple different engagements with James, Rickert and Latour, none of these three philosophers receives a full introduction at any one point in the text. James is mostly introduced in the section 'James's approach to wonder and metaphysics' (pp. 28–40) in Chapter 2. Rickert is introduced in both the section 'Rickert's approach to judgement' (pp. 62–8) in Chapter 3 and the section 'Rickert's philosophy of value' (pp. 96–102) in Chapter 4. Meanwhile Latour is introduced in the sections 'Latour's empirical approach to values' (pp. 86–91), 'Latourian values in scientific, religious and political practices' (pp. 91–6) and 'Latour's philosophy of value further described and assessed' (pp. 106–10) in Chapter 4. The reader is referred to the index to locate specific topics related to the three philosophers.

A brief note on translation from German sources: all quotations (including those from German sources) are in English; where no published translations existed, I have produced my own translations. I have added some important German words in italics between parentheses, so that the interested reader can see which terms were used in the original.

I received much institutional support, financially, practically and morally, from UCL. For this I am thankful to two Deans of the Faculty of Engineering Sciences (Anthony Finkelstein and Nigel Titchener-Hooker) and two Heads of the Department of Science, Technology, Engineering and Public Policy (Jason Blackstock and Joanna Chataway). Many other UCL colleagues have been highly supportive of the project. Let me mention three because they stood out, each in their different ways. Daniel Hogendoorn made many suggestions for themes to study and books to buy; he also agreed that I should spend a large part of my funded PI time on writing this book – hence I also acknowledge the support by the UK's Economic and Social Research Council (ESRC), grant number ES/N018834/1 from 2016–2019, under the Open Research Area (ORA) for the Social Sciences agreement. Sarah-Louise Quinnell was probably the only colleague who fully read the submitted doctoral thesis; she subsequently found a way to incorporate a whole stream on philosophy of culture, based on this book, within the department's new BSc in Science and Engineering for Social Change (which took in its first students in September 2023). Chris Penfold, commissioning editor at UCL Press, saw the merits of the book when I approached him in December 2022, made some very helpful suggestions for the book proposal and shepherded it to Board approval. It is an honour to publish this book with UCL Press – open access publishing is the future.

For comments on drafts of chapters and/or substantive suggestions on the argument, I am grateful to the following people: Michael Burdett, Jeremy Carrette, Albert Cath, Hans de Knijff, Ariel Dempsey, Wim Drees, Daniel Hogendoorn, Mike Hulme, Casper Bruun Jensen, Christian Krijnen, Alister McGrath, Atsuro Morita, Ken Oye, Andrew Pinsent, Henk Plomp, Jerry Ravetz, Dan Sarewitz, Lenny Smith, Bethany Sollereder, Peter Tomson, Luco van den Brom, Koo van der Wal, Graham Ward, Kenneth Wilson, Arjen Zegwaard, Margreet Zwarteveen and two anonymous reviewers for UCL Press. The usual disclaimer applies.

1
Introduction

In his *Facing Gaia: Eight lectures on the new climatic regime* ([2015] 2017), French thinker Bruno Latour (1947–2022) provides a penetrating analysis of the philosophical implications of climate change and its associated uncertainties. He proposes an alternative approach to metaphysics as well as related 'anthropological' readings of the practices of science, religion and politics – practices which he claims have become entangled in modernity through inaccurate philosophical images and which should be more clearly distinguished in terms of how they are each confronted with their own type of uncertainty. Latour aims to disentangle these practices, starting with a non-religious reading of the self-organising processes on this Earth, under the banner of James Lovelock's 'Gaia':

> Gaia is presented here as the occasion for a return to Earth that allows for a differentiated version of the respective qualities that can be required of sciences, politics, and religions, as these are finally reduced to more modest and more earthbound definitions of their former vocations. (Latour [2015] 2017, 4)

In order to capture these 'qualities', Latour builds on his voluminous study *An Inquiry into Modes of Existence: An anthropology of the Moderns* ([2012] 2013b), which he claims 'turned out to be under the more and more pervasive shadow of Gaia' ([2015] 2017), 2–3):

> [T]he anthropology of the Moderns that I have been pursuing for forty years turns out to resonate increasingly with what can be called the *New Climate* [*sic*, '*Climatique*' in the original] *Regime*.

> I use this term to summarize the present situation, in which the physical framework that the Moderns had taken for granted, the ground on which their history had always been played out, has become unstable. As if the décor had gotten up on stage to share the drama with the actors. (Latour [2015] 2017, 3)

According to Latour, the similarities and differences between the practices of science and religion are relevant for dealing with climate change in the practices of politics. For instance, the supposed religious disenchantment of nature is a misreading of the practices of science, and new poetics (and 'liturgy') to motivate climate action may result from a turn to myth based on the science of Gaia. Also, any unchallenged scientific authority given to climate models is a misreading of science (a misreading that, according to Latour, lends a 'religious' certainty to science); this in turn leads to disbelief in alternative views at the science–policy interface that fully incorporate uncertainty in the practices of science. Furthermore, political disregard for non-modern worldviews in climate-change policy is for Latour the result of a misreading of the way science and religion are (not) open to the future and of a lack of sensitivity to alternatives in metaphysics.

While I agree that these problems of 'modernity' in the context of climate change are all real and important, the philosophical approach followed by Latour deserves critical scrutiny. This book philosophically clarifies and, if I may boldly say, qualifies – that is, goes *beyond* – Latour's thought. On the one hand, I assess what climate change means for philosophy and argue in that context that Latour's work can be considered a major contribution to science-and-religion, a field that emerged in the 1950s and 1960s but with which Latour hardly engages; on the other hand, I make a methodological intervention on the sort of naturalism that guides both Latour's work and a large part of the field of science-and-religion. In order to accomplish this task, I develop a cultural philosophical approach that I call 'transcendental naturalism'.

In January 1965 the conference 'A Reconsideration of the Relation of Theology to the Sciences' was held in Chicago.[1] The scholars who came together in that conference were re-imagining the linkages between science and religion – with the latter taken as either religious practices or 'theology', defined by the organisers as 'those critical, intellectual attempts to understand and reform the beliefs and practices of a given religious community' (Burhoe and Tapp 1966b, 11).[2] The threat of nuclear annihilation – connected with an unwise use of scientific powers – was casting its shadow over the emerging field of science-and-religion;[3]

the hope of most of the speakers was that by adopting a critical approach to religious 'values', the 'rich, emotional and aesthetic resources of the various religions may join to serve all humankind' (Burhoe and Tapp 1966b, 12).

In February 2013 Bruno Latour gave his series of Gifford Lectures 'Facing Gaia: A new enquiry into natural religion' in Edinburgh, of which *Facing Gaia* is a reworked and expanded version. Also Latour was re-imagining the linkages between science and religion, this time under the shadow of climate change. Many of the themes that Latour addresses – including the religious disenchantment of nature, the scientific disbelief in a plurality of value-laden perspectives and the disregard for non-modern worldviews in politics – have been major topics in the wider science-and-religion discussion, as I will show in Part II of this book. There is also continuity between the naturalistic approach taken by most speakers in the 1965 conference and the approach taken by Latour. Latour is very much in agreement with them in criticising what I call *scientistic* naturalism, but still he is after a sort of naturalism, I claim.

I take it to be an important tenet of the 'naturalism' that I will work with and further qualify in this book – in dialogue with the works of William James, Heinrich Rickert and Bruno Latour – that 'science and religion are dealing with the same reality, and not with two different and mutually exclusive realities' (Harrington 1966, 99). Still, science and religion constitute different types of practices; they are led by different values: '[s]cience is essentially informative where religion is primarily celebrative', as a central speaker in the 1965 conference portrayed it (Harrington 1966, 99). A crucial component of naturalism is its openness to uncertainty and wonder. Theologian John Hayward described this as follows:

> All scientists, all the king's horses and men, and all the devotees of the arts and humanities, each in their own voice, try to express their own meanings. But right along with every achievement of meaning is a pervasive, annoying, never-assuaged sense of mystery which keeps the whole machinery driving. (Hayward 1966, 31–2)

At the same time this openness to uncertainty is connected to the creativity of judgement or 'valuing consciousness', as theologian Henry Nelson Wieman describes it:

> Th[e] indefinite expansion of the valuing consciousness is the greatest good ever to be attained in the universe. Only in this way is

> the universe endowed with the values of truth, beauty, love, justice, freedom, and responsible power, because these values emerge only when some valuing consciousness brings them into being by its capacity for appreciation and responsibility. But even in human existence these values cannot be progressively created unless our existence is brought under the control of the creativity which expands the valuing consciousness. (Wieman 1966, 85)

Like many speakers in the 1965 conference, Latour is proposing a 'rational' approach to science-and-religion (and more widely, as we will see, to all 'modes of existence'). However, in his metaphysical work *An Inquiry into Modes of Existence* he gives his own reading of what constitutes 'rationality':

> Our project is thus in fact a rational project (if not rationalist) from start to finish, provided that we agree to define reason as what makes it possible to *follow* the various types of experience *step-by-step*, tracking down truth and falsity in each mode [of existence] after determining the practical conditions that allow us to make such a judgment in each case. (Latour [2012] 2013b, 19)

For religion, naturalism obviously means for Latour that there is no place for the 'supernatural' in the philosophical analysis of religious practices:

> Led astray by the supernatural, itself a delayed reaction to the invasion of 'nature', they are no longer in a position to do their duty by *defending materiality, unjustly accused, against matter, unduly spiritualized*. They need to be reminded of the celebrated evangelical injunction, inverted: 'What use is it if you save your soul, if it means losing the world?' (Latour [2015] 2017, 210–11)

In this book – which, at the service of assessing what climate change means for philosophy, features a methodological intervention with respect to naturalism in the science-and-religion discussion – I will critically reflect on the metaphysical assumptions embedded in the approaches of James and Latour (and in many other versions of naturalism) and argue, along with Rickert, for the separate ontological status of values. In summary, paraphrasing the above quotation from Wieman: *values are unreal (even though they do exist inside and not outside of this world) and cannot be 'created' by judgement; it is the valuations in judgement that are real (and uncertain) and that determine which values get realised.* The philosophical point is subtle (it is also related to a methodological point about the status of metaphysics in philosophy), but it is important enough, I argue, to be developed and defended as part of my metaphilosophical discussion of philosophy under climate change.

Some of the speakers in the 1965 conference engaged explicitly with William James. For instance, F. S. C. Northrop (author of the 1962 book *Man, Nature and God*) describes the escape from 'naïve realism', with its substance thinking, to a combination of 'radical empiricism' (as defined by William James, but ultimately attributed by Northrop to David Hume) and what he calls 'hypothetical logical realism', under which he classes the emphasis on the importance of 'models' in various practices.[4] This is how Northrop describes 'radical empiricism':

> [M]ost of us are apt, like Kant, Einstein, and Whitehead, among many others, to need to read and reflect deeply on Hume in order to become clear about what the character of mere directly observed experience is. Because he concentrated on determining this, he is called a 'radical empiricist'. To his findings must be added those of the radical empiricist William James, more recently those of Whitehead, and in classical Asia those of the Buddhist and non-dualistic Vedantic Hindu epistemologists. All agree that radically empirical immediacy does not warrant belief in a substance of any kind, be it material or mental. Thereby one escapes from the primitive confusion and linguistic distortions of naïve realism in both science and the humanities. (Northrop 1966, 26)

This book will include an investigation of some philosophical limitations of radical empiricism, specifically the forms used by James and Latour, from the perspective of what I call 'transcendental naturalism'.

In Part I my interest lies in emphasising, along with Latour, James and Rickert, the positive emotion of wonder (experienced in judgement and pointing at values) about the ineffable, deeply uncertain reality that cannot be modelled; reality goes beyond – but is necessarily approached, in a tentative way, via – the models that actors use in their respective cultural practices. I set out the case for developing a philosophy of culture in the form of a transcendental naturalism that refrains from metaphysics. In Part II I use transcendental naturalism to offer interpretations of some of the alleged problems of modernity already mentioned: the religious disenchantment of nature, the scientific disbelief in a plurality of value-laden perspectives and the disregard of non-modern worldviews in politics. All are pertinent in the context of climate change and are discussed in dialogue with Latour's *Facing Gaia*, in which these three themes play an important role. Throughout the book I relate my philosophical approach to climate change to Latour's work – even though I am critical of details in its philosophical methodology.

I have used several terms up to this point that I wish to define in the remainder of this introductory chapter for later use in the text: 'science', 'religion', 'culture', 'practice', 'values', 'worldviews', 'uncertainty', 'philosophy', 'methodology', 'metaphysics', 'naturalism' and, of course, 'transcendental naturalism' (plus also other terms that will follow in laying out the philosophical framework, such as 'criticism', 'epistemology', 'ontology' and 'anthropology'). Along the way my research approach is outlined, the research questions are described and, finally, the structure of the book is introduced.

The practices studied, criticism, values, worldviews and uncertainty

I focus in this book mainly on the natural sciences as a subset of 'science' as *Wissenschaft* (this latter Germanic term, like the Dutch *wetenschap*, includes the natural sciences, the social sciences and the humanities).[5] With regards to 'religion', the net is again cast wide; I include not only theistic religion centred on God(s), but also religious worldviews that emphasise the Transcendent. What 'science' and 'religion' actually consist of are relevant topics in philosophy under climate change, hence my refraining from getting into definitional issues for both types of practices at this early point.

In their Foreword to the edited volume *Navigating Post-Truth and Alternative Facts: Religion and science as political theology* (Baldwin 2018), which is the second title in a book series on 'Religion and Science as a Critical Discourse', Lisa Stenmark and Whitney Bauman (the series editors) explain that they would like to see the science-and-religion discourse move away from too much focus on theory towards injecting a prophetic voice and a planetary perspective into public debate. Their series aims to offer a scholarly platform for doing just that. The editors express 'concerns about the status of scientific claims, and the totalizing tendency of scientific claims over and against religions and other knowledge systems' (Stenmark and Bauman 2018, vii). I share these concerns and will be using my engagement with Latour's work to bring his voice more explicitly into the science-and-religion discussion.

Stenmark and Bauman's main thrust with their book series is to instil more 'criticism' and 'critical discourse' into the science-and-religion discourse: 'This discourse lacks a (self) critical perspective, and this series attempts to address it through a somewhat fuzzy use of the idea of critical discourses' (Stenmark and Bauman 2018, vii). Then follows a long list of types of critical discourse, not taken to be limitative: 'By critical discourse, we mean all of these, and more, because none of these approaches is sufficient, but all of them are crucial for thinking about the planetary community and our moral and ethical responsibilities to human and earth others' (Stenmark and Bauman 2018, viii).

The latter normative goals stated by Stenmark and Bauman make their view of critique less sensitive to the risks that Latour has highlighted in his influential essay 'Why has critique run out of steam? From matters of fact to matters of concern':

> [T]he critical mind, if it is to renew itself and be relevant again, is to be found in the cultivation of a *stubbornly realist attitude* – to speak like William James – but a realism dealing with what I will call *matters of concern*, not *matters of fact*. The mistake we made, the mistake I made, was to believe that there was no efficient way to criticize matters of fact except by moving *away* from them and directing one's attention *toward* the conditions that made them possible. But this meant accepting much too uncritically what matters of fact were. This was remaining too faithful to the unfortunate solution inherited from the philosophy of Immanuel Kant. Critique has not been critical enough, in spite of all its sore-scratching. Reality is not defined by matters of fact. Matters of fact are not all that is given in experience. Matters of fact are only very partial and, I would argue, very polemical, very political renderings of matters of concern and only a subset of what could also be called *states of affairs*. It is this second empiricism, this return to the realist attitude, that I'd like to offer as the next task for the critically minded. (Latour 2004, 231–2)

The risk of 'criticism' is that it focuses too much on science and (deconstructing) its theoretical truth.[6] There are many a-theoretical aspects to culture (including to science) that also need to be reflected on in critical analysis. My choice in this book of using the philosophy developed by Heinrich Rickert to shed light on Latour – and through him on philosophy under climate change – is largely due to Rickert's attempt at a systematic extension of Kantian 'criticism'[7] to all cultural domains. While Rickert is not really counted among (precursors of) postmodern philosophers, his fundamental emphasis on uncertainty, as well as his acknowledgement of the need for openness of philosophical systems, makes him, I claim, a marker of the transition from modern to postmodern thought. Hence 'criticism' in this book has a more limited meaning than as used by Latour or Stenmark and Bauman (I use it philosophically to denote transcendental philosophy). However, it *does* have relevance, at a methodological level, for what Latour labels as 'matters of concern' (see my treatment of the issues of disenchantment, disbelief and disregard in Part II).

Following Andrew Pickering (1992, 3), I use the term 'culture' to denote the 'field of resources' that practitioners in a practice draw on, with 'practice' defined as 'the acts of making (and unmaking) that they perform in that field'.[8]

I take 'values' not to be limited to the ethical domain. Instead, with Rickert, I consider 'values' to be the ideal (that is, unreal) objects that give meaning and structure to all the different domains within culture. Furthermore, I distinguish, again with Rickert, between subjectively held values and values that are supposed to be objectively valid (which does not mean that we are certain of them).[9] There are thus different sets of values that give meaning to the different domains of science, religion, politics, etc. As part of my engagement with Latour and Rickert, I aim to further the science-and-religion dialogue by proposing a philosophy of culture that highlights the role of values in judgements in different cultural domains, that is, a philosophy of value.

I do not separate, as some authors (e.g. Drees 2010) do, 'worldviews' from values (where 'worldviews' pertain to how the world works), but I follow Hedlund-de Witt in considering 'worldviews' to be 'inescapable, overarching systems of meaning and meaning making that to a substantial extent inform how humans interpret, enact, and co-create reality' (Hedlund-de Witt 2013, 156). This definition of 'worldview' is in line with Rickert's notion of *Weltanschauung*. He equates it with a 'conception of life' (*Lebensauffassung*), in which a human being's attitude towards life is expressed (Rickert 1934a, 2).

With respect to 'uncertainty', most formal definitions of the term 'uncertainty' refer to the 'absence of certainty' or the 'lack of knowledge'; they thus refer to some qualification of our state of knowledge.[10] In my book *Simulating Nature* I presented a typology of uncertainty in scientific simulation (Petersen ([2006] 2012, Chapter 3, 49–64).[11] I include 'recognised ignorance' as a type of uncertainty. This concerns those uncertainties about a phenomenon that we realise, in one way or another, are present, but for which we cannot establish any useful estimate, for example, due to limits of predictability and knowability ('chaos') or due to insufficiently known processes.[12]

The topic of uncertainty has been studied in philosophy for at least the past 2,500 years. So, in proposing a philosophical framework for analysing the role of uncertainty in different cultural practices, it makes sense to connect to existing philosophical schools. Given the attention that I will pay to the creative role of uncertainty in different cultural practices, it is proper to avoid *dogmatic* metaphysics and philosophy, and to opt instead for an *open* approach to metaphysics and philosophy.

Transcendental naturalism and philosophical methodology

As I have indicated, an important aspect of what is inspiring about science and religion is that their practices are full of uncertainty. It is this uncertainty that drives these creative enterprises, as well as other cultural domains. Any philosophy and metaphysics that aspire to be regarded as appropriate for analysing science and religion, as well as their intersections with one another and with other domains such as politics, need to capture the importance of this uncertainty, while avoiding (extreme) relativism. The transcendental naturalistic philosophy that I argue for, as a corrective to Latour's philosophy, is compatible with both a theistic and an atheistic metaphysics, as well as with an 'agnosticism' that does not consider the question about belief in God or the Transcendent answerable (or even an appropriate question) – an 'agnosticism', by the way, that at the same time considers its own position to be 'compatible with a religious way of life and outlook' (Le Poidevin 2010, xiii).[13] Obviously this philosophy is also able to accommodate Latour's own proposal for an alternative metaphysics. However, that metaphysics is then qualified as not belonging to theoretical philosophy but being a matter of faith.

'Metaphysics' is thus taken here as theory about what lies beyond experience and philosophy. Since metaphysics is 'theoretical', as opposed to the 'a-theoretical' which characterises most cultural domains, it may be correlated with 'religion' but is not identical to it. Metaphysics requires 'faith' that goes beyond reason; *Wissenschaft* – as I take it in its wide sense – includes philosophy, is theoretical, but does *not* include metaphysics. Any philosophy that aims to be a rendering of 'all there is' makes metaphysical assumptions (which thus indicates that I ultimately take all *Wissenschaft* also to involve faith).

'Transcendental' philosophy is philosophy that, in a similar vein as Immanuel Kant (1724–1804) and inspired by David Hume (1711–1776), aims to get rid of (classical) metaphysical assumptions underpinning experience and concepts. Instead it uses a transcendental approach that focuses on the possibility conditions of knowledge. As many subsequent philosophers have observed, Kant can be interpreted as having made his own metaphysical assumptions in his philosophy, such as about the *Ding an sich*, which has led to questions about how far the transcendental approach can be taken. I wish simply to note here that a transcendental approach can also be formulated without metaphysically laden *Dinge an sich*, and in the present book I investigate the approach that Rickert developed to take the transcendental project as far as is possible.

Rickert worked with an 'ontology' (theory of modes of being) in which values – which play a crucial role in his formulation of the transcendental approach – do not reside in a world beyond experience. 'Epistemology' (theory of knowledge) and ontology are intrinsically connected, given that judgements are required to predicate being. Rickert's transcendental approach acknowledges that uncertainty is involved in arriving at judgements, which makes his philosophy very well suited to analysing the limitations of knowledge in all domains of culture. Furthermore, Rickert acknowledges that at some point (not for deploying the transcendental approach, but rather for bringing unity in one's view of the world) one has to have a metaphysics. However, as I already indicated, obtaining or defending that metaphysics is not really part of philosophy proper, that is, of philosophy as a *Wissenschaft*.

One of the metaphysical assumptions that Latour, James and Rickert all fight against is that of 'scientistic naturalism'[14] – an assumption *against* supernaturalism and *for* natural science as the basis of all knowledge – which they see many scientists make but which they cannot stomach philosophically. The discussion surrounding various forms of 'naturalism' has been a core topic in the science-and-religion dialogue as it took off in the 1950s and 1960s. In this book, which seeks to formulate an appropriate philosophy under climate change, a distinction is made between philosophically appropriate and inappropriate forms of 'naturalism'. It is important to remain aware that defining 'naturalism' is a very tricky business (cf. Flanagan 2006). Often the definition is a negative one, with the common core between various definitions being that 'naturalism' objects to the following form of 'supernaturalism':

> (i) there exists a 'supernatural being or beings' or 'power(s)' outside the natural world; (ii) this 'being' or 'power' has causal commerce

> with this world; (iii) the grounds for belief in both the 'supernatural being' and its causal commerce cannot be seen, discovered, or inferred by way of any known and reliable epistemic methods. (Flanagan 2006, 433)

Typically, the different extant versions of naturalism are atheistic. This is necessarily so for scientistic versions, but most non-scientistic versions of naturalism, even those which can be considered 'religious', are also atheistic.

An example of an atheistic religious naturalism can be found in the works of Donald Crosby, for example his books *A Religion of Nature* (2002) and *Nature as Sacred Ground: A metaphysics for religious naturalism* (2015). Crosby considers nature as metaphysically ultimate and an appropriate focus of religious concern. Another key proponent of atheistic[15] religious naturalism is Ursula Goodenough, who explicitly claims that she is engaged in 'religiopoiesis', that is, the crafting of religion. According to Goodenough:

> [e]ach religion is grounded in its myth, and each myth includes a cosmology of origins and destiny. The scientific worldview coheres as such a myth and calls for a religiopoietic response. (Goodenough 2000, 561)

Goodenough is convinced that behavioural directives 'only work if they flow from belief' and that, for instance, 'the most enduring form' of environmentally beneficial behaviour will result 'from a theological and spiritual apprehension of our place in the scheme of things [and] [s]cientists have important things to tell us here' (Goodenough 2000, 565).

There are also theistic and agnostic versions of naturalism.[16] Recently, for instance, Fiona Ellis (2014) has developed a 'theistic naturalism'. She identifies the restriction of what are 'known and reliable epistemic methods' to natural science alone (which is what I mean with the label 'scientistic naturalism')[17] as philosophically unwarranted. On the basis of expanding the category of 'known and reliable epistemic methods' to social science, Ellis argues for values also being part of nature (in a version of naturalism that Ellis calls 'expansive naturalism')[18]. Subsequently, she argues, following Emmanuel Levinas (1906–1995), that relating to God need not be interpreted supernaturalistically (that is, by regarding God as a 'thing' outside the natural world). Interpretation of that relationship can rather be done in a way that is similar to how humans relate to values, with the specific additional element being that God should be considered as radically other than nature. Note that Ellis is conscious of straddling into theology here (but she maintains that the possibility of her position can be argued for philosophically):

> The position at which we have arrived involves a rejection of the claim that philosophy and theology are distinct disciplines with distinct subject-matters – that they add up to two in this sense. Likewise, we have rejected the idea that theology is to be dispensed with on scientific or philosophical grounds or because its subject-matter – God – resists all attempts to be comprehended. These contested claims rest upon the assumption that God and the world add up to two, leaving it open for the atheist to reject the first term of this distinction, and, with it, the discipline which takes this term as its subject-matter. God and world do not add up to two, but nor are they to be identified, for God is distinct from the world, albeit not as a distinct thing, and in such a way that He remains omnipresent to all things. So the world is irreducibly God-involving, but God is not reducible to the world. The idea that God is not reducible to the world suggests that we need to uphold a distinction between theology and philosophy, and it is no part of my position that the two disciplines are to be conflated. On the contrary, we can philosophize about things in the world without mentioning God, just as we can take as our focus God Himself. The conclusions we draw in this latter context will be confined to God as He is in relation to the world, for even if we endeavour to talk about God outside His relation to the world, such talk involves an implicit and irreducible reference to the one who is seeking to comprehend Him in this manner. The mistake is to suppose that this imposes an irredeemable limitation. (Ellis 2014, 198–9)

Ellis demonstrates with her considered position that a theistic naturalism is possible. In doing so she poses a challenge to Owen Flanagan, who asserts that naturalism necessarily

> is not friendly to theism. The epistemological humility called for is not so humble that it tolerates agnosticism. Theological claims do not work and for that reason they are something akin to nonsense, lacking in cognitive significance, as they used to say in the old days. (Flanagan 2006, 437)

I take it that both theism and agnosticism, as well as atheism, are live options that can be understood in a transcendental naturalistic philosophy as ultimately a-theoretical commitments.

'Transcendental naturalism', the position that I explore in this book, does not feature in overviews of 'naturalism' (e.g. Flanagan 2006; Drees 2006; Leidenhag 2018). In short, I take transcendental naturalism to (1) respect the methods and claims of science, but not succumb to scientism (in the sense which assumes that only science can lead to knowledge) and (2) derive no certainty from *a priori*[19] values, but still admit them into ontology and epistemology. To phrase it more positively: transcendental naturalism is based on combining an expansive concept of 'nature' (which encompasses the actual world and the transcendental, unreal values that also belong to the world 'on this side') with an emphasis on the separate ontological status of transcendental values. Its metaphilosophical position is that philosophy should limit itself to theorising only about the world that is 'on this side', and not try to specify any other world 'beyond'.

The label 'transcendental naturalism' has been used before by other authors but with different meanings. Sami Pihlström made use of the phrase 'transcendental naturalism' in his book *Naturalizing the Transcendental: A pragmatic view* (2003), but he does not have my expansive concept of nature nor my recognition of the ontological status of values. While Pihlström also brings together transcendental and pragmatist[20] philosophy, he does so mainly through Kant and Wittgenstein (instead of through Rickert and James);[21] he also 'naturalises' the *a priori* into the *a posteriori*, which I claim is unwarranted (see Chapter 3). I instead follow Rickert's strict transcendental approach and allow for uncertainty pertaining to the *a priori*. Somewhat further away from my reading of 'transcendental naturalism' sits Colin McGinn's book *Problems in Philosophy: The limits of inquiry* (1993). McGinn uses the phrase to denote the following thesis:

> [P]hilosophical perplexities arise in us because of definite inherent limitations on our epistemic faculties, not because philosophical questions concern entities or facts that are intrinsically problematic or peculiar or dubious. Philosophy is an attempt to get outside the constitutive structure of our minds. Reality itself is everywhere flatly natural, but because of our cognitive limits we are unable to make good on this general ontological principle. Our epistemic architecture obstructs knowledge of the real nature of the objective world. (McGinn 1993, 2)

While this is definitely an important and interesting thesis, it is not what this study is about.

Willem Drees has made the instructive point that both pragmatism and (neo-)Kantianism might be useful schools of thought for the study of naturalism. Observing that dealing with values is hard for naturalism, he concludes:

> In a naturalistic approach, arguing for a normative position, whether in morality or in epistemology, will always be an unfinished project. It is a project in which naturalism can benefit from other philosophical styles, such as pragmatism (with its sensitivity to the way in which our norms are rooted in our practices) and Kantianism (with its reflection on the never fully accessible, always elusive, transcendent regulative ideals). (Drees 2010, 92–3)

In its search for an appropriate philosophy under climate change, this book contributes to this 'unfinished project of naturalism' by amending a pragmatist – or, more precisely, radically empiricist – approach, used by Latour and James, from the perspective of a particular neo-Kantian approach (as distinct from a still metaphysically laden Kantian approach) used by Rickert.

Let me here capture the 'methodology' of transcendental naturalism, which I base on Rickert's description of his take on the methodology of philosophy more generally.

It is not possible to 'experience' the world as a whole: 'One can only feel something particular, like one can only want something particular' (Rickert 1934a, 8). Theoretical truth is not necessarily the highest good; it can even be considered 'dangerous' from the perspective of, e.g., religious (or other types of) truth. But this should not prevent philosophy from trying to obtain knowledge about the world as a whole (*Erkenntnis des Weltganzen*). Obtaining theoretical clarity concerning a-theoretical worldview questions can have an influence on one's practical life.

The largest difficulty for philosophy is how to get started, without losing the ideal of *one* philosophy *vis-à-vis* a plurality of philosophies; another, lesser, difficulty is how to deal with infinity (*Unendlichkeit*):

> The fact that definitive knowledge of the world can never be reached, because in its whole it presents itself as an inexhaustible manifold, says nothing about the possibility of obtaining scientific knowledge about it. (Rickert 1934a, 12)

Uncertainty will always remain, but this does not mean that all knowledge is impossible (*contra* extreme relativism).

'World' has two meanings: 'everything that exists' (*alles, was es überhaupt gibt*)[22] and 'world' versus 'human being' (Rickert 1934a, 13). This leads to philosophical questions about the world as a whole ('ontology'), the human being as a whole ('anthropology') and the relationship between the human being as a whole and the world as a whole known by them ('epistemology'). Philosophy aims to offer 'a perspective on *all* worldviews' (*einen Überblick über* alle *Weltanschauungen*), enlightening the grounds of characteristic differences between worldviews. If this enterprise is successful, then clarity is reached on the human being's position in the world as a whole. Philosophy thus offers a service to human beings' cultural life (*Kulturleben*) by enlightening theoretically our consciousness (*Bewußtsein*) in that cultural life. Philosophy is thus not dangerous to life: even though it 'kills' life through concepts, it is at life's service.

Besides ontological and anthropological problems, philosophy addresses the methodological problem: 'Which resources do we have available to theoretically grasp with our thinking as much as possible the world as a whole, in which we live … ?' (Rickert 1934a, 20). Theoretical researchers build systems of concepts to obtain knowledge about the wholes that they study. Philosophers should heed the temptation to close their system:

> The conscientious researcher will expressly point out gaps [in our knowledge] and, in consideration of them, always keep his system 'open', that is, shape it in such a way that new material, which will only be discovered through subsequent research, finds a place in it. (Rickert 1934a, 24)

According to Rickert, materialism (a form of 'scientistic naturalism') offered a philosophically useless theory of the world as whole. Materialists cannot explain how in a world that is *just* material one can obtain knowledge about matter: it must remain a mystery. Any theory of the world that limits itself to known objects cannot be philosophy: such a theory will not allow one to think of the world as a whole in its totality. Nor does intuitionism (under which Rickert also classed James, as I will discuss in this book) work: 'Only intuition in conjunction with something else, which we call thinking and on principle have to distinguish from intuition, produces true knowledge' (Rickert 1934a, 35).

A final methodological point is that one cannot have an

individualising theory of the world as a whole, only a generalising one. Rickert's methodology makes use of what he calls the 'heterological principle' (e.g. Rickert 1934a, 45–7) to characterise the whole (which cannot be conceptualised directly): the concept of the world as a whole can only be conceived in our thinking when we are able for each negation of a statement to substitute a positive element. This in turn leads to a pair of concepts (e.g. subject–object, immanence–transcendence, theoretical–a-theoretical) under which everything falls (in the manner of 'either–or').

The structure of this book

This book is structured around seven questions that I aim to answer, my overall aim being to formulate – in the context of dealing with climate change – a transcendental naturalistic philosophy of culture that enables adequate reflection on uncertainty in science and religion. Each question is treated in a separate chapter (Chapters 2 through 8) – divided over two parts of the book:

Part I

1. How does *wonder* relate to uncertainty?[23] (Chapter 2)
2. How does *judgement* relate to uncertainty? (Chapter 3)
3. How do *values* relate to uncertainty? (Chapter 4)
4. How do *models* relate to uncertainty? (Chapter 5)

Part II

5. How do *poetics* relate to uncertainty, and what are the implications for dealing with climate change? (Chapter 6)
6. How do *authorities* relate to uncertainty, and what are the implications for dealing with climate change? (Chapter 7)
7. How do *futures* relate to uncertainty, and what are the implications for dealing with climate change? (Chapter 8)

Chapter 9 provides a conclusion and assesses the book's progress in reaching the stated aim. That final chapter includes a reflection on the usefulness of Latour's recent philosophical work for contributing to the task at hand.

Part I ('Philosophical framework – transcendental naturalism') contains four chapters. In Chapter 2 ('Wonder') I introduce the phenomenon of 'wonder' and interpret it philosophically, using William James's *The Principles of Psychology*, *The Will to Believe* and the metaphysical approach to experience that he developed in his later doctrine of pure experience. After exploring the Jamesian philosophical approach to experience, I analyse Bruno Latour's approach, as contained in his *An Inquiry into Modes of Existence* and *Facing Gaia*. Subsequently I propose positive readings of uncertainty (through wonder and intimations of metaphysical transcendence) in the practices of science and of religion. In Chapter 3 ('Judgement') I introduce a philosophical analysis of 'judgement', starting with Heinrich Rickert's transcendental approach to judgement, and offer examples of judgement in scientific and religious practices. I make use of interpretations of Immanuel Kant's *Critique of the Power of Judgment* (Kant [1790] 2000) by Rickert and other commentators. I highlight how Rickert extended the Kantian project in analysing the fundamental openness to uncertainty in practices, emphasising the role of freedom in judgements that link perceptual being to *a priori* values. In Chapter 4 ('Values') I dissect the role of values in cultural practices, starting with Bruno Latour's empirical approach to values in his work on 'modes of existence'. This provides the initial impetus for understanding the driving values in scientific, religious and political practices. I engage with Heinrich Rickert's philosophy to arrive at a transcendental naturalistic analysis of the role of values in cultural practices. In Chapter 5 ('Models') I first highlight the role of models in Latour's mode of reference and mode of religion. Models in science and religion are both the result of transformations, but, making reference to both philosophy of science and philosophy of religion, their roles are shown to be different. I end with an overview of philosophy of science debates on models, including the debate on 'instrumentalism', a 'pragmatist' philosophy of science that started around the beginning of the twentieth century. For transcendental naturalism, I argue that a position of weak 'referential realism' is defensible, which entails the basic acknowledgement that there is a world independent of the human mind. This chapter concludes the laying out of the philosophical framework in Part I.

Part II ('Themes in science and religion, applied to climate science and politics') contains three chapters. They deal with themes that are connected with problems caused by scientistic forms of naturalism and that also play important roles in Latour's *Facing Gaia* (which aims to come to terms philosophically with climate change). These themes consist of the religious disenchantment of nature, the scientific disbelief in a plurality of value-laden perspectives and the disregard for non-modern worldviews in politics. Chapter 6 ('Poetics and climate: modern myth and disenchantment') takes up as a first theme, along with James, Latour and Santayana, the supposed process of 'disenchantment' of the world and the role that science has been claimed to play in this process *vis-à-vis* religion. A central present-day question in science-and-religion is whether a science-compatible modern myth can be construed – theistic, agnostic or atheistic in kind – that replaces or amends classical religious myths and can 're-enchant' the world? As my entry point to this theme I focus on 'poetics', a term that encompasses but has a wider sense than 'poetry' and refers to the coming together and effects of textual elements, in the context of uncertainty. I first show how different values (scientific and religious) are at stake in poetics and science-and-religion, starting with the state of play at the end of the nineteenth century and continuing with other contributions in the contemporary science-and-religion discussion. I end with present attempts to address the ecological crisis, including climate change, through modern myths based on science, identifying some problems connected with aiming for ecological conservation based on a religious interpretation of science. The theme of Chapter 7 ('Authorities and climate: modern rationality and disbelief') is the role of 'authority' or 'authorities' in the practices of science and religion, and its implications for climate science and politics. I first engage with the perspectives of James, Latour and Rickert on authorities in connection with science-and-religion. This informs my subsequent analysis of authorities in the context of how this is discussed in other contributions in the contemporary science-and-religion literature. I end with the example of science advice within the Intergovernmental Panel on Climate Change (IPCC), which exemplifies the problematic role of a notion of expert judgement that is based on modern rationality at the crossing of the practices of science and politics. Chapter 8 ('Futures and climate: modern planning and disregard') deals with the role of the 'future' or 'futures' in the practices of science, religion and public policy. After engaging with the perspectives of James, Latour and Rickert on futures in connection with science-and-religion, I analyse the role of futures in contemporary science-and-religion discussions. I conclude with two recent examples of mutual disregard by on the one hand modern planning and science, and on the other by non-modern cultures – again in the context of the crossing of the practices of climate science and politics.

In the final chapter, Chapter 9 ('Conclusion: a transcendental naturalistic approach beyond Bruno Latour'), the elements discussed in the different chapters of the book are brought together and some concluding reflections are given on Latour's work. I frame this work as a contribution to science-and-religion that can be restructured as a philosophy of value which fits within transcendental naturalistic philosophy in the context of climate change. I continue with a brief reflection on what the heightened attention to uncertainty in the transcendental naturalism proposed in this book can bring more widely to the science-and-religion debate on the religious outlooks (theistic, atheistic and agnostic) of naturalism. I conclude with a final assessment of the book's argument.

Notes

1 The articles and commentaries written for this conference were published in the first issue of *Zygon: Journal of Religion and Science* in March 1966.

2 In this book I will use 'religion' to stand for religious practices, not for 'theology'.

3 While environmental problems as such were not yet separately categorised in the early 1960s, nuclear war was seen to have environmental consequences; also the 'population explosion', with significant environmental consequences, was included in the Editorial by Burhoe and Tapp (1966a).

4 In this book the latter component is captured by the transcendental side of 'transcendental naturalism'.

5 When I use 'science' without a qualifier from here onwards, it should be taken to mean 'natural sciences'. Given that the natural sciences are embedded in a heavily technological environment, I take the natural sciences here to include the engineering sciences.

6 Note that Latour does not adopt a notion of what neo-Kantians call 'theoretical truth' in his work (see Chapter 4).

7 Kantian criticism, in brief, is a philosophical method inspired by Hume that systematically assumes the fallibility of theoretical knowledge and analyses its consequences. See also below, in the section 'Transcendental naturalism and philosophical methodology' (pp. 9–16), and Chapter 3.

8 Rickert's philosophy of culture includes a further specification of what can philosophically be understood to be included in the notion of 'field of resources' (see Chapter 4).

9 I argue in this book that this notion of 'values' does not necessarily get one into 'metaphysics' (although it *does* make up part of a separate sphere in 'ontology'). See the following section for my definition of 'metaphysics' (in which I again follow Rickert).

10 Note that defining uncertainty as lack of knowledge does not imply that the lacking knowledge can be gained in principle or that the uncertainty is necessarily epistemic. See my notion of 'ontic uncertainty' in Petersen ([2006] 2012).

11 I have always made the following disclaimer: no typology of 'uncertainty' exists that includes all of its meanings (even in the context of the natural sciences) in a way that is clear, simple and adequate for each potential use of such a typology. Still I claim that many of the elements of my proposed typology are applicable more generally to all sciences, both natural and social sciences, and even to all cultural practices. This is not a topic for the present book, however.

12 'Unrecognised ignorance' does not count as 'uncertainty' since it concerns 'pure ignorance' (unknown unknowns) about which we cannot say anything determinate – hence the distinction used in this book between 'uncertainty' (which includes 'recognised ignorance', or 'border with ignorance' as it is called by Funtowicz and Ravetz 1990) and 'ignorance' (taken to mean 'pure ignorance' that can be recognised at a metalevel to exist but that is not recognised and characterised with some positive determinations from a situatedness at the border with uncertainty). Note that recently Rik Peels (2023) has produced the first full epistemological exploration of the notion of 'ignorance'. Using his terminology, I surmise that the theoretical kinds of uncertainty that I am considering in this book can be classed as 'suspending ignorance' (where one suspends judgement on the truth of a proposition), which is one of six varieties of 'propositional ignorance'. Alternatively, especially when one considers different groups of individuals who may take different positions, the uncertainty may be classed as 'undecided ignorance'.

13 The philosophical framework explored in this book can also provide a deeper understanding of the science–policy interface approach that I have been co-developing since 2001. Such an approach is reflexive about uncertainties in the science and engineering base that is brought

to bear on societal problems beset with value plurality – this involves a so-called 'post-normal science' problem-solving strategy (Funtowicz and Ravetz 1993; Petersen et al. 2011; Petersen 2014b).

14 They all simply use the word 'naturalism' instead of 'scientistic naturalism'.

15 Goodenough actually describes her position as 'nontheistic' (see, e.g., Goodenough [1998] 2023).

16 An example of an agnostic version of naturalism is given in Chapter 9.

17 Ellis calls this 'scientific naturalism'.

18 Ellis's focus is on moral values. In this book I take a broader set of values into account.

19 The way I use '*a priori*' in this book is to denote that which is independent from sense experience. As is explained in Chapter 4, the sphere of the *a priori* values, which are central to the transcendental position laid out in this book, lies within the sphere of the unreal, the world of meaning and value. In Chapter 3 it is noted that the *a priori* for Kant is often understood as having a metaphysical interpretation and associated certainty, which is not how the *a priori* is conceived in this book.

20 Note that for Pihlström the label 'pragmatism' denotes a broad stream of philosophy (from Peirce and James through to Rorty). He also notes that pragmatism has always contained a transcendental element: '[P]ragmatism, the single originally American philosophical movement, was formed as a synthesis of Kant and Darwin – of the two most important European background figures of American thought. Nevertheless, Kant's crucial influence on pragmatist thinkers has often been neglected, even by those thinkers themselves' (Pihlström 2003, 16–17). In company with Richard Gale, I take 'pragmatism' to be 'a theory of both meaning and truth'; Gale specifies this as follows, in his interpretation of James: 'An idea's meaning is a set of conditionalized predictions, with its truth consisting in the actual fulfillment or verification of these predictions, as is required by this assumption' (Gale 1999, 153). In this book I will both deal with the pragmatist notion of 'truth' (versus 'theoretical truth') and with the metaphysical assumptions involved in 'radical empiricism' (versus 'transcendental empiricism').

21 Pihlström does not mention Rickert.

22 When one substitutes 'nature' for 'world' it should become clear why I characterise Rickert's philosophy as a very open form of 'naturalism'.

23 'Uncertainty' in these questions refers both generically to practices and specifically to the practices of science and religion.

Part 1
Philosophical framework – transcendental naturalism

2
Wonder

Introduction

Where to begin our exploration of the proper place of uncertainty in philosophical approaches to the practices of science and religion? A natural starting point is in the experience of uncertainty, particularly in the emotion of wonder. In science, the complexity of the world overwhelms us humans. In religion, the situation is similar. For instance, Jerome Miller, author of *In the Throe of Wonder: Intimations of the sacred in a post-modern world* (1992), delves into the philosophical depth of the experience of the unknown:

> [P]hilosophy requires us to recognize as unknown precisely the familiar which we thought we knew. At the very beginning it situates us in the middle of a whole which we know only as wholly unknown. ... Because the unknown is not assimilatable into the given, we can become aware of it as unknown only by acknowledging its difference, and the impossibility of homologizing its otherness with what we have heretofore thought of as the already known. (Miller 1992, 3)

In this chapter I philosophically examine the phenomenon of 'wonder' as a type of human emotional experience that is associated with uncertainty, and that may (but need not) involve intimations of metaphysical transcendence.[1] Wonder may arise in all cultural practices (e.g. science, religion, art, politics, etc.) and, as I will argue in Chapter 6, a non-scientistic notion of wonder based in transcendental naturalism can be used philosophically to underpin ecological action in the context of climate change.

Let me start my exploration of wonder with a complex case, taken from Bruno Latour's depiction of a scene from Pierre Daubigny's play *Gaia Global Circus* in his book *Facing Gaia* ([2015] 2017). A climate scientist experiences wonder (and fear) when she, being aware of what is known about anthropogenic climate change, is confronted with climate denialism. She is subsequently left at once uncertain and inspiringly stirred by what is happening and what the future – including her own actions – could look like:

> For several seconds, in suspense, Virginia [climate scientist] explores other solutions, each one more calamitous than the one before. This is when, in a moment of inspiration and panic, she cries out against Ted [climate sceptic], whom the spectators are on the verge of driving out of the room: 'Go tell your masters that the scientists are on the warpath!'
>
> However, in the next scene she admits sheepishly that she doesn't know what that means. For scientists, in fact, the warpath doesn't exist. … We are touched in our most intimate being by the hope that humanity will never have such capability [of changing the climate]. We are constantly at risk of conspiring with our enemies [climate-change deniers and their funders]. This is what it really means to find ourselves at war: to have to decide, without any pre-established rules, which side we're going to have to be on. (Latour [2015] 2017, 30–1)

There is already quite a bit to unpack in this passage, but Latour adds even more complexity for consideration. It is not just the 'crossing' between the practices of science and of politics that concerns Latour in the book. Above all, he is taking his cue from climate change to address existential uncertainty pertaining to our worldview, including our position *vis-à-vis* the practices of religion. He uses a plethora of experiences of wonder that through his systematic analyses – laid out in detail in his magnum opus *An Inquiry into Modes of Existence* ([2012] 2013b) and based on an occasionalist[2] empiricist approach – leads him to propose a new approach to doing metaphysics:

> Let's be careful: let's not rush into saying that we're already familiar with the list of existents and the way they are related to one another, for example, by saying that there exist two and only two forms – causal relations and symbolic relations – or by claiming that all existents form a Whole that can be encompassed by thought.

> This would amount to stuffing them all back into the single frame of Nature/Culture, which we are seeking, precisely, to circumvent. No, we have to agree to remain open to the dizzying otherness of existents, the list of which is not closed, and to the multiple ways they have of existing or of relating among themselves, without regrouping them too quickly in some set, whatever it might be – and certainly not in 'nature'. It is this opening to otherness that William James proposed to call the *pluriverse*. (Latour [2015] 2017, 36)

'Remain[ing] open to the dizzying otherness of existents' is the invitation to wonder that also inspires the present book – which as part of a larger search for a philosophy fit to address climate change sets out to clarify and limit what one can argue philosophically about the object of wonder. As I explained in Chapter 1, my aim for the entire book is to unpack the crossing between science and religion, and their respective uncertainties, in the context of climate science and politics, while at the same time developing 'transcendental naturalism' (in discussion with Latour's work). A beginning will be made with this task here by first examining the phenomenon of wonder philosophically, while also focusing on the settings of the practices of science and religion.

In the present chapter, I mainly analyse the work of the American philosopher William James (1842–1910) and compare Latour's way of thinking to James's. I explain how James, in his doctrine of 'pure experience', pluralistically addressed the 'metaphysics of experience',[3] and that Latour, while moving further along philosophically in terms of pluralism, essentially extended James's doctrine of pure experience. I also initially compare James's analysis of the metaphysics of experience to transcendental philosophy – a topic that will be developed more fully in the next three chapters, on 'judgement', 'values' and 'models' respectively. These analyses are all performed in the context of answering the basic question for this chapter: How does wonder relate to uncertainty? Or, both more broadly and in some specific detail: How do emotion and the metaphysics of experience – and corresponding intimations of transcendence – relate to the irreducible uncertainty that characterises both science and religion?

As Haralambous and Nielsen show, 'wonder' has deep roots in the history of philosophy:

> In Theaetetus (155d3), Plato calls '*wonder*' (*thaumazein*) the *origin of philosophy* (and Aristotle follows Plato in this assessment in

> *Metaphysics* 2.982 b). Philosophers have since debated whether Plato meant wonder as puzzlement and intrigue or wonder in its sublime mode as something that inspires awe and reverence. (Haralambous and Nielsen 2014, 219)

What connects both notions of 'wonder' is that they are both responses to uncertainty (which can be reduced or not). My suggestion is that the two notions are linked: not being able to solve a puzzle can lead to awe, and the associated emotions will feature continuity. In the context of the role of wonder in fiction, wonder can be seen to act

> as a door or gateway; when present, wonder enables the inquirer as gatekeeper to open a flow of movement between fact and fiction, one that enables them to merge with each other so that facts become wondrous. (Haralambous and Nielsen 2014, 220)

The existence of wonder – an individual phenomenon – is itself a cultural product (not in the sense of culture versus nature, but in the sense of culture being a historical product of nature/the world). Sarah Tindal Kareem observes in her study on *Eighteenth-century Fiction and the Reinvention of Wonder* that '[w]onder is part of a broad and shifting semantic field in late seventeenth- and eighteenth-century psychology and aesthetics that at various times includes surprise, curiosity, admiration, suspense, stupor, awe, amazement, and astonishment' (Kareem 2014, 7). She argues that 'the wonder that ... eighteenth-century fictions engage encompasses both wonder *at* and wonder *about* objects' (Kareem 2014, 8). Again, as stated above, these two notions of wonders can be connected in practice.

However, Lisa Sideris, in her book *Consecrating Science: Wonder, knowledge, and the natural world*, pleads for keeping the two notions analytically distinct, since wonder about objects may disappear and/or does not necessarily lead to awe. She describes the phenomenon of wonder as follows:

> What does it mean to wonder? Wonder is almost routinely exalted as a laudable state, but perhaps not all expressions of it deserve to be celebrated. Wonder seems to exist at the border of sensation and thought, aesthetics and science. It has the power to transfix as well as transport us. It is characterized both as a childlike capacity, closely aligned with sensory and emotional engagement, and as a kind of scientific virtue. (Sideris 2017, 14)

It is especially in the context of her discussion of scientistic naturalism and ecology (to which this book turns in detail in Chapter 6) that Sideris wishes to maintain a clear distinction between wonder as puzzlement and wonder as awe and reverence. In regard to the latter sort of wonder, she notes:

> The experience of loss of self, of *letting go* of ego-dominated rationality, is one of the links between wondering responses and experiences often termed religious, as theorists such as William James have noted. ... In such moments of profound receptivity to the unexpected, we may sense our connection to something that is ontologically or spiritually *more* (as James termed it) than what is given in our daily experience of the world or the world as filtered through familiar categories of knowledge. (Sideris 2017, 15)

With regards to 'wonder as puzzlement', she claims that something odd happened in the seventeenth and eighteenth centuries:

> [T]he period from roughly the mid-seventeenth to the mid-eighteenth century saw a brief efflorescence of wonder, as well as a temporary rapprochement between wonder and curiosity. Interestingly, this same period saw the rise of 'modern' science, and of the mechanical worldview promulgated by Descartes and Bacon, and often censured by environmentalists, religion scholars, and historians, for its radical disenchantment of the natural world. ... How is it that this 'age of wonder' was simultaneously an age of disenchantment? (Sideris 2017, 22)

She concludes that 'wonder as puzzlement' had developed into a wonder that is 'not the beginning but the *result* of inquiry, a response to *knowledge obtained* rather than to the puzzling, awesome, or mysterious phenomenon itself' (Sideris 2017, 23–4). In the conclusion of this chapter I will evaluate this claim.

In the next two sections, I elucidate the Jamesian and Latourian approaches to wonder and the metaphysics of experience respectively. I continue the chapter with analyses of the role of wonder, emotion and the metaphysics of experience *vis-à-vis* uncertainty in scientific practices (using examples from natural science) and in religious practices (using examples from liturgical ritual).

James's approach to wonder and metaphysics

James is a founding father of the discipline of psychology, especially through the publication of his *The Principles of Psychology* in 1890. At Harvard University he was first appointed as a Professor of Psychology from 1889–1896 before being re-appointed as a Professor of Philosophy in 1897. James's philosophical approach to metaphysics had reached its initial form already in the mid-1890s and was published in its most elaborated form in *A Pluralistic Universe* in 1909 (based on his Hibbert Lectures to Manchester College, Oxford in 1908).[4] In this section I will analyse how, in James's philosophy, judgements that have the emotion of wonder associated with them can intimate metaphysical transcendence. Before I deal with James's doctrine of 'pure experience', which he outlined in his 1904 articles 'Does "consciousness" exist?' and 'A world of pure experience' (republished posthumously in *Essays in Radical Empiricism* (James [1912] 1976), I set the scene by introducing some relevant elements of James's thought that derive from his *The Principles of Psychology* and by briefly highlighting his approach to wonder in *The Will to Believe* (James [1897] 1979).[5]

In the *Principles* chapter on 'The consciousness of self', James is highly critical of what he calls 'Transcendentalist theory' (associated with Kant and his followers). James includes the following in his summary of Kant's transcendental philosophy, specifically of Kant's notion of the 'transcendental Ego':

> All things, then, so far as they are intelligible at all, are so through combination with pure consciousness of *Self*, and apart from this, at least potential, combination nothing is knowable *to us* at all.
>
> But this self, whose consciousness Kant thus established deductively as a *conditio sine qua non* of experience, is in the same breath denied by him to have any positive attributes. ... These declarations on Kant's part of the utter barrenness of the consciousness of the pure Self, and of the consequent impossibility of any deductive or 'rational' psychology, are what, more than anything else, earned for him the title of the 'all-destroyer'. The only self we know anything positive *about*, he thinks, is the empirical *me*, not the pure *I*; the self which is an object among other objects and the 'constituents' of which we ourselves have seen, and recognized to be phenomenal things appearing in the form of space as well as time. (James [1890] 1981, 342–3)

James argues on the basis of his understanding of transcendental philosophy that there is no need for him to revise his own concept of 'a remembering and appropriating Thought incessantly renewed' (James [1890] 1981, 343). He contrasts Kant's and his own metaphysical views:

> On the whole, a defensible interpretation of Kant's view would take somewhat the following shape. Like ourselves he believes in a Reality outside the mind of which he writes, but the critic who vouches for that reality does so on grounds of faith, for it is not a verifiable phenomenal thing. Neither is it manifold. The 'Manifold' which the intellectual functions combine is a mental manifold altogether, which thus *stands between* the Ego of Apperception and the outer Reality, but still stands inside the mind. In the function of knowing there is a multiplicity to be connected, and Kant brings this multiplicity inside the mind. The Reality becomes a mere empty *locus*, or unknowable, the so-called Noumenon; the manifold phenomenon is in the mind. We, on the contrary, put the Multiplicity with the Reality outside, and leave the mind simple. Both of us deal with the same elements – thought and object – the only question is in which of them the multiplicity shall be lodged. (James [1890] 1981, 343)

It is not my aim at this point significantly to engage in Kant interpretation (various Kant interpretations are discussed in the next chapter).[6] Suffice it here to flag that Heinrich Rickert wrote about metaphysical Kant interpretations like James's:

> One might be inclined … to connect this domain of being, of the indispensable presuppositions of an object world, with the domain of 'intelligible' being that Kant took over from the tradition, and think that with the concept of a non-psychic subject we would arrive in the realm of metaphysics. But how would we come to consider a theoretically completely problematic being as the domain that should include the not-at-all problematic, but theoretically indispensable, presupposition of all object knowledge? It can only be a kind of being *on this side* [*diesseitigen Seins*], whose acceptance is required for purely theoretical reasons, and which we call *pro-physical* in order to distinguish it from any metaphysical kind of being that lies beyond the world of experience. (Rickert [1934b] 1999, 378)

In Chapters 3 and 4 I will give a detailed treatment of Rickert's non-metaphysical approach to transcendental philosophy. I will analyse transcendental values as having a separate ontological status in constituting an element of judgement. As I will show below, James offered a glimpse of such a transcendental approach in his last chapter of the *Principles*, on 'Necessary truths and the effects of experience'.

On the topic of the emotion of wonder, James provides an analysis in his chapter on 'Association'. Wonder for James belongs to the problem-related class of thought: 'voluntary thinking' (which comprises 'the mode of recalling a thing forgotten' and 'the voluntary quest of the unknown', James [1890] 1981, 551):

> [I]n the theoretic as well as in the practical life there are interests of a more acute sort, taking the form of definite images of some achievement, be it action or acquisition, which we desire to effect. The train of ideas arising under the influence of such an interest constitutes usually the thought of the *means* by which the end shall be attained. If the end by its simple presence does not instantaneously suggest the means, the search for the latter becomes an intellectual *problem*. The solution of problems is the most characteristic and peculiar sort of voluntary thinking. ...
>
> [W]e see in the philosophy of desire and pleasure, that ... nascent excitements, spontaneously tending to a crescendo, but inhibited or checked by other causes, may become potent mental stimuli and determinants of desire. All questioning, wonder, emotion of curiosity, must be referred to cerebral causes of some such form as this. The great difference between the effort to recall things forgotten and the search after the means to a given end, is that the latter have not, whilst the former have, already formed a part of our experience. (James [1890] 1981, 550–1)

Note that James does not require the problem to be solved (or solvable). So if the 'means' is not found to solve the 'problem', wonder may persist and become a continuing or recurring emotion with respect to a particular intellectual interest that involves an unresolvable uncertainty.

How do thoughts relate to 'desire and pleasure'? James addresses this question more precisely in his chapter on 'The perception of reality', in which he assesses the genesis and philosophical status of what he calls 'beliefs' (and what I will call 'judgements').[7] Judgements can range from uncertain to certain: they come in 'every degree of assurance' (James [1890] 1981, 913). At the outset of the chapter James makes the very important claim that '[i]n its inner nature, belief or the sense of reality, is a sort of feeling more allied to the emotions than anything else' (James [1890] 1981, 913), highlighting the importance of including emotion in analysing judgements in practices (see my discussion below of his chapter on 'The emotions').

The relation between judgement and wonder is subtle, however, and is not addressed by James in his *Principles*. The emotion in judgement involves consent to the content ('an idea which is inwardly stable'), while the emotion in wonder may involve the emotion associated with continuing doubt and inquiry, which James describes as 'opposites of belief', with 'the content of our mind … in unrest' (James [1890] 1981, 914). This analytical tension can be resolved by categorising remaining doubt pertaining to stable content as an uncertain judgement that one sticks with (consents to). That sort of doubt will emotionally have a more positive connotation (that is, it could be wonder) than when contents have not been stabilised (again, what James describes as 'doubt').

Judgements can be about what James describes as 'real' or 'unreal' things (and prima facie 'unreal things', when they are attended to, can get the status of 'real' too, albeit in different fashions – see below): '[t]he total world of which the philosophers must take account is … composed of the realities *plus* the fancies and illusions' (James [1890] 1981, 920). In the section 'The many worlds' in the chapter on 'The perception of reality', James clarifies:

> [T]here are various categories both of illusion and of reality, and alongside of the world of absolute error (i.e., error confined to single individuals) but still within the world of absolute reality (i.e., reality believed by the complete philosopher) there is the world of collective error, there are the worlds of abstract reality, of relative or practical reality, of ideal relations, and there is the supernatural world. (James [1890] 1981, 920–1)

With respect to propositions and judgements on these many worlds, James states:

> Propositions concerning the different worlds are made from 'different points of view'; and in this more or less chaotic state the consciousness of most thinkers remains to the end. Each world *whilst it is attended to* is real after its own fashion; only the reality lapses with the attention. (James [1890] 1981, 922–3)

Note here, crucially, that for James the 'reality' of things depends on their being actively affirmed, and thus 'each thinker, ... [having] dominant habits of attention[,] ... practically elect[s] from among the various worlds some one to be for him the world of ultimate realities' (James [1890] 1981, 923). Humans, being finite creatures, cannot fully grasp all the many worlds:

> [I]n the strict and ultimate sense of the word existence, everything which can be thought of at all exists as *some* sort of object, whether mythical object, individual thinker's object, or object in outer space and for intelligence at large. Errors, fictions, tribal beliefs, are parts of the whole great Universe which God has made, and He must have meant all these things to be in it, each in its respective place. But for us finite creatures, ''tis to consider too curiously to consider so.' (James [1890] 1981, 923–4)

The latter quote from *Hamlet*[8] resonates with the Psalmist's exclamation 'Such knowledge is too wonderful and excellent for me: I cannot attain unto it' (Psalm 139:5).[9] Humans are limited to a focus on their 'practical reality', and thus for the purposes of James's discussion in the *Principles*, 'whatever excites and stimulates our interest is real' (James [1890] 1981, 924).

James explicitly agrees with Kant that the act of judgement does not enrich content in an 'inward way': 'it leaves it inwardly as it finds it, and only fixes it and stamps it in to *us*', which makes 'ourselves' the 'fons et origo of all reality' (James [1890] 1981, 925). Contrasting us with 'bare logical thinkers', James concludes that 'as thinkers with emotional reaction, we give what seems to us a still higher degree of reality to whatever things we select and emphasize and turn to *with a will*' (James [1890] 1981, 925–6). 'Belief in objects of theory' for James is connected to their roles in our practical reality:

> That theory will be most generally believed which, besides offering us objects able to account satisfactorily for our sensible experience, also offers those which are most interesting, those which appeal most urgently to our aesthetic, emotional, and active needs. (James [1890] 1981, 940)

In his *Principles*, James retains to a large extent an agnostic position concerning different philosophical systems, given his aim to provide a comprehensive psychological description of belief, that is, judgement. I argue that James's approach in the *Principles* can be considered 'naturalistic' – not in the scientistic sense (since in that sense 'naturalism' is too much closed and limited to the worldview associated with the sciences) – because he does not allow for a *causal* link between supernatural being and practical reality, that is, experience.

In his celebrated chapter on 'The emotions', James proposes to move beyond 'the merely descriptive literature of the emotions', which 'is one of the most tedious parts of psychology' (James [1890] 1981, 1064). After analysing the 'coarser' emotions of grief, fear, rage and love, he arrives at the 'subtler' emotions, 'the moral, intellectual, and aesthetic feelings' (James [1890] 1981, 1082), and starts off with examples of aesthetics in mathematical or legal judgement:

> A mathematical demonstration may be as 'pretty', and an act of justice as 'neat', as a drawing or a tune, although the prettiness and neatness seem to have nothing to do with sensation. We have, then, or some of us seem to have, genuinely *cerebral* forms of pleasure and displeasure, apparently not agreeing in their mode of production with the 'coarser' emotions we have been analyzing. (James [1890] 1981, 1082)

Still, importantly, the aesthetics of judgement (on which more will be said in Chapter 3) is thoroughly embodied for James; crucially, it is *not* the case that the bodily expression of emotion 'comes later and is added on' to a supposedly immediate emotional feeling (James [1890] 1981, 1082). James recognises that

> where long familiarity with a certain class of effects, even aesthetic ones, has blunted mere emotional excitability as much as it has sharpened taste and judgment, we do get the intellectual emotion, if such it can be called, pure and undefiled. (James [1890] 1981, 1085)

This can lead to the situation that 'The "marvels" of Science, about which so much edifying popular literature is written, are apt to be "caviare" to the men in the laboratories' (James [1890] 1981, 1086). Such can also be true for the emotion of wonder in the face of uncertainty; it may be more or less lived insofar as more or less bodily emotion comes with the intellectual emotion. In the less lived case of wonder, one can say with James that '[e]motion and cognition seem then parted'; 'and cerebral processes are almost feelingless, so far as we can judge, until they summon help from parts below' (James [1890] 1981, 1086). Thus emotions of wonder, like other emotions, 'blunt themselves by repetition more rapidly than any other sort of feeling' (James [1890] 1981, 1089):

> The more we exercise ourselves at anything, the fewer muscles we employ; and just so, the oftener we meet an object, the more definitely we think and behave about it; and the less is the organic perturbation to which it gives rise. The first time we saw it we could perhaps neither act nor think at all, and had no reaction but organic perturbation. The emotions of startled surprise, wonder, or curiosity were the result. Now we look on with absolutely no emotion. (James [1890] 1981, 1089)

Again, it must be added that if we are confronted with an unresolvable uncertainty, the emotion of wonder may persistently return once we attend to the still (or again) puzzling object of thought.

Based on James's *The Principles of Psychology* and his later work, including *The Varieties of Religious Experience*, Jeremy Carrette (2008) usefully outlines a three-stage picture of James's theory of emotion. 'Stages' here refer to the development of James's thought. Stage one (James's 'organic theory') focuses on the 'coarser' or 'standard' emotions. Without doubt the central basis of James's theory of emotion is grounded in the body, as I pointed out in the above. Stage two (James's 'cognitive theory') deals with the 'subtler' or 'complex' emotions, also addressed in the *Principles* and discussed above, which are related to the moral, intellectual, spiritual (mental) and aesthetic dimensions of life. Stage three (James's 'social theory') refers to the 'religious' and 'metaphysical' emotions. These three types of emotion (as described by the three theories) can occur in combination, that is, a social emotion can have cognitive and organic emotions associated with it. I will return to James's theories of emotion in my discussion of religious practices below.

Moving beyond the philosophical analysis of emotion – and, as I will argue, highly relevant for the philosophical investigation that I aim to undertake in this book – are the philosophical reflections that James included in the final chapter of his *Principles*, entitled 'Necessary truths and the effects of experience'. He sums up one of his two main results at the end of that chapter:

> The causes of our mental structure are doubtless natural, and connected, like all our other peculiarities, with those of our nervous structure. Our interests, our tendencies of attention, our motor impulses, the aesthetic, moral, and theoretic combinations we

> delight in, the extent of our power of apprehending schemes of relation, just like the elementary relations themselves, time, space, difference and similarity, and the elementary kinds of feeling, have all grown up in ways of which at present we can give no account. (James [1890] 1981, 1280)

He thus upholds, as he himself writes, 'a naturalistic view' of the cause of our mental structure (James [1890] 1981, 1216). However, he also fights an excessively one-sided focus on experience in what he labels 'Experience-philosophy': 'the coupling of terms within the mind' are not 'simple copies of corresponding couplings impressed upon it by the environment' (James [1890] 1981, 1280). James highlights, to complement his naturalism, crucial aspects of mental structure which are supposed by 'the so called *apriorists* to be of transcendental origin' (James [1890] 1981, 1215). I argue that in the final chapter of his *Principles* James has effectively hinted at a transcendental naturalistic approach, though he did not develop it.[10] While James does not formulate transcendental naturalism, and certainly not as a philosophy of 'value', as I will do following Rickert (see Chapter 4), he introduces his discussion as follows:

> The first thing I have to say is that all schools (however they otherwise differ) must allow that the *elementary qualities* of cold, heat, pleasure, pain, red, blue, sound, silence, etc., are original, innate, or *a priori* properties of our subjective nature, even though they should require the touch of experience to waken them into actual consciousness, and should slumber, to all eternity, without it. (James [1890] 1981, 1216)

Among what he identifies as 'elementary qualities' James includes value-pairs, such as pleasure–pain (and, I would argue, he could also have added beauty–ugliness, goodness–badness, and so on),[11] and he identifies that such values belong to another ontological domain (my term) than sense experience. He continues: 'The warfare of philosophers is exclusively relative to their forms *of combination*' (James [1890] 1981, 1216), and then explains the difference between empiricism and transcendental philosophy:

> The empiricist maintains that these forms can only follow the order of combination in which the elements were originally awakened by the impressions of the external world; the apriorists insist, on

the contrary, that *some* modes of combination, at any rate, follow from the natures of the elements themselves, and that no amount of experience can modify this result. (James [1890] 1981, 1216–17)

It is important to note here that James thus ultimately sides with transcendental philosophy against empiricism on the question of understanding the philosophical status of judgement. This does not invalidate anything that he said earlier in the *Principles* on the role of emotion and aesthetics in judgement. However, it does add an important philosophical ingredient: there are ideal values embedded in judgements.

In the same final chapter of the *Principles*, James also provides a brief analysis of 'The genesis of the natural sciences', in which he demonstrates how values (my term) in scientific practices result in the order of scientific thought:

> What we experience, what *comes before us*, is a chaos of fragmentary impressions interrupting each other; what we *think* is an abstract system of hypothetical data and laws.
>
> This sort of scientific algebra, little as it immediately resembles the reality given to us, turns out (strangely enough) applicable to it. That is, it yields expressions which, at given places and times, can be translated into real values, or interpreted as definite portions of the chaos that falls upon our sense. It becomes thus a practical guide to our expectations as well as a theoretic delight. But I do not see how any one with a sense for the facts can possibly call our systems immediate results of 'experience' in the ordinary sense. Every scientific conception is in the first instance a 'spontaneous variation' in some one's brain. For one that proves useful and applicable there are a thousand that perish through their worthlessness. Their genesis is strictly akin to that of the flashes of poetry and sallies of wit to which the instable brain-paths equally give rise. But whereas the poetry and wit (like the science of the ancients) are their 'own excuse for being', and have to run the gauntlet of no farther test, the 'scientific' conceptions must prove their worth by being 'verified'. This test, however, is the cause of their preservation, not that of their production. (James [1890] 1981, 1231–3)

James observes that natural scientific practice, over its longer genesis, is led by a value of keeping congruent reference to the world when translating experience of the natural world into forms that withstand the test of verification, while the results of this practice can lead to 'theoretic delight' (e.g. in the form of wonder, which can also lead to intimations of metaphysical transcendence).[12] The notion of maintaining congruence is described by James as follows:

> [T]he peculiarity of those relations among the objects of our thought which are dubbed 'scientific' is this, that although they no more are inward *reproductions* of the outer order than the ethical and aesthetic relations are, yet they do not conflict with that order, but, once having sprung up by the play of the inward forces, are found – some of them at least, namely the only ones which have survived long enough to be matters of record – to be *congruent* with the time- and space-relations which our impressions affect. (James [1890] 1981, 1235–6)

And here is how James uses the language of 'translation' for describing what happens in science:

> [T]hough nature's materials lend themselves slowly and discouragingly to our translation of them into ethical forms, but more readily into aesthetic forms; to translation into scientific forms they lend themselves with relative ease and completeness. The translation, it is true, will probably never be ended. The perceptive order does not give way, nor the right conceptive substitute for it arise, at our bare word of command. (James [1890] 1981, 1236)

The final statement here clarifies that for James uncertainty will continue to reign in the practice of science. The uncertainty that I am referring to here is the probably everlasting uncertainty on whether the scientific theories that we have arrived at provide a perfectly 'congruent' translation of 'nature's materials'.[13] A safe assumption is that the ultimate truth in science will never be reached. Still, as I will address below in the section on 'Wonder and intimations of metaphysical transcendence in scientific practices' (pp. 46–52), what we take for scientific truths can evoke aesthetic judgements of beauty and tentatively intimate 'big' metaphysical transcendence (e.g. notions of God or the Transcendent), thus involving an emotion of wonder that leads into (big) metaphysics.

In his address 'The will to believe', given in 1896, James compares the difference between wonder at 'small' metaphysical transcendence and wonder at 'big' metaphysical transcendence, using as examples the practices of science and religion respectively. In science, James says, '[t]he most useful investigator, because the most sensitive observer, is always he whose eager interest in one side of the question [that is, reaching a judgement] is balanced by an equally keen nervousness lest he become deceived' (James [1897] 1979, 26). That wonder is triggered by the uncertainty of whether the scientific judgement reached will still stand as 'verified' in the future (James [1897] 1979, 27). In religious matters, when focusing on big metaphysical transcendence – exemplified with the statement that 'the best things are the more eternal things, the overlapping things, the things in the universe that throw the last stone, so to speak, and say the final word' (James [1897] 1979, 29) – wonder is associated with a will to believe and a right to believe a 'live hypothesis which may be true' (James [1897] 1979, 31). In the latter case, instead of wondering about whether and how to verify a scientific hypothesis, wonder pertains to the question: is the live religious hypothesis that one holds 'prophetic and right' (James [1897] 1979, 31)?

In terms of explicating a (small) metaphysics, James is at his boldest in his 1904 articles in the *Journal of Philosophy, Psychology, and Scientific Methods*. In 'Does "consciousness" exist?', he reflects on the 'bipolar relation' between 'thoughts' and 'things' as two different types of being ('two sorts of object') – correlated with the polarities between 'spirit' and 'matter' and between 'soul' and 'body' – and aims to amend what he assumes Kant had changed with respect to traditional metaphysics, that is, to bring in the 'transcendental ego' to undermine the soul and throw the bipolar relation 'off its balance' (James [1912] 1976, 3).[14] James proposes now to deny the transcendental notion of 'consciousness' the status of existence, and to find another metaphysical way to resolve the bipolarity of 'thought' and 'thing', both of which do exist. In his article, he therefore develops his notion of '"pure" experience':

> The instant field of the present is at all times what I call the 'pure' experience. It is only virtually or potentially either object or subject as yet. For the time being, it is plain, unqualified actuality, or existence, a simple *that*. In this *naïf* immediacy it is of course *valid*; it is *there*, we *act* upon it; and the doubling of it in retrospection into a state of mind and a reality intended thereby, is just one of the acts. (James [1912] 1976, 13)

In his subsequent article 'A world of pure experience', he adds about the substitution of one experience by another that

> [a]ccording to my view, experience as a whole is a process in time, whereby innumerable particular terms lapse and are superseded

> by others that follow upon them by transitions which, whether disjunctive or conjunctive in content, are themselves experiences, and must in general be accounted at least as real as the terms which they relate. (James [1912] 1976, 31)

This brings James to his notion of the 'more' and the associated transcendence (in the form of 'mini-transcendences', as I will argue below):[15]

> Whosoever feels his experience to be something substitutional even while he has it, may be said to have an experience that reaches beyond itself. From inside of its own entity it says 'more', and postulates reality existing elsewhere. For the transcendentalist, who holds knowing to consist in a *salto mortale* across an 'epistemological chasm', such an idea presents no difficulty; but it seems at first sight as if it might be inconsistent with an empiricism like our own. Have we not explained that conceptual knowledge is made such wholly by the existence of things that fall outside of the knowing experience itself – by intermediary experiences and by a terminus that fulfils? Can the knowledge be there before these elements that constitute its being have come? And, if knowledge be not there, how can objective reference occur?
>
> The key to this difficulty lies in the distinction between knowing as verified and completed, and the same knowing as in transit and on its way. (James [1912] 1976, 33–4)

Counter to the metaphysics that he attributes to transcendentalism, James puts his proposal for 'radical empiricism',[16] which features centrally the 'conjunctive transition [that is] the very original of what we mean by continuity, it makes a continuum wherever it appears' (James [1912] 1976, 34–5). The 'postulat[ing] of reality existing elsewhere' that James refers to here concerns the happening of 'meaningful acts' under uncertainty that bridge 'mini-transcendences'.[17] I argue that, on this account, where hesitation occurs and the uncertainties that are at play become fully reflected on, the emotion of wonder may arise. Applying James's metaphysics to the short-term dynamics of science, for instance, wonder may arise where 'knowing' is still 'in transit and on its way' and mini-transcendences need to be 'made' continuous. Such wonder about whether there is reference may disappear when a state of 'knowing as verified' is reached. Still, as said above, wonder at ready-made science through intimations of big transcendence, a 'metaphysical emotion', is also a definite philosophical possibility for James.

This concludes my initial engagement with James's radical empiricism.[18] In the next chapter I will address the important similarities with and differences from Rickert's transcendental empiricism. Here I first address a more directly connected approach, that of Bruno Latour, which through comparison with James's can be analysed more clearly.

Latour's approach to wonder and metaphysics

To introduce Bruno Latour's occasionalist empiricism, which he first most extensively shared with the public in his *An Inquiry into Modes of Existence: An anthropology of the Moderns* ([2012] 2013b) after 25 years of development, let me first quote the author-approved summary of this work on the book's dust jacket:

> In this new book, Bruno Latour offers answers to questions raised in *We Have Never Been Modern*, a work that interrogated the connections between nature and culture. If not modern, he asked, what *have* we been and what values should we inherit? Over the past twenty-five years, Latour has developed a research protocol different from the actor-network theory with which his name is now associated – a research protocol that follows the different types of connectors that provide specific truth conditions. These are the connectors that prompt a climate scientist challenged by a captain of industry to appeal to the *institution* of science, with its army of researchers and mountains of data, rather than to 'capital-s Science' as a higher authority. Such modes of extension – or modes of existence, Latour argues here – account for the many differences between law, science, politics, and other domains of knowledge.
>
> Though scientific knowledge corresponds to only one of the many possible modes of existence Latour describes, an unrealistic vision of science has become the arbiter of reality and truth, seducing us into judging all values by a single standard. Latour implores us to recover other modes of existence in order to do justice to the plurality of truth conditions that Moderns have discovered throughout their history. This systematic effort of building a new philosophical anthropology presents a completely different view of what Moderns have been, and provides a new basis for opening diplomatic encounters with other societies at a time when all societies are coping with ecological crisis.

As I will discuss in Chapter 4, Latour's metaphysics includes 14 real 'modes of existence' and one fake one.[19] Latour frames the development of his metaphysics as an 'inquiry', with a large role given to an imagined anthropological investigator who constantly wonders about how the different modes work, how to name the 'connectors' and their 'truth conditions', what the 'beings' are that they 'institute' and how this is all related to the way that actors deal with uncertainty in the multitude of practices – or within 'many worlds', to use James's expression – in which they are engaged. One might even call Latour's philosophy a 'philosophy of uncertainty and wonder'.[20] Latour's investigator also constantly wonders about the differences between modes of existence (and their 'crossings'). For instance, in the first chapter in his book, on 'Defining the object of inquiry', Latour has her 'wondering … if Science is a domain distinct from Politics or The Economy or Religion' (30). Later in the chapter he has religious actors wondering about the mode of religion:

> Here again we find a hiatus, an agonizing one during which a priest, a bishop, a reformer, a devout practitioner, a hermit, wonders whether the innovation he believes necessary is a faithful inspiration or an impious betrayal. (43)

And so it goes on.

In order to arrive at a characterisation of Latour's metaphysics, let us return to the opening scene of this chapter and specifically highlight Latour's description of one of the modes of existence, the mode of reference **[REF]**.[21] Both in *An Inquiry into Modes of Existence* and in *Facing Gaia*, Latour enlists his own vast body of work on the practices of science to emphasise and support what climate scientists are increasingly doing in response to the 'rationalist' strategy of climate deniers: to show that the practice of science essentially consists of maintaining 'constants through transformations' in order to 'reach remote entities',[22] and that the 'institution' of climate science involves 'large numbers of researchers', a 'complex system for verifying data' through 'articles and reports' and 'peer evaluation', a 'vast network of weather stations, floating weather buoys, satellites, and computers that ensure the flow of information' and 'models' (Latour [2012] 2013b, 3; see also Chapter 5 of the present book, 'Models').

Latour starts his treatment of the mode of reference in *An Inquiry into Modes of Existence* with a warning of how different his image of 'science' is to that of 'Science':

> If debates over the definition of the rational and the irrational are so vigorous, if the prospect of negotiating the form of institutions finally cut out for the work of reason seems so remote, it is because of a major problem in the anthropology of the Moderns: the enigma posed for them by the irruption of the sciences, starting in the seventeenth century and continuing today. This enigma has been made insoluble by the immense abyss that developed, in the course of the Moderns' history, between the theory of Science and the practice of the sciences, an abyss further deepened with the emergence of ecology, which obliges us to take into account what is called the 'known and inhabited world' in an entirely new way. (Latour [2012] 2013b, 70)

After identifying the central role for 'chains of reference' in the practices of science, he enters into metaphysics:

> The lines traced by these chains will now allow us to unsettle the ordinary notion of correspondence. In fact, what are usually called the 'knowing mind' and the 'known object' are not the two extremes to which the chain would be attached; rather, they are *both* products arising from the lengthening and strengthening of the chain. A knowing mind and a known thing are not at all what would be linked through a mysterious viaduct by the activity of knowledge; they are the progressive result of the extension of chains of reference. (Latour [2012] 2013b, 80)

We here can see that there is a remarkable similarity with James's depiction of his doctrine of 'pure experience'.[23] One can indeed view James's doctrine of pure experience as a precursor of Latour's mode of reference, where real subjects and objects arise from 'the instant field of the present' which 'is at all times ... the "pure" experience' (James [1912] 1976, 3). In addition, James's description of the dynamics of science, in the last chapter of his *Principles*, shows important similarities with Latour's approach (though it does not so much focus on all the actants that act in the laboratory and that form a crucial and highly original ingredient in Latour's work).[24]

The uncertainty associated with the mode of reference is connected with fundamental limitations in knowledge obtained through 'trajectories' of chains of reference, which Latour describes as follows:

> [T]here is a limitation that follows this knowledge wherever it extends, albeit one that is in a sense *internal* to its expansion.

Once again, the trace of its trajectories provides a much better identification of this internal frontier: however far they go, however well equipped they are, however fine the mesh, however complete their 'coverage', however competent their operators, chains of reference can never be *substituted* in any way for what they know. Not at all because the known 'eludes' knowledge in principle and resides in a world 'of its own', forever inaccessible, but quite simply because existents *themselves are also going* somewhere, but *elsewhere*, at a *different pace*, with a different *rhythm* and an entirely different *demeanor*. Things are not 'things in themselves', they belong 'to themselves' – a different matter altogether. Still, none of this deprives knowledge of access. On the contrary, it accedes marvellously well to whatever network, whatever reason, it has to grasp. There is thus, properly speaking, no *beyond* of knowledge: either knowledge is truly beyond us – along a trajectory *different* from that of chains of reference – and then we are not dealing with equipped and rectified knowledge – or else there is access – by a new method, a new instrument, a new calculus – and we remain in fact *within* the limits of knowledge, not at all beyond. (Latour [2012] 2013b, 84)

'Chains of reference can never be substituted for what they know': here is where we encounter Latour's notion of 'transcendence' (or 'mini-transcendence'). Each mode of existence has a 'particular form of hiatus, of discontinuity, of transcendence' associated with it (Latour [2012] 2013b, 266). On the website that accompanies his book, modesofexistence.org, Latour has provided notes on several technical terms that he uses in the book, such as 'hiatus' and 'transcendence'.[25] About 'hiatus', Latour writes in his online explanation:

All continuations of a course of action suppose a discontinuity that must be overcome in order to define a trajectory. It is this discontinuity, and the fact of getting over it, that we call a hiatus, or gap, threshold or break – the actual term is unimportant. This term belongs to the metalanguage of the investigation and allows for a definition of the mini-transcendence required for any definition of the being-as-other.

And he explains 'transcendence' as follows:

The inquiry needs to distinguish between two types of transcendence: the first, called 'bad' transcendence, seeks a foundation in a substance by breaking with courses of action and trajectories; the second, called 'good' or, better, 'small' transcendence, seeks to focus attention on the hiatus, the discontinuity, the step, the threshold by which all existents must pass in order to subsist. This latter is strictly synonymous with immanence. The paradox is only apparent since the very notion of immanence is shared between a justified polemical meaning (contrary to bad transcendence) and a meaning which corresponds exactly to what we refer to here as trajectory, hiatus and, therefore, good transcendence.

James, in his doctrine of pure experience, and Latour, in his doctrine of modes of existence, have both opted for a metaphysics of small transcendence, which I argue is characteristic of radical empiricism. A major difference between the two philosophers is the number of modes that they include in their philosophies, reflected in different 'levels' of plurality that they include in their respective metaphysics. For Latour there are 14 real modes while James, in outlining his doctrine of 'pure experience', tackled only one – similar in many respects to Latour's 'mode of reference'. This is not to say, however, that James could not have been sympathetic to the approach taken by Latour.[26]

What is crucial about all the 14 modes of existence described by Latour is that '[c]lassifying the modes allows us to articulate well what we have to say' (Latour [2012] 2013b, 376). Speaking well within scientific practices does not imply that one can also speak well in religious practices; these two different types of practices are driven by different values, leading to different truth conditions or ways to evaluate whether one is speaking well (different in all cases from a rationalist notion of speaking 'literally'):

> If you claimed to be speaking 'literally', to what mode would you be alluding? To reference **[REF]**? But if researchers finally end up going straight, they all know only too well that they proceed by impressive leaps over obstacles. When an engineer is finally effective, it is through the dizzying zigzags of technology **[TEC]**. If politicians **[POL]** speak frankly and directly, it is by following twisted paths. And if you settled for 'speaking figuratively', to what mode would you be alluding? To that of the beings of fiction **[FIC]**? But it seems that their demand to be 'held', their demand for 'style' and 'tension', put you under a much greater obligation than one might think in hearing you laud the advantages of metaphor. As if it were enough to 'express oneself freely' to produce a work

> of art! And those who speak about the beings sensitive to the one who enunciates them in order to bring them into presence **[REL]** – must we say that they speak 'in figures and parables' – yes, undoubtedly – or that they speak as literally as can be about what is, what was, and what is coming – which is true as well? Isn't God himself said to 'write straight with crooked lines'? And how are we to qualify the formidable drift of lines of force and lineages **[REP]**? Will you say of life itself that it goes on 'literally' or 'figuratively'? It would be good to know, for everyone who visits aquariums and zoos and museums of natural history wonders about this. As for the beings of influence and possession **[MET]**, who has ever managed to address them by approaching them head on? (Latour [2012] 2013b, 377)

Taking seriously the different modes of existence identified by Latour allows one to 'remain open to the dizzying otherness of existents' (see the introductory section of this chapter, p. 25). Note here that Latour also reflects at a meta-level upon his own philosophical wonder about whether he has captured things correctly:

> When he wakes up in the morning, at the end of his labors, the author, uneasy, wonders whether what he has just put together from bits and pieces, gathered over many years without ever being shown to the public, looks like a gingerbread house, or a painting by Le Douanier Rousseau: a hodgepodge of curiosities that says a lot about the odd tastes of the autodidact who collected them, but very little about the world he claims to be describing. Try as he might to reassure himself by telling himself that the questionnaire that is the basis for the study has 'held up' for a quarter of a century, that he has never 'let go' of it along the way, that he has always drawn from it clarifying effects that have often enchanted him, he knows how fragile this testimony is and how many ruses the Sphinx is capable of deploying to deceive the one it places before the enigma of the 'work of art to be done'. (Latour [2012] 2013b, 476)

My response to Latour's wonder is that the metaphysical assumptions embedded in his way of thinking require critical reflection from the perspective of transcendental philosophy. This is what I will undertake in the next three chapters.

Wonder and intimations of metaphysical transcendence in scientific practices

In this section I will consider wonder and intimations of metaphysical transcendence in scientific practices. For that purpose, in line with the philosophers already discussed, I analyse science as a practice instead of a set of disembodied beliefs. As I indicated above, Latour was far from being the first scholar to criticise the suggestion that one could 'speak literally' in science. Take historian of science Thomas Kuhn, for instance, who in his seminal 1962 book *The Structure of Scientific Revolutions* radically criticised the philosophical views of science in his day. Philosopher of science Joseph Rouse (1987, 30–40) has shown how radical Kuhn's approach was by providing an interpretation of that book which emphasises scientific practices at the expense of scientific beliefs. For instance: 'Paradigms are not primarily agreed-upon theoretical commitments but exemplary ways of conceptualizing and intervening in particular empirical contexts' (Rouse 1987, 30). He notes how Kuhn had replaced representing and observing with 'constructing, tinkering, and noticing as exemplars of scientific practice' (Rouse 1987, 40).

Scientific practice is beset with uncertainty:

> All paradigms confront obstacles (anomalies) at all times. … The recognition of anomalies is … an awareness that something significant is not understood or not being dealt with adequately, but it is not yet a clear awareness of what the problem is. … How scientists respond to such ambiguous difficulties often depends upon whether the problems they present seem localizable. (Rouse 1987, 32–3)

In the cases where a crisis ensues because the anomalies do not get resolved, the intelligibility and reliability of many research practices and achievements are placed in doubt:

> [I]t is not that scientists do not know what to believe; scientists are professionally accustomed to uncertainty of *that* sort. It is that they are no longer quite sure how to proceed. What investigations are worth undertaking, which supposed facts are unreliable artifacts, what concepts or models are useful guides for their theoretical or experimental manipulations? (Rouse 1987, 33–4)

There are even direct parallels that can be drawn to religious conversion: 'Changing from one paradigm to another is not like a conversion to new beliefs, but is like a conversion to a new form of life' (Rouse 1987, 34). As Rouse relates, science is a thoroughly communal activity:

> [T]here are no generally applicable standards of rational acceptability in science. There is only a roughly shared understanding of what can be assumed, what can (or must) be argued for, and what is unacceptable for any given purpose and context. Both purposes and contexts are quite varied and undergo significant transformations over time. They reflect the judgments of a community concerning what is credible and reliable in the context of their ongoing work. (Rouse 1987, 124)

Furthermore, when there is no crisis scientists proceed not on the basis of what they believe, but on the basis of how they do things.

Now emotion is central in all significant human activities (as I described in the above following James's *The Principles of Psychology*), and I would argue that this is also the case in the core activities of the practice of science. However, particularly in science there is a suspicion of emotion, even though this has not always been the case. Jack Barbalet (2004, 248–9) and others have shown that in the early days of the scientific revolution passion played a central role in the performance of science. Scientists were explicit that they were overcome by emotional turmoil caused by the puzzlement they experienced, arising from their extraordinary curiosity. In their writing they narrated their surprises and related when they were at a loss in explaining particular phenomena. According to Lorraine Daston and Katherine Park:

> [m]using admiration, startled wonder, then bustling curiosity – these were the successive moments of seventeenth-century clichés describing how the passions impelled and guided natural philosophical investigations. (Daston and Park 2001, 303)

The emotions of uncertainty and anxious curiosity can only be cured by scientific engagement and finding explanations, which can in turn result in joy.

From the late eighteenth century, Francis Bacon's early seventeenth-century counter-position – that for science to proceed all emotions must be expelled, and from all scientific activities, not only from the communication of science – became dominant. However, from his analysis of scientific practice, Michael Polanyi has concluded that '[s]cientific passions are no mere psychological by-product, but have a logical function which contributes an indispensable element to science' (Polanyi [1958] 1998, 134). Positive passions affirm that something is precious. According to Polanyi:

> [t]he excitement of the scientist making a discovery is an *intellectual* passion, telling that something is *intellectually* precious and, more particularly, that it is *precious to science*. (Polanyi [1958] 1998, 134)

Emotion thus serves 'as a guide in the assessment of what is of higher and what of lesser interest; what is great in science, and what relatively slight' (Polanyi [1958] 1998, 135). Such appreciation 'depends ultimately on a sense of intellectual beauty' (Polanyi [1958] 1998, 135). So indeed emotion plays a central role in scientific practice.

When a correspondence is attained between the values of the scientific thought collective and the particular conditions encountered in research, this 'evokes the emotions of joy, delight and pleasure' (Barbalet 2004, 269). Making reference to the work of Joseph De Rivera, Jack Barbalet concludes that this joy 'is precipitated as a feeling of self-actualisation and of the meaningfulness of one's activities, indeed being', and that '[i]n this regard, joy and wonder are parallel emotions' (Barbalet 2004, 269). Thus the emotion of wonder in science, which may result in the emotion of joy, is a 'metaphysical emotion' in the sense of James's social theory of emotion (see above) and can lead to intimations of metaphysical transcendence.

The cognitive referent of metaphysical emotion – the appreciation of beauty, for instance – can thus reside in matching scientific values. In physics, an example of such values could be the following:

> Scientific values consist in the continual and increasing recognition of the uniformity of nature (Chandrasekhar 1987, 4)

This statement appeared in a 1946 lecture on 'The scientist' by S. Chandrasekhar. With respect to the motivation of scientists, in the same lecture he 'reject[s] the view that the motivation springs from a conscious or subconscious belief that everything he does will eventually find use in the amenities of daily life' (Chandrasekhar 1987, 12–13). Yet he 'also do[es] not accept the view that scientists are urged on in their work by a "holy passion" for truth or a "burning curiosity" to unravel the "secrets" of nature' (Chandrasekhar 1987, 13). In Chandrasekhar's view, scientists are attracted to elegance in theorising. He adds:

> What actually does give substance and reality to the efforts of a scientist is his desire to participate actively in the progress of his science to the best of his ability. And if I have to describe in one word what is the prime motive which underlies a scientist's work, I would say *systematization*. (Chandrasekhar 1987, 13)

Only 'people who are acquainted with the subject have no difficulty in recognizing or appreciating' the scientist's contribution, even as beauty in art cannot be defined (Chandrasekhar 1987, 13).

Nearly 40 years later, in a 1985 lecture titled 'The pursuit of science: Its motivation', Chandrasekhar has come to the conclusion that:

> the motives of the individual scientists ... are as varied as the tastes, the temperaments, and the attitudes of the scientists themselves. Besides, their motivations are subject to substantial changes during the lifetimes of the scientists; indeed, it is difficult to discern a common denominator. (Chandrasekhar 1987, 15)

He then asks the following questions:

> [A]fter a scientist has reached maturity, what are the reasons for his continued pursuit of science? To what extent are they personal? To what extent are aesthetic criteria, like the perception of order and pattern, form and substance, relevant? Are such aesthetic and personal criteria exclusive? Has a sense of obligation a role? I do not mean obligation with the common meaning of obligation to one's students, one's colleagues, and one's community. I mean, rather, obligation to science itself. And what, indeed, is the content of obligation in the pursuit of science *for* science? (Chandrasekhar 1987, 26)

These are deep questions. For some scientists, the answers may be related to intimations of (big) metaphysical transcendence.

For being able to intimate metaphysical transcendence, it is not necessary to hit on what will be accepted as true by the scientific community. Chandrasekhar (1987, 21–3) illustrates this with two episodes from Werner Heisenberg's career. After the laws of quantum mechanics had come to a sharp focus in his mind, Heisenberg relates:

> I was far too excited to sleep and so, as a new day dawned, I made for the southern tip of the island, where I had been longing to

climb a rock jutting out into the sea. I now did so without too much trouble and waited for the sun to rise. (Heisenberg 1971, 61)

Some 30 years later his ideas on particle physics were rejected, but Heisenberg had experienced similar excited emotions at the time when he formulated these ideas, which he explicitly connected with metaphysical transcendence:

> That these interrelationships display, in all their mathematical abstraction, an incredible degree of simplicity is a gift we can only accept humbly. Not even Plato could have believed them to be so beautiful. For these interrelationships cannot be invented; they have been there since the creation of the world. (Quoted in Heisenberg 1984, 144)

And Elisabeth Heisenberg, Heisenberg's wife, relates:

> With smiling certainty, he once said to me: 'I was lucky enough to look over the good Lord's shoulder while He was at work'. That was enough for him, more than enough! It gave him great joy, and the strength to meet the hostilities and misunderstandings he was subjected to in the world time and again with equanimity, and not to be led astray. (Heisenberg 1984, 157)

Note that my interest here lies with the emotion of wonder in science and the sort of philosophical or indeed metaphysical claims that are made in connection with this emotion. I am less interested here in assessing whether such claims are later evaluated as being 'true'.

Many examples – and counter-examples – can be given of intimations of metaphysical transcendence in relation to design in nature. It will be difficult to find a pattern, however. As James has already written in his book *Pragmatism* about this argument: '[God's] designs have grown so vast as to be incomprehensible to us humans' (James [1907] 1975, 57–8). We do not really know what we mean when we talk about design. However, talk about design in nature *can* intimate metaphysical transcendence:

> 'Design', worthless tho' it be as a mere rationalistic principle set above or behind things for our admiration, becomes, if our faith concretes it into something theistic, a term of *promise*. (James [1907] 1975, 59)

This shows that James could support a position of 'design without fixity', which takes seriously the emergence of complex designs from natural processes, rejects both crude naturalism and an absolute designer-God with a fixed plan and supports faith in a more open and uncertain role in creation for a loving God who is not all-powerful and all-knowing in the traditional philosophical senses (see the following section and also Chapter 8).

Stephen Jay Gould ([1990] 2000), in his history of paleontological discovery and interpretation in the Burgess Shale, describes 'wonder' as having two aspects: '[wonder] at the beauty of the organisms themselves, and at the new view of life that they have inspired' (Gould [1990] 2000, 14). In the community of paleontologists, Gould finds a 'joint love for knowledge about the history of our wonderful life' (Gould [1990] 2000, 19). However, he is not overwhelmed by a notion of design:

> Wind back the tape of life to the early days of the Burgess Shale; let it play again from an identical starting point, and the chance becomes vanishingly small that anything like human intelligence would grace the replay. (Gould [1990] 2000, 13–14)

In contrast with Gould, in the context of physics and astronomy a couple of centuries earlier, Isaac Newton wrote in his *Principia*:

> This most elegant system of the sun, planets, and comets could not have arisen without the design and dominion of an intelligent and powerful being. … He rules all things, not as the world soul but as the lord of all. (Newton [1713] 1999, 940)

Here we have hit on the theism that was so strongly opposed by James.

Concerning the issue of theism and design, let us take a brief look at a contemporary philosopher, Alvin Plantinga, who asks whether science offers positive support for theistic (Christian) belief (Plantinga 2011, 193–264). Plantinga first notes the striking fact that several of the basic physical constants must fall within very narrow limits for intelligent life to develop. Depending on one's beliefs, the coincidences can evoke different emotions (or: depending on one's emotions, this can evoke different beliefs). One possible reaction – and this is Plantinga's view – is 'to see them as substantiating the theistic claim that the universe has been created by a personal God and as offering the material for a properly restrained theistic argument' (Plantinga 2011, 197). He proceeds to explore biological arguments that can evoke the belief in design.

With respect to 'intelligent design', Plantinga's impression is that the arguments for it are reasonably powerful. Nevertheless he concludes that

> it is unclear that the difference in probability [for the presence of protein machines based on assuming either unguided or guided evolution] is sufficient to constitute serious support for the existence of an intelligent designer. (Plantinga 2011, 236)

While probabilistic reasoning may not be able on its own to support guided evolution, Plantinga holds that there are other warrants for that theistic belief.

The wonder generated by the realisation of uncertainty *vis-à-vis* nature can be a genuine experience that intimates (big) metaphysical transcendence and that has real meaning for people – it can mean the world to them and affect their behaviour (and thus have practical implications). I will argue in Chapter 4 that Latour in his metaphysics cannot meaningfully reflect on this type of wonder. In my transcendental naturalistic approach built on Rickert's philosophy, I will show that Latour's modes of experience lack a mode of mystics; they also, more generally, lack room for reflection on contemplation rather than activity.

Wonder and intimations of metaphysical transcendence in religious practices

The emotion of wonder and the metaphysics of experience are also associated with intimations of the sacred in religious practices. Again, also for the practices of religion, Latour was not the first scholar to emphasise that religion is not about 'speaking literally',[27] but it must be flagged again that he does not address a mode of mystics. To discuss the phenomenon of wonder and intimations of (big) metaphysical transcendence in religious practices, let me first give an example from the Judaeo-Christian tradition of the recitation or singing of Psalms. I here pick in particular a Psalm that explicitly stresses wonder (Psalm 139). The first verses read as follows:

> O Lord, thou hast searched me out and known me : thou knowest my down-sitting and mine up-rising, thou understandest my thoughts long before.

> Thou art about my path, and about my bed : and spiest out all my ways.
>
> For lo, there is not a word in my tongue : but thou, O Lord, knowest it altogether.
>
> Thou hast fashioned me behind and before : and laid thine hand upon me.
>
> Such knowledge is too wonderful and excellent for me : I cannot attain unto it.
>
> (Psalm 139:1–5, Coverdale's translation, Book of Common Prayer)

When such a Psalm is part of a liturgical ritual, such as evensong or any other form of worship or prayer, the narrative (in older Bible translations, such as the one used above, or in newer Bible translations) can evoke the emotion of wonder in the worshipper. This it can obviously also do – but often to a lesser extent – in the private reader. Liturgical ritual can lead people to 'creep into God':

> '[C]reeping into God' is [for most people] something we must learn. It involves a momentary withdrawal from the natural world so as to project our thoughts beyond it. That is why special phrases, liturgies and hallowed language are necessary: they are the guarantee that we are addressing … [an] Other, and not just talking somewhat pompously to ourselves. (Scruton 2012, 8–9)

For different people in different cultures and religions there are different ways for the 'numinous' (Otto [1917] 1923) – the non-rational (not irrational) dimension of the 'holy' Other – to be experienced. Celia Deane-Drummond (2006) gives the example of the importance of silence in liturgy (e.g. in the Eucharist), since 'silence acts like a matrix within which the Word is embedded and through which a theology of wonder arises' (Deane-Drummond 2006, 140). The emotion of wonder may be triggered by becoming aware of the breaking in of the reign of God.

Many more examples may be given, including those from other than Christian religions. However, the matter that concerns me here is to illustrate that the relationships between emotions, the metaphysics of experience and intimations of the sacred in religion cannot fully be reflected on from the specific modes of existence that Latour identified in his metaphysics. A deeper philosophical reflection will be needed – one that I claim is not itself metaphysics and that can be based on transcendental naturalism, as I will demonstrate in the next few chapters.

Returning now to James, it is important to note that according to him there is no general religious emotion:

> There is religious fear, religious love, religious awe, religious joy, and so forth. But religious love is only man's natural emotion of love directed to a religious object; religious fear is only the ordinary fear of commerce, so to speak, the common quaking of the human breast, in so far as the notion of divine retribution may arouse it; religious awe is the same organic thrill which we feel in a forest at twilight, or in a mountain gorge; only this time it comes over us at the thought of our supernatural relations; and similarly of all the various sentiments which may be called into play in the lives of religious persons. (James [1902] 1985, 31)

As was argued by Carrette (see above), religious emotion has an organic basis, a cognitive structure and a social dimension, 'insofar as the religious object is shaped in the religious context' (Carrette 2008, 429).

The social dimension is crucial for religious emotion and corresponding metaphysical experiences and intimations of the sacred. Therefore religion cannot be confined to the subjective and private domain of personal experience. While many writers in the tradition of pragmatist philosophy (e.g. Rorty 1997, 85) have interpreted James as having 'privatised' religion, and as thus having resolved the tension between science and religion as one between 'co-operative endeavors' and 'private projects', others (e.g. Lamberth 1999; Miedema 2002; Carrette 2008) would disagree. James's self-assessed 'crasser' or 'piecemeal' (as opposed to universalistic) supernaturalism (James [1902] 1985, 410) includes an inalienable social dimension. And even though James seems to give primacy to personal religious experience over the institutional side of religion, I would argue that religious institutions (such as liturgical ritual) can be regarded as 'human systems evolving in consequence of human needs' (James [1907] 1975, 78).

Note that by believing too much in *models* of God we inevitably get further removed from experience and substantiation in experience becomes virtually impossible. This also holds for James's model of God. Where James criticises the theistic conception of God on the basis that it does not connect with religious experiences, he portrays God as 'intimate soul and reason of the universe' (James [1909a] 1977, 18), 'the indwelling divine' (James [1909a] 1977, 19) and as 'finite, either in power or knowledge, or in both at once' (James [1909a] 1977, 141). So, in James's model of God, God is not all-powerful and all-knowing, but still this God – whom we can intimate, who is Other, but who is continuous with us – can show us 'a world in which all is well, *in spite* of certain forms of death, indeed *because* of certain forms of death' (James [1909a] 1977, 138). Individuals can intimate metaphysical transcendence through judgement,[28] which can only problematically be collectively shared in terms of models, for which it remains uncertain how well they can capture the underlying reality. I will more fully address this issue in Chapter 5, on 'models'.

The sense of wonder – both in religion and science – should not be considered as merely a cognitive affair, but as one involving the whole person engaged with a community. This sense of wonder is a precious gift that can be learned – and should preferably not be unlearned – through education, the primary aim of which, following Miedema, is 'directed to the development of the whole person, that is, that all domains of human potentiality and ability – be they cognitive, creative, moral, religious, expressive, or the like – should be taken into account' (Miedema 2002, 87).

Conclusion

This brings us back to Sideris's claim mentioned in the introduction to this chapter: that 'wonder as puzzlement' has become solely a response to 'knowledge obtained' rather than to 'the puzzling, awesome, or mysterious phenomenon itself'. I have stressed the link between the two notions of wonder that she distinguishes. Through philosophically recognising the limitations of reason and the roles of emotion and the sense of wonder in driving scientific and religious practices, the meaning of 'uncertainty' can be assessed in a positive register (where even when one thinks that one has solved an important piece of the puzzle, this can go along with feeling a sense of mystery and associating remaining uncertainty with the super-rational). Analogous to religious practices, the emotion of wonder and the metaphysics of experience can play an important role in science.

Aside from these questions of 'big transcendence' and the associated wonder, the main result of this chapter, with the introduction of James's and Latour's philosophical approaches to radical empiricism, has been to highlight how their philosophies of 'small' transcendence show how uncertainty and wonder are intrinsic features of any cultural practice. Still I maintain that both their philosophies face difficulty with reflexively including within their radical empiricisms any intimations of metaphysical 'big' transcendence in both scientific and religious practices.

The transcendental naturalism that will be developed in the next few chapters will be more open to that possibility, even though particular metaphysical beliefs cannot be demonstrated philosophically. When we compare religious and non-religious wonder, we must admit, however, that while some religious persons can read in both scientific and religious practices possibilities to co-create the world in partnership with God (and being certain of there being meaning in God as creator),[29] other people may be left with a less specified intimation of metaphysical transcendence (one that does not imply the existence of a creator-God). In my exploration of transcendental naturalism in this book, I consider it an asset to be able to keep open the possibilities of theism, agnosticism and atheism (thus not to make any of these specific metaphysical choices in advance).

In the following three chapters, I further lay out the philosophical framework for this book by taking a closer look at judgement, values and models respectively. In this chapter, the emotion of wonder was seen to be associated with uncertain judgements, with James offering relevant insights into the embodiment and aesthetics of judgement. The next chapter will fully concentrate philosophically on what is involved in judgement, and will propose a correction to both James's and Latour's radical empiricism with respect to judgement.

Notes

1 Note that below, following Latour ([2012] 2013b), a distinction will be introduced between 'big transcendence' (only captured with a negative connotation by Latour as 'bad transcendence' which assumes 'substance') and 'mini-transcendences' ('good transcendence' which assumes 'subsistence'). In the transcendental naturalistic position that I am defending in this book as a methodological position in the science-and-religion debate, I am not following Latour in labelling one type of metaphysics, that associated with 'big transcendence', as 'bad' and another type, that associated with 'small transcendence', as 'good'. I rather claim that both types of metaphysical position can be taken on faith (or not), but cannot be philosophically argued for (or against).

2 I here follow Harman's (2016) labelling of Latour's metaphysics as 'occasionalism'.

3 I take the phrase 'metaphysics of experience' (which was not used by James) from Lamberth (1999).

4 This is established by David Lamberth in his 1999 book. Lamberth also offers an enriched interpretation of James's most famous work, *The Varieties of Religious Experience*, which was published in 1902 (based on his Gifford Lectures to the University of Edinburgh in 1901–2). He furthermore shows how James's book *Pragmatism*, published in 1907 (based on his Lowell Lectures to the Lowell Institute, Boston in 1906), contains important clues on his metaphysics.

5 Three essays in *The Will to Believe* are dealt with in more detail in Part II of this book.

6 It must be said that James is thoroughly aware of the difficulties of interpreting Kant. Also, on interpreting the transcendental ego as an actual agent, he notes that 'there is reason to think that at bottom he [Kant] may have had nothing of the sort in mind' (James [1890] 1981, 345). After making that observation, James concludes uncontroversially that *if* an agent interpretation of Kant's transcendental ego were correct, *then* one could qualify Kant's theory as bad, non-empirical psychology.

7 James writes that others, such as Brentano, used the label 'judgment' for what he himself prefers to call 'belief' (James [1890] 1981, 916).

8 Horatio, in Act V, Scene 1 of the play, says: ''Twere to consider too curiously, to consider so.'

9 The first five verses of this Psalm feature at the end of this chapter.

10 James explicitly indicates that he is siding with transcendental or 'apriorist' philosophy, see, e.g. in his following remarks: 'On the whole, then, the account which apriorists give of the *facts* is that which I defend' (James [1890] 1981, 1216); 'The word experience has a halo of anti-super-naturalism about it; so that if anyone express dissatisfaction with any function claimed for it, he is liable to be treated as if he could only be animated by loyalty to the catechism, or in some way have the interests of obscurantism at heart. I am entirely certain that, on this ground alone, what I have erelong to say will make this a sealed chapter to many of my readers' (James [1890] 1981, 1222–3); 'There is thus no denying the fact that the mind is filled with necessary and eternal relations which it finds between certain of its ideal conceptions, and which form a determinate system, independent of the order of frequency in which experience may have associated the conception's originals in time and space. … Shall we continue to call these sciences [of classification, logic, and mathematics] "intuitive," "innate," or "*a priori*" bodies of truth, or not? Personally I should like to do so. But I hesitate to use the terms, on account of the odium which controversial history has made the whole of their connotation for many worthy persons' (James [1890] 1981, 1255); 'The popular notion that "Science" is forced on the mind *ab extra*, and that our interests have nothing to do with its constructions, is utterly absurd. The craving to believe that the things of the world belong to kinds which are related by inward rationality together is the parent of Science as well as of sentimental philosophy; and the original investigator always preserves a healthy sense of how plastic the materials are in his hands' (James [1890] 1981, 1260); 'Where harmonies are asserted of the real world, they are obviously mere postulates of rationality, so far as they transcend experience. Such postulates are exemplified by the ethical propositions that the individual and universal good are one, and that happiness and goodness are bound to coalesce in the same subject' (James [1890] 1981, 1268); 'There is … a large body of *a priori* or intuitively necessary truths. As a rule, these are truths of *comparison* only, and in the first instance they express relations between merely mental terms. Nature, however, acts as if some of her realities were identical with these mental terms. So far as she does this, we can make *a priori* propositions concerning natural fact. The aim of both science and philosophy is to make the identifiable terms more numerous. So far it has proved easier to identify nature's things with mental terms of the mechanical than with mental terms of the sentimental order' (James [1890] 1981, 1269); 'The widest postulate of rationality is that the world is rationally intelligible throughout, after the pattern of *some* ideal system' (James [1890] 1981, 1269).

11 He could also have added the Rickertian notion of theoretical truth in a truth–falsehood value-pair. As we will see in this book, James did not deny such a notion of theoretical truth; however, he did not see much philosophical value in expanding on it.

12 James also indicates that the genesis of 'every scientific conception', the short-term dynamics of scientific practice, cannot be reduced to experience.

13 Or, as Latour would describe this translation: as leading to true 'reference', see below.

14 As I showed above, Rickert is critical of interpreting Kant's transcendental ego metaphysically, which I will return to in the next chapter.

15 As flagged in the above, I take the term 'mini-transcendence' from Latour ([2012] 2013b); I will investigate it further below.

16 James introduces the doctrine of 'pure experience' as part of what he calls 'radical empiricism' in his article 'A world of pure experience'. In the 'Preface' to his later book *The Meaning of Truth*, he explains what he understands by 'radical empiricism', consisting of, first, a postulate, next, a statement of fact, and, finally, a generalised conclusion: 'The postulate is that the only things that shall be debatable among philosophers shall be things definable in terms drawn from experience. … The statement of fact is that the relations between things, conjunctive as well as disjunctive, are just as much matters of direct particular experience, neither more so nor less so, than the things themselves. … The generalized conclusion is that therefore the parts of experience hold together from next to next by relations that are themselves parts of experience. The directly apprehended universe needs, in short, no extraneous trans-empirical connective support, but possesses in its own right concatenated or continuous structure' (James [1909b] 1975, 6–7).

17 I take the term 'meaningful act' (*Aktsinn*) from Rickert (1921) and will investigate it further in the next chapter.

18 Elsewhere (Petersen 2014a), I have endeavoured to connect James to phenomenological thought, which from Heidegger onwards shows remarkable similarities to the phenomenological implications of James's metaphysics, in particular when one focuses on uncertainty. James distinguishes two components of knowing: immediate knowing and conceptual knowing. Immediate knowing (direct acquaintance) lacks mediation by concepts and conceptual knowing (knowledge about) involves the substitution of conceptual paths of conjunction for perceptual ones. Any bit of pure experience contains an inexhaustible wealth of detail and knowing, according to James's pluralism, and has to leave open space for factual novelty. In Petersen (2014a), I have demonstrated that phenomenological thought is fit for the task to explore further this aspect of uncertainty.

19 The fake mode of existence is called 'Double Click' by Latour. He describes it as a rationalist epistemology that is afraid of the 'hiatuses' featured in his own occasionalist metaphysics, that tries to 'displac[e] without translation' and 'speaks literally'; an epistemology that wishes to 'maintain the same despite the other'; see Table 4.2.

20 And a 'philosophy of value', as I will argue in Chapter 4. The different modes of existence are related to different value domains, the unfolding of which in practices does not need to be interpreted metaphysically (see my description of 'transcendental naturalism'), as Latour does in his occasionalism.

21 As is visible from the first column in Table 4.2, Latour denotes the modes either by their full name, e.g. 'reference', or by a shorthand with the first three letters in small caps and bold face, e.g. **[REF]**. I will follow this practice in this book. A fuller treatment of other modes of existence than that of reference will have to wait until Chapter 4.

22 See Table 4.2.

23 As far as I have been able to discover, only one other commentator on Latour has made a similar observation (de Vries 2016, 167–9). Commentators usually emphasise a philosophical link between Latour and Alfred North Whitehead, with Isabelle Stengers often being mentioned as a mediator (e.g. Schmidgen [2011] 2015, 82; Harman 2016, 132). For instance, Graham Harman (2016) – who links Latour's modes of existence philosophy to 'occasionalism', which he defines as 'see[ing] the world as made up of *gaps* that need to be bridged, rather than taking it for granted that everything is already in contact with other things' (129) – explicitly mentions precursors such as Aristotle and Whitehead, but he does not mention James. Of course, Whitehead's process philosophy had been thoroughly influenced by James.

24 As we saw in the above, James describes the uncertainty involved with extending chains of reference as follows: while the 'genesis [of scientific conceptions] is strictly akin to that of the flashes of poetry and sallies of wit to which the instable brain-paths … give rise', these '"scientific" conceptions must prove their worth by being "verified"', with the ultimate truth condition being how 'congruent' the conceptions are with more direct experience of 'what comes before us', being 'a chaos of fragmentary impressions interrupting each other' (1231–3).

25 These terms are typeset differently in the book and the website was considered by Latour to be intrinsically linked to the book, which itself is also fully available online through open access.

26 However, it must be added here that James, after publishing his metaphysics of pure experience, moved towards an idealistic metaphysical position in his final years, in which he abandoned his doctrine of pure experience (see, e.g. Gale 1999).

27 In the above section on 'Latour's approach to wonder and metaphysics', we saw that he wrote: 'And those who speak about the beings sensitive to the one who enunciates them in order to bring them into presence **[REL]** – must we say that they speak "in figures and parables" – yes, undoubtedly – or that they speak as literally as can be about what is, what was, and what is coming – which is true as well? Isn't God himself said to "write straight with crooked lines"?' (Latour [2012] 2013b, 377).

28 'Judgement' is addressed in the next chapter.

29 Theologian Philip Hefner proposed the term 'created co-creator' (Hefner 1984). In a later article he summarised: 'Homo sapiens is God's created co-creator, whose purpose is the stretching/enabling of the systems of nature so that they can participate in God's purposes in the mode of freedom' (Hefner 1988, 263).

3
Judgement

Introduction

How is judgement arrived at? What should one assume philosophically that is involved? How does judgement relate to uncertainty? The issue of uncertainty affects not only the manner in which we actually make judgements (see Chapter 2) but also, more deeply, how we philosophically conceive the process of judgement. As we will see in this chapter, judgement has multiple philosophical meanings. Here the particular interest lies in a meaning that sits in between the actual realisation (the real psychophysical act of judgement) and the unreal contents of judgement: judgement as making a tentative, uncertain connection between the real and the unreal. Using transcendental philosophy, I will show how important the power of judgement is for creating (fallible) realisations of cultures and how the radical empiricism of both Latour and James comes with a metaphysical load that cannot be argued for philosophically.

In the previous chapter, James's metaphysical thesis of pure experience was presented, as well as Latour's similar line of thought in his work on the modes of existence. Their 'radical empiricist' positions on judgement are critically reflected on in the present chapter. I show how neo-Kantian Heinrich Rickert (1863–1936) philosophically identified a domain of being, the 'pro-physical', which on the surface seems to have a similar function as James's 'pure experience', or Latour's equivalent of that, but which does not come with the same metaphysical load.[1] Rickert urges philosophers to acknowledge that they cannot theoretically settle the question of whether, for instance, 'pure experience' is *really* the one primal entity that exists in the world from which the rest then follows.

After outlining Rickert's neo-Kantian transcendental approach to the analysis of judgement, which underpins the position of transcendental naturalism defended in this book, the role of aesthetics and emotion in judgement is expanded on in the context of interpretations of Kant's critique of the power of judgement by Rickert and more recent commentators.

I would argue that if one philosopher offers all the ingredients for thematising the topic of uncertainty in the context of a philosophy of what one can and cannot know, without using the term 'uncertainty', it was the German philosopher Immanuel Kant (1724–1804). While much attention has often been paid to how Kant sought to reach certainty in connection with the *a priori* principles that legitimate both theoretical and practical knowledge,[2] in this chapter I highlight how Rickert extended the Kantian project by analysing the fundamental openness to uncertainty in practices and emphasising the role of freedom in judgements that link perceptual being to *a priori* values. I pay particular attention to how subjects who are cognitively and emotionally engaged in cultural practices (such as those of science or religion) deal with tentative, uncertain knowledge. One key element here is not to confuse '*a priori*' with 'certain'. Instead we need to take *a priori* justification of knowledge in its intended sense, as justification that its *a priori* contribution does not rely on sense experience in making a judgement.[3]

In this chapter thus the humble side of Kant is emphasised, through a Rickertian lens. Note that the extensive references to Kant in this chapter are made mainly for explanatory and illustrative purposes. I agree with Rickert's plea in arguing for transcendental philosophy as a philosophy of value (to be developed more fully in the next chapter):

> Philosophy in the Kantian sense must ... strive in all its parts to expressly, fully and in an orderly manner bring to consciousness the values that give meaning to the various areas of life. This means that 'criticalism' (*Kritizismus*) is characterised in every respect, whether dealing with the subjective or the objective, as a philosophy of values. Of course, it can also be interpreted differently historically, and the correctness of the systematic thoughts outlined here does not in any way depend on the question of what is Kantian about it. It would be bad for a philosophy to require an appeal to 'authorities'. The reference to Kant is intended only for explanation, not justification. (Rickert 1921, 159)

I will therefore not enter into full-blown Kant exegesis in this chapter. Instead I will refer to a variety of existing Kant interpretations, as well as further developments of his philosophy, particularly those of Rickert.

While in Chapter 2 James was found to be reacting to 'Transcendentalist theory', under which label he grouped Kantian and neo-Kantian thought,[4] and criticised it for being bad psychology (if read as psychology), Rickert emphasised that transcendental philosophy building on Kant (and in many respects moving beyond Kant) actually aims at being very careful in its discussions of, for instance, science, ethics and religion not to overstep the bounds of reason that Kant elucidated in his Critiques.[5] The purpose of transcendental philosophy, as developed initially in Kant's Critiques,[6] is, to be clear, not the same as putting everything in doubt and denying specific propositions. Transcendental philosophy rather studies the conditions for the *possibility* of knowledge. One of the driving forces for Kant and his followers is their consideration that civilisation has a basis – and that philosophy should aim, as far as is possible, to find, one could say, the 'method' of civilisation, or, as Rickert and other neo-Kantians would say, of 'culture'.

Kant's approach to this task constituted an epochal break in philosophy. As theologian Karl Barth aptly describes it: 'The Enlightenment before Kant was the absolute and boundless self-affirmation of reason, which, as such an affirmation, was ultimately bound to be uncertain of itself' (Barth [1947] 2001, 258). The predicament of modern man now is that he has to deal with deep uncertainty, which will never go away:

> [T]he courage (*Mut*) demanded here from him is not meant to be arrogance (*Hochmut*), let alone faintheartedness (*Schwachmut*), but – lying midway between the two – humility (*Demut*), enabling man to subject himself to a searching criticism of his capacities which will show him the right course and which, precisely because it is searching and showing the right course, will clarify and confirm his ability to subject himself to, and, once he has done this, to be guided by the results of this self-criticism. (Barth [1947] 2001, 256)

So what does a Kantian proposal for a humble approach and self-criticism ultimately amount to?

Referring in particular here to Kant's third Critique, on the power of judgement, this power of judgement (*Urteilskraft*) turns out to be a crucial element in the faculty for thinking (*Denkungsvermögen*). I claim that a humble approach to transcendental philosophy fully hinges on it. The scope of Kant's proposed 'power of judgement' encompasses all domains of knowledge: 'all our judgments, in accordance with the order of the higher cognitive faculties, can be divided into *theoretical*, *aesthetic*, and *practical*' (*Power of Judgment*, 20, 226).[7] Theoretical knowledge (also abbreviated by Kant simply to 'cognition', *Erkenntnis*) is coupled by Kant to the faculty of understanding (*Verstand*); it pertains to knowing what is true about objects (*Gegenstände*) in nature (broadly understood, that is, including human nature). Practical knowledge (of morals) depends on the faculty of reason (*Vernuft*) and correlates with a desire (*Begehrung*) to do what is good. Last but not least, aesthetic knowledge (for instance, judgements of taste, but also reflecting judgements more generally) results from the power of judgement; it is connected with the feelings of both pleasure and displeasure (*Gefühl der Lust und Unlust*).

What Kant had argued is that (theoretical) knowledge about nature is not (practical) knowledge of ideas and vice versa, even though both domains of knowledge are indissolubly interconnected – the power of judgement provides the linking pin between those two domains, as he elaborates in the introduction to the *Critique of the Power of Judgment*: 'the power of judgment makes possible the transition from the domain of the concept of nature to that of the concept of freedom' (*Power of Judgment*, 5, 196). As I will show in this chapter, the power of judgement has an even more fundamental function than that: it is what makes it possible to reach judgement under uncertainty in any sphere of value, for example in science and in religion.

In this chapter, Rickert's approach to judgement will be explored first, after which we will delve more deeply into Kant's power of judgement. The chapter then continues with some brief Kantian and Latourian explorations of the operation of the power of judgement in the practices of science and religion.

Rickert's approach to judgement

Heinrich Rickert was one of the most famous and influential philosophers in Germany – and all over the world where German philosophers were read – around the turn of the twentieth century.[8] His influence waned quickly in his later years (encompassing the period after the First World War until 1936, the year in which he died), along with the demise of neo-Kantianism more generally. Rickert is associated with the Southwestern (or Baden) school of neo-Kantianism, which emphasised Kant's third Critique (on the power of judgement) as a crucial modification and extension of his first Critique (on pure reason).[9] Rickert has made what

I deem to be a seminal contribution to the analysis of judgement in transcendental philosophy through his ontological chapter 'The third domain' (*Das dritte Reich*)[10] in his *System of Philosophy* of 1921. The problem that confronts Rickert there is how reality and validity can philosophically be considered to be connected with each other. He thoroughly rejects metaphysical solutions to the problem, for instance the one proposed by 'intuitionism' (under which he classes James):

> In the opinion of some thinkers, the unified, identical world essence should be revealed through direct *intuition*. It is believed that intuitionism can solve our problem. The unity of value and reality must then be found in the conceptually unbroken 'experience'. The separation into the two realms of real being and unreal validity would be a split between the immediate and the absolute, which 'only' owes its existence to our intellect or faculty of understanding. (Rickert 1921, 247–8)

Rickert deems such an approach, to which James's doctrine of pure experience can also be said to belong, *un*philosophical:

> By *simply* forgetting the separating concept formation and *returning* to immediacy one is by no means done in *philosophy* when one is concerned with the comprehensive totality of the world (*das umfassende Weltall*).
>
> ... We separate the real from the valid. The reality of experience is not the *world* of experience in its entirety. Despite this we can still speak of it [the reality of experience] as a unity on the basis of our understanding. If, on the other hand, we attempt to bring *everything*, both the real and the valid, into the one thought of the *world* of experience, we have either returned to something empty of content, the theoretical object in general, or we have to follow consistent mysticism in declaring the unity of the universe, which we believe we have found, to be completely incomprehensible and ineffable. But that would not bring us any further in our *knowledge*. What is still missing is the *concept* of world unity, which we seek where we philosophise, and thus unity in a *theoretical* sense. (Rickert 1921, 248)

While one cannot philosophically disprove the doctrine of pure experience, it is something that must be taken on faith and therefore belongs to the domain of metaphysics.

Also, some of the extant metaphysical interpretations of Kant's *Dich an sich* do not work for Rickert. He therefore opts to propose a refined ontology that is associated with the transcendental approach. Like James, he finds a middle ground where – in a way structurally similar to how James positioned his 'pure experience' *vis-à-vis* 'thought' and 'thing' – 'reality' and 'validity' are transcendentally assumed but not yet separated in the meaning that is bestowed in the act of a valuing judgement:

> In short, the meaning (*Sinn*) attached to the act of valuation is not, on the one hand, real psychological being, but rather points beyond this to valid values. On the other hand, it is not a valid value either, because it only points to values. The ambiguity of the expression 'meaning' ('*Sinn*') is an evil that should not be denied, but we see no way of eliminating it.
>
> … The immanent meaning (*Sinn*) of judgement is not valid truth itself, but a component of that intermediate realm, which coincides neither with the transcendent theoretical value, nor with the reality of real judgment, which is merely real and insofar devoid of meaning.
>
> From this we see that the word 'judgement' is not used in two but in *three* senses (*Bedeutungen*), which correspond to the three realms of our world, and we now grasp not only real judgement and valid judgement, but also the meaning-bestowed-in-the-act (*Aktsinn*) of judging as something separate. (Rickert 1921, 262–4)

These passages are crucial for understanding philosophically the interconnection between what happens in actual reality (the psychological act of judgement) and the unreal realm of values (where valid judgements reside). Instead of a third domain with an independent type of existence, Rickert construes the domain of meaning-bestowed-in-the-act-of-judgement as world-in-between-worlds (the world of 'pro-physics' as opposed to 'metaphysics', the latter of which constitutes a fourth world, the beyond)[11] as being thoroughly dependent on the worlds of reality and validity. As we saw in Chapter 2, James depicted 'pure experience' as follows:

> The instant field of the present is at all times what I call the 'pure' experience. It is only virtually or potentially either object or subject as yet. For the time being, it is plain, unqualified actuality, or existence, a simple *that*. In this *naïf* immediacy it is of course *valid*;

> it is *there*, we *act* upon it; and the doubling of it in retrospection into a state of mind and a reality intended thereby, is just one of the acts. (James [1912] 1976, 13)

From the perspective of Rickert's philosophy, this should be considered an unreflective metaphysical amalgam of reality and validity through its references to, on the one hand, being in 'the present', 'as yet', 'actuality' and 'existence', and, on the other hand, being 'valid'. Again, one cannot disprove the doctrine of pure experience philosophically, but by accepting it one entirely closes off one domain of philosophy, that of pro-physics, which I argue represents the crux of transcendental philosophy.[12]

While we saw that in the last chapter of *The Principles of Psychology* James sided with transcendental philosophy versus 'Experience-philosophy' in his understanding of the role of the *a priori* in judgement, he continued to struggle with the proper place of the *a priori* in philosophy. I showed in Chapter 2 how in an earlier chapter of *The Principles* James dismissed a metaphysical interpretation of Kant, especially his *Ding an sich*. In his discussion on 'Percept and concept' in the posthumously published *Some Problems of Philosophy*, James still finds it difficult to define the proper role of the *a priori* in his own metaphysics of judgement. According to James, 'the *a priori* world is full of [synthetic concepts]' (James [1911] 1979, 47). This I interpret to mean that in what he counts among the '*a priori*' sciences (mathematics, logic, ethics, aesthetics), '[n]othing *happens*' (James [1911] 1979, 41) other than that 'rational relations' are 'found' that 'are all products of our faculty of comparison and of our sense of "more"' (James [1911] 1979, 40). James summarily dismisses the Kantian transcendental approach since he claims that it does not agree as well with our experience as his own account:

> The account I give directly contradicts that which Kant gave and which has prevailed since Kant's time. Kant always speaks of the aboriginal sensible flux as a 'manifold' of which he considers the essential character to be its *disconnectedness*. (James [1911] 1979, 33)

According to James, Kant denies that there is a role for the faculty of understanding (*Verstand*) in making the connections. It is especially the *Dinge an sich*, Kant's 'noumena', that James is targeting as problematic in Kant's transcendental procedure: 'reality is sought … outside both of the perceptual flow and of the conceptual scheme. Kant lodges it before the flow, in the shape of so-called "things in themselves"'. James adds to this that Kant apparently had a 'moral need of somehow rebuking "sinnlichkeit"' (James [1911] 1979, 48).

The case that I aim to make here is that James's issues with (his interpretation of)[13] Kant's instantiation of the transcendental procedure to solve the problem of linking percept and concept do not apply to Rickert's solution. Rickert refuses to make a metaphysical assumption, as Kant and James did in their different ways, in linking percept and concept:

> We have reason to separate our attempt, at least for the moment, with sharpness from all the tendencies that are rightly called '*meta*physical'. In doing that, we do not want to claim anything against metaphysics at all. We only do not seek the solution to *the* problem that concerns us now in the metaphysical direction. (Rickert 1934a, 111)

This is how Rickert introduces his notion of the 'pro-physical' in his 1934 book that aims to be an introduction to the fundamental problems of philosophy, when he asks:

> Is there something that does not lie beyond, but definitely on this side, and that nevertheless is something fundamentally different from the split object world, namely, something that, even before the objectivising split into perceptible and intelligible being, is its 'presupposition' in the true sense, and therefore cannot be grasped by a *meta*physics, but only by a theory which, in contrast, we have to designate as *pro-physics*, which expresses in its name what it strives for? (Rickert 1934a, 111)

The theory of a pro-physical 'front world' (*Vorderwelt*) prevents us from having a metaphysical solution of a 'back world' (*Hinterwelt*). As one Rickert commentator says, 'it is the logical predecessor of reality and values, and of our knowledge of them' (Zijderveld 2006, 183). The same commentator further explains how this works for Rickert:

> This 'front world' is not an abstract, far away reality, but it is part of our everyday world, since we constantly, though usually unconsciously, interpret the meaning of what we and the others do and say in terms of values. Or, in more modern terms, we are essentially meaning bestowing, that is communicating beings. It is the task of philosophy to conceptualize this activity. That is

> precisely what the not meta-physical but pro-physical theory of the three independent, yet heterologically connected realms [of reality, validity, and pro-physics] does. (Zijderveld 2006, 183)

Let me emphasise that the pro-physical approach advocated by Rickert does not contradict James's emphasis on the 'great difference between percepts and concepts' (James [1911] 1979, 32). James and Rickert agree that the conceptual cuts we make are purely ideal. However, for Rickert there is too much metaphysics in 'pure experience' being 'a big blooming buzzing confusion, as free from contradiction in its "much-at-onceness" as it is all alive and evidently here' (James [1911] 1979, 32) for it to belong to the type of transcendental philosophy advocated by him. The 'manifold' that we perceive in our experience – which Kant assumed as metaphysically needing a 'beyond' (in the things-in-themselves, the *Dinge an sich*) and which James assumed as itself being metaphysically prior as it constitutes 'pure experience' – is still there for Rickert. However, he aims to give it its appropriate place in his theory of pro-physics, which lies 'on this side' and which gives a proper role to *a priori* values, also lying 'on this side' (which does not imply that they can be grasped and applied with certainty; on the contrary, though they may be said to be 'experienced', this is happening in an indirect way: they are pointed to and assumed to be valid in fallible judgements).

James's biggest problem with rationalist approaches is that they put too much emphasis on 'concept' versus 'percept', which leads to the risk of 'intellectualism':

> Whenever we conceive a thing we '*define*' it; and if we still don't understand, we define our definition. Thus I define a certain percept by saying 'this is motion' or 'I am moving'; and then I define motion by calling it the 'being in new positions at new moments of time'. This habit of telling what everything is becomes inveterate. The farther we push it, the more we learn *about* our subject of discourse, and we end by thinking that knowing the latter always consists in getting farther and farther away from the more perceptual datum. This uncriticized habit, added to the intrinsic charm of the conceptual form, is the source of 'intellectualism' in philosophy. (James [1911] 1979, 47–8)

I would add that Rickert could not agree more. He also identifies 'the problem of the intellectualist worldview' (*das Problem der intellektualistischen Weltanschauung*):

> Where [intellectualism] rules, one thinks *one-sidedly*. One sees the meaning of human life chiefly in scientific (*wissenschaftlichen*) culture; indeed, one sometimes seeks to interpret even the 'essence' of the world in its totality from this perspective. The influence of Greek intellectualism can be felt well into modern times. All the more, one should bear in mind that the 'whole human' never lives *only* thinking theoretically, and that therefore a comprehensive anthropology in no way has the scientific (*wissenschaftliche*) right to determine the meaning of the entire culture from science (*der Wissenschaft*). (Rickert 1934a, 160)

Rickert agrees with commentators on Kant who had found Kant's criticism of intellectualism unsatisfying. He identifies the need to delineate more clearly 'new' ways to do metaphysics:

> Yes, one can point out that Kant himself has not adhered to the limits he drew. He speaks of the 'in itself' of the world and basically knows very well what he means by it and by 'God'. But this knowing can only be based on theoretical knowledge, and thus is criticism by no means free from a theoretical apprehension of the absolute. It is thus important to further develop the approaches to a new metaphysics found in Kant. (Rickert 1924, 163)

According to Rickert, Kant, in specifying his transcendental procedure, conflated the unknowable (*das Unerkennbare*), about which we remain ignorant, with potentially reducible uncertainty (*das noch Unerkannten*). Having here again arrived at Kant interpretation, let me now turn to more detailed examples of Kant's way of philosophising transcendentally, especially in his *Critique of the Power of Judgment*, with the aim of illustrating the workings of what Rickert classes under 'pro-physics', focusing in particular on arriving at meaning-bestowed-in-the-act-of-judgement. What does it mean philosophically to judge under uncertainty?

Kant's power of judgement

As is explained in this section, the power of judgement, via its aesthetic judgements, assists humans in reaching theoretical judgements (*Erkenntnisurteile*) – including in situations (which humans often find themselves in) where no algorithmic rules (or even heuristics) are available for arriving at theoretical judgements that are true. Analogously, moving beyond Kant, I tentatively suggest that for *all* value domains, or modes of existence, a-theoretical 'judgements' are reached in practices that in a pro-physical analysis can be shown to be dependent on aesthetic judgements.

Kant spent a large portion of his *Critique of the Power of Judgment* on dealing with judgements of taste in the particular context of the beautiful and sublime in nature and the arts. Recent Kant interpreters who have focused on the role of emotion, especially in the third Critique, have taken his focus on the arts (which covers most of the Critique) to serve mainly didactic purposes. They have argued that his analysis applies to *all* cultural practices (typically science and ethics are emphasised by these interpreters) as involving judgements of taste (e.g. Wieland 2001; Nuzzo 2014).

In the Preface to his Critique, Kant first introduces the tension between the understanding and the power of judgement:

> It can ... easily be inferred from the nature of the power of judgment (the correct use of which is so necessary and generally required that nothing other than this very faculty is meant by the name 'sound understanding') that great difficulties must be involved in finding a special principle for it (which it must contain in itself *a priori*, for otherwise, it would not, as a special faculty of cognition, be exposed even to the most common critique), which nevertheless must not be derived from concepts *a priori*; for they belong to the understanding, and the power of judgement is concerned only with their application. (*Power of Judgment*, 5, 169)

He subsequently brings aesthetic judgements pertaining to beauty and the sublime in nature and art to the fore:

> This embarrassment about a principle (whether it be subjective or objective) is found chiefly in those judgings that are called aesthetic, which concern the beautiful and the sublime in nature or in art. (*Power of Judgment*, 5, 169)

It is crucial here to understand that Kant's own use of the word 'aesthetic' pertains more broadly to the sphere of sensibility (aesthetics being at that time the science of sensibility). It is not limited to the evaluation of beauty and the sublime in nature and art, contexts to which the word 'aesthetic' is nowadays normally restricted.

In his Critique, Kant demonstrates clearly for the example of judgements of taste how the power of judgement is intrinsically connected with the spheres of emotions, feelings and sensations. I explored a Jamesian approach to emotion and cognition in Chapter 2. Here I observe that already for Kant the spheres of emotions, feelings and sensations are also important in cases where the power of judgement contributes to the genesis of, for instance, theoretical knowledge. A contemporary Kant interpreter, Angelica Nuzzo, portrays the role of emotion in Kant's transcendental philosophy as follows:

> Just as the power of judgment taken into consideration in the third *Critique*, emotions are fundamentally related to beliefs, motivations, and desires, yet they are not directly identical with them. When referred to judgment, I suggest, a certain emotional structure or disposition is the transcendental condition that allows for a different cognitive and practical attitude with regard to ourselves and to the world – a new, humanly richer *Denkungsart* (or mental disposition) towards both our cognitive and moral life. … But what are these emotions transcendentally connected with the power of judgment? They are, I suggest, what I call 'participatory' and 'reflective' emotions, that is, emotions that are informed by the peculiar feeling of pleasure and displeasure characterizing the aesthetic experience, and are such as to disclose the subject's new position as part of and participant in the natural and human world – no longer as a detached legislator over and above it but as an active and engaged member of what is now recognized a broader living whole. (Nuzzo 2014, 89)

Leaving aside the question of how Kant's Critiques should be interpreted as a whole, it is clear that his last Critique contributes a crucial element to transcendental philosophy.

By working from a transcendental philosophical perspective, Kant is at the same time able to formulate the grounds of what the objectivity of theoretical knowledge consists in (he did that in particular in his first Critique, which focused on the *a priori* conditions of lawfulness applied by the understanding) and to avoid losing sight of uncertainty in empirical laws. The power of judgement is necessarily called upon to deal with uncertainty and to construct provisional models (which Kant called *Entwurfe*) of the world (Picht 1989, 73). Let me explain how this works and how feelings offer an ineliminable element of dealing with uncertainty in a variety of practices. First, however, we should deal with Kant's grand narrative for the power of judgement, which relates to Kant's dream pertaining to progress in theoretical knowledge (which he regards as a system) and the obstacles that stand in the way in practice:

> [A]lthough experience constitutes a system in accordance with *transcendental laws*, which contain the condition of the possibility of experience in general, there is still possible such an *infinite multiplicity* of empirical laws and such a *great heterogeneity of forms* of nature, which would belong to particular experience, that the concept of a system in accordance with these (empirical) laws must be entirely alien to the understanding, and neither the possibility, let alone the necessity, of such a whole can be conceived. (*Power of Judgment*, 20, 203)

The grand assumption under which the power of judgement operates, according to Kant, is thus the purposiveness of nature.

This bold move by Kant, to posit that we necessarily regard nature as purposively put together, that is as artfully made, may be seen – and Kant does not disagree – as a leap of faith. It must therefore be remembered that this grand assumption cannot be empirically proven:

> [T]he representation of nature as art is a mere idea, which serves as a principle, merely for the subject, for our investigation of nature, so that we can where possible bring interconnection, as in a system, into the aggregate of empirical laws as such, by attributing to nature a relation to this need of ours. (*Power of Judgment*, 20, 205)

Even if we would not go along with Kant's full-fledged teleological narrative, he still makes the important point that when we strive for unification of empirical laws, we must assume that nature 'allows' for such unification to be found. We cannot then assume experience to be a mere aggregate, but must assume its systematicity:

> [I]t is a mere presupposition of the power of judgment, in behalf of its own use, always to ascend from empirical, particular laws to more general but at the same time still empirical ones, for the sake of the unification of empirical laws. (*Power of Judgment*, 20, 210–11)

There is, of course, no guarantee that full unification in the sphere of theoretical knowledge will ever be reached. Kant himself was sceptical about this. There is so much that we will remain uncertain about.

When one does not give up and keeps trying to learn more and generalise, however, one is operating under the *a priori* principles of the power of judgement.

This leads us to a more detailed investigation of the power of judgement. Generally speaking, it is a faculty for subsuming under universals (rules, principles, laws). Either the judgement subsumes under an existing universal (the 'determining' power of judgement) or, if only the particular is given, it must find the universal (the 'reflecting' power of judgement). I will focus here in particular on the latter kind, the reflecting judgements. The product of the reflecting power of judgement is art (or *an* art, broadly defined), which is discussed by Kant in the context of theoretical knowledge:

> The reflecting power of judgement thus proceeds with given appearances, in order to bring them under empirical concepts of determinate natural things, not schematically, but *technically*, not as it were merely mechanically, like an instrument, but *artistically*, in accordance with the general but at the same time indeterminate principle of a purposive arrangement of nature in a system, as it were for the benefit of our power of judgment, in the suitability of its particular laws (about which understanding has nothing to say) for the possibility of experience as a system, without which presupposition we could not hope to find our way in a labyrinth of the multiplicity of possible empirical particular laws. (*Power of Judgment*, 20, 213–14)

I suggest that a similar argument can be constructed for other value domains. In judgements reached in those domains, the role of the reflecting power of judgement is to arrive at meaningful contributions to the practices of different cultural domains that can withstand the test of the 'truth conditions' valid for those domains.

Now in Kant's transcendental philosophy it often seems that *certainty* of ideas (and of laws, for that matter) is required in order for them to fulfil their *a priori* function; the possibility of ideas (and laws) being *uncertain* is thus difficult for him to thematise. Interestingly, Kant seems generally to be much more willing to grant that laws of nature are uncertain than that ideas are. Still, Kant is also aware of the uncertainty of ideas and of maxims that can be deduced from them. He has exposed flaws in the old metaphysics that went before him and in his *Prolegomena to Any Future Metaphysics* he acknowledges that the correct system of ideas that will emerge from the sustained 'efforts of the learned'

(*Prolegomena*, 4, 382) and constitute the new metaphysics may not be his own; it may well result from 'attacks, revisions, and qualifications' (*Prolegomena*, 4, 382) of his theses. However, Kant does maintain that

> through critique our judgment is afforded a standard by which knowledge can be distinguished with certainty from pseudo knowledge; and, as a result of being brought fully into play in metaphysics, critique establishes a manner of thinking that subsequently extends its wholesome influence to every other use of reason. (*Prolegomena*, 4, 383)

So, once we are considering an idea, we should be able to test its 'robustness' by applying the critical method to it. All this still begs the question of how we arrive at both the highest-level ideas (the psychological, cosmological and theological ideas) and the lower-level maxims connected to them. In contemporary transcendental philosophy, as we will see in Chapter 4, there is both less metaphysical baggage and many more cultural value domains than Kant had distinguished (he only referred to the theoretical, practical and aesthetic domains). Practices in all of these value domains are faced with uncertainty.

Let us continue to delve into what is involved philosophically in arriving at a judgement, be it an aesthetic, a theoretical or a practical judgement. Making a judgement always involves an emotion[14] – a feeling that refers to the freedom experienced in relating a particular to the sphere of the *a priori*, and which is therefore philosophically relevant in analysing what Rickert calls pro-physics. As Wieland (2001, 19–20) points out, emotions have the ability to open up particular aspects of the world that cannot be fully captured in theories (nor, I would add, other types of knowledge in the different cultural domains).[15] These include, for instance. much of what happens in the interpersonal relationships between people, non-propositional knowledge and the unspeaking background that provides coherence and shape to explicit knowledge.

A crucial step in Kant's critique of judgement is that there is always an aesthetic judgement, with accompanying emotion, preceding a theoretical (or other type of) judgement. The emotion that is triggered in making an aesthetic judgement is the direct and undisguised feeling experienced in the judgement of taste. It is this reflective pleasure of judgement that opens up the possibility to arrive at universals. As long as the process of reflection is continuing and a universal result has not yet been reached, the feeling of pleasure continues: it is not the result that gives pleasure, but rather the process of a free play of the faculties of cognition. As Kant observes in relation to theoretical knowledge, this feeling of pleasure is 'with regard to cognition in general, but without being restricted to a particular cognition' (*Power of Judgment*, 5, 222). This state ends as soon the universal has been found – that is, when a theoretical or practical decision has been made.[16]

One of the strongest examples considered by Kant of how emotions stir thinking is that of poetry:

> [t]he *art of poetry* ... expands the mind by setting the imagination free and presenting, within the limits of a given concept and among the unbounded manifold of forms possibly agreeing with it, the one that connects its presentation with a fullness of thought to which no linguistic expression is fully adequate, and thus elevates itself aesthetically to the level of ideas. (*Power of Judgment*, 5, 326)

Now the emotion involved in the power of judgement is in most cases not as strong as in the case of poetry leading to judgements arriving at universals (this being an eminent example of reflective pleasure mediated by an aesthetic idea). However, as Wieland (2001, 374) argues, such eminent examples and more subtle discoveries of ingenuity share a common root. In Chapter 6 I will return to the importance of poetics in dealing with uncertainty. Let me in the remainder of this chapter exemplify the philosophical approach to judgement that I have suggested here by focusing on the practices of science and religion, providing examples from Kant as well as from Latour.

Judgement in scientific practices

In the *Critique of the Power of Judgment*, Kant extensively discusses the power of judgement in the context of natural science, but more with respect to his grand narrative and unification than in terms of the role of emotion and aesthetic judgement in scientific practice. Kant claims that scientists cannot but assume the necessity of natural laws, even though they cannot understand this necessity because of an infinite number of empirical laws (see also previous section):

> Thus we must think of there being in nature, with regard to its merely empirical laws, a possibility of infinitely manifold empirical laws, which as far as our insight goes are nevertheless contingent (cannot be cognized *a priori*); and with regard to them we judge

> the unity of nature in accordance with empirical laws and the possibility of the unity of experience (as a system in accordance with empirical laws) as contingent. (*Power of Judgment*, 5, 183)

So the reflecting power of judgement is needed to deliver methodological principles, such as parsimony, continuity, simplicity, etc., which guide the unification of the multitude of empirical laws – even though in reality a final unification of all empirical laws will never be reached (Friedman 1992, 191).[17]

This means that there remains a deep uncertainty attached to any universal empirical law. Here I will give examples, taken from Kant's writings on natural science, of how judgement plays a crucial role in the construction of models (in Kant's terms here 'mathematical representations') to underpin universal empirical laws. Kant makes an important distinction between models and concepts:

> [M]athematicians represent the repulsive forces of the parts of elastic matters as increasing or decreasing, in accordance with a certain proportion of their distances from one another, at greater or lesser compression of these parts. … [O]ne completely misses their meaning, and misinterprets their language, if one ascribes that which necessarily belongs to the procedure of constructing a concept to the concept in the object itself. (*Metaphysical Foundations of Natural Science*, 4, 505)

For instance, in the mathematical construction of the ideal gas law, which states that the product of pressure and volume remains constant (for constant temperature), Newtonian physics presupposes the existence of two kinds of forces: repulsive and attractive forces. In Kant's theoretical underpinning of the Newtonian worldview, repulsive forces can only be conceptualised as contact forces and attractive forces only as volume forces that work at a distance. Now Kant allowed models to not be true: the supposition of an atomic structure of matter, for instance, can be useful (or even indispensable) to formulate an adequate mathematical representation of repulsive forces, without this supposition needing to be true. This shows clearly how uncertain elements in scientific practice can nonetheless be productively harnessed by the reflecting power of judgement to arrive at universals, which need to be evaluated on their own merits.[18]

Kant was ambivalent *vis-à-vis* the atomic hypothesis. At the very least he demanded that models should not be mistaken for theoretical concepts (*Begriffe*). Nevertheless, he did acknowledge the heuristic role of models. The mechanistic, atomistic philosophy that he criticised has had a large influence on the development of natural science, especially because it was most amenable to mathematical treatment. Kant also remained ambivalent with regard to the certainty that could be delivered by the use of mathematics in natural science. But in the *Metaphysical Foundations of Natural Science* he does employ mathematical methods in the construction of models.

A second example of Kant's own construction of models is his use of infinitely small distances between material objects in the derivation of repulsive contact forces (*Metaphysical Foundations of Natural Science*, 4, 520–3). Because in reality, according to Kant, there are no distances between discrete objects (since matter is a continuous quantity), meaning that the infinitely small distances that feature in the mathematical representation should be distinguished from every actual distance. Kant realises that there are such issues attached to his mathematical construction, but urges the reader not to object to a concept itself because of difficulties in constructing it. He claims that the validity of the result of the work of reflective judgement, the metaphysical concept (of repulsive force, for example), is not dependent on the (potentially problematic) mathematical constructions that led to it.[19]

Still, one should always be prepared for universal empirical laws to turn out to be false. This was not easy for Kant with respect to the universal law of gravitation. He considered that law to be one of very few examples for which there was certainty on the mathematical form:

> [the rule of the] physical law of reciprocal attraction, extending to all material nature, ... is that these attractions decrease inversely with the square of the distance from each point of attraction, exactly as the spherical surfaces into which this force spreads itself increase, something that seems to reside as necessary in the nature of the things themselves and which therefore is customarily presented as cognizable *a priori*. (*Prolegomena*, 4, 321)

In the *Metaphysical Foundations of Natural Science* (4, 517–18), Kant offers metaphysical speculations on the reasons for this mathematical form. However, in the end he admits both that success in the unification of empirical laws is not guaranteed and that the universal law of gravitation must be inferred, using the reflecting power of judgement, from data of experience (*Metaphysical Foundations of Natural Science*, 4, 534).

Finally, on Kant and scientific practices, moving from the importance of unification in science (and the necessary role of the power of judgement there) to the more general issue of the constructive role of emotion in scientific practices, we can see that Kant's acknowledgement of the importance for scientific discovery of the spheres of emotions, feelings and sensations resonates with views discussed in Chapter 2 on the guidance provided by emotion and the appreciation of beauty. From Kant we can learn about the central role of aesthetic judgements, including when we would not associate them with what is commonly understood by 'beauty'. The deep questions asked by Chandrasekhar (quoted in Chapter 2) – about the reasons for a scientist's continued pursuit of science, the role of aesthetic criteria (such as the perception of order and pattern, form and substance) and a possible sense of obligation in the pursuit of science for science – are very much Kantian questions, which we are still grappling with today.

We now turn briefly to Latour. Near the end of his *Inquiry* chapter on the mode of reference he describes the practice of scientific research, in which emotionally engaged scientists find themselves not only 'transformed' and 'surprised', but also very much 'on edge', by the 'connections' that they are producing through the use of reflective judgement:

> [A]s long as the event of discovery lasts, no researcher is unaware of the potential dangers of establishing a correspondence between the dynamics of things and the work of reference. They all know that they are transformed by the event, they themselves and the things on which, finally, after so many failures, they have a grip – provided that they contain these things firmly all along the path of experimentation, modelization, re-creation, and calculation. The danger of 'missing the connection' is what keeps researchers on edge at work. …
>
> Wasn't it the most famous scientist of them all who used to say that 'the most incomprehensible thing in the world is that the world is comprehensible'? The second part of the aphorism is true, unquestionably: the world is comprehensible. But Einstein was mistaken in saying that it is incomprehensible that this should be so. There is no mystery, no miracle: there has been a series of risky events in which at each point we can see the emergence of a double discontinuity, in the reproduction of the world and in the extension of reference along with the pas de deux through which the encounter with 'thought collectives' – to borrow Ludwig Fleck's

> lovely expression – adapts. It is on the basis of such collective events that we must understand the surprise of knowledge that marks the scientist transformed by her discovery just as much as it marks the object grasped by the scientist. (Latour [2012] 2013b, 90–1)

It is very clear that for Latour scientific research is a creative enterprise in which actors are constantly grappling with uncertainty and staking claims. Latour, in his 2016 *Reset Modernity!* exhibition, makes the connection with Kant's *Critique of the Power of Judgment* explicit (he even had the title page of that work on display in the exhibition); he quotes a passage on experiencing nature as the sublime and then retorts:

> Every feature of such a situation is now gone … The Anthropocene subject is no longer a spectator because there is no safe place any more. (Latour 2016, 169)

Now, through the discoveries of the earth sciences, Latour observes:

> [Y]ou realize, at least if you consider the earth, that you, you the human agent, have become so omnipotent that you have been able to inflict definitive damages on its system. (Latour 2016, 169)

However, Latour does not make the connection that I have explored in this section between Kant's power of judgement and jumping the uncertainty 'gaps' in his mode of reference.

Judgement in religious practices

Religion, for Kant, is connected with practical knowledge. Kant distinguishes religion (or, better, his religion of reason) from morals not in its content but merely in its form. Religion represents morals in a certain way, inasmuch as it gives to the idea of God, which is evolved from morality itself, an influence upon the human will for the fulfilment of every human duty (cf. Barth [1947] 2001, 262). As I argued above, the reflecting power of judgement also plays a role in arriving at practical knowledge, including religious knowledge. In *Religion within the Boundaries of Mere Reason* (6, 87–8), Kant compares the practical affairs of natural scientists who try to arrive at natural laws with the practical affairs of human beings who aim for moral improvement (which for Kant is a main function of religious practices). Kant highlights the deep uncertainties that are associated with both types of practice.

Although there can in a technical sense perhaps be no theoretical knowledge about God, since God is not an object of our theoretical knowledge and is not to be comprehended simply as existent reality, we are also uncertain about our models of God (which belong to practical knowledge) even as we are uncertain about our models of the world (which belong to theoretical knowledge). Since the relationship between God and creation lies 'before' experience, there is no worldly analogy for this relationship. Nevertheless, we do build models of God and our relationship to Him:

> [I]t is in no way reprehensible to say that every human being *makes a God* for himself, indeed, he must make one according to moral concepts ... in order to honor in him *the one who made him*. (*Religion*, 6, 168)[20]

In § 87 ('On the moral proof of the existence of God') of the *Critique of the Power of Judgment*, Kant had stated that:

> [W]e must assume a moral cause of the world (an author of the world) in order to set before ourselves a final end, in accordance with the moral law; and insofar as that final end is necessary, to that extent (i.e., in the same degree and for the same reason) is it also necessary to assume the former, namely, that there is a God. (*Power of Judgment*, 5, 450)

In a note he added to the second edition, he clarifies the distinction between 'objective' (theoretical) knowledge and 'subjective' (practical) knowledge:

> This moral argument is not meant to provide any *objectively* valid proof of the existence of God, nor meant to prove to the doubter that there is a God; rather, it is meant to prove that if his moral thinking is to be consistent, he *must include* the assumption of this proposition among the maxims of his practical reason. – Thus it is also not meant to say that it is necessary to assume the happiness of all rational beings in the world in accordance with their morality *for* morals, but rather that it is necessary *through* their morality. Hence it is a *subjective* argument, sufficient for moral beings. (*Power of Judgment*, 5, 450–1)

Kant's so-called proof of the existence of God is therefore not really a proof of the *existence* of God, but rather of the necessity to assume this existence so that we can be moral. Still, this *a priori* argument does not address the crucial question of how to arrive at maxims consistent with the idea of God: how do we know how God's will is to be honoured (cf. *Religion*, 6, 103)? We have no way to know for certain (and thus claim we are doing right) whether our deeds are well-pleasing to God.[21]

Let us now consider what the rational status of religious ritual is in the eyes of Kant. Barth recognises in Kant at least some appreciation of statutes such as the (Christian) church:

> [T]he pure religious faith has need of a statutory church faith as its vehicle. ... [T]here must be, as against this divine constitution, a statute on the human side, which, even if it is not to be considered as divinely statutory, is yet an equivalent raised publicly to the status of a basic law; a humanly inalterable, humanly qualified statute, as it were: the Scripture, beside which, however, no tradition and no symbols must then be set up as equal to it in value. (Barth [1947] 2001, 276)

Obviously, this 'statute' 'becomes subject to the limitations of sentient human nature' (Barth [1947] 2001, 277). According to Barth:

> Kant ... dispute[s] ... the idea that the reality and possibility of revelation, its availability as data for human reason and its perception by human reason, are things which can be accounted for by philosophical means ... [and] he disputes the philosopher's right to deny revelation because it cannot be accounted for by philosophical means. (295–6)

In *The Conflict of the Faculties*, Kant separates the job of the biblical theologian from that of the philosopher: 'The biblical theologian proves the existence of God on the grounds that He spoke in the Bible' (*Conflict of the Faculties*, 7, 23). And the human will for good comes from grace (according to Kant, a supernatural and at the same time a moral influence), 'which the human being can obtain only by an ardent faith that transforms his heart – a faith that itself, in turn, he can expect only through grace' (*Conflict of the Faculties*, 7, 24).

Fallibility and uncertainty are associated both with the institution of the church and religious rituals embedded in its practices. Ideally, for Kant, they should not be necessary for the rational religion.

However, rituals based on revelation can have pedagogical value, as a mere means – though a precious one – to bring the ignorant closer to rational religion (*Religion*, 6, 165). Still, Kant remains quite sceptical of the value of religious ritual, especially if one believes that through participation in religious ritual one can justify oneself before God (*Religion*, 6, 174).

It may be his (over-)reaction to his pietistic upbringing, but Kant qualifies supposed contact with God as religious enthusiasm (*Religion*, 6, 174). I argue, however, that an important role can be played in religious ritual by the power of judgement and accompanying emotions. Like poetry, religious ritual can expand the mind, set the imagination free and present models of God. There is a whole world of aesthetics in the practical knowledge sphere of religion that deserves further exploration and will be addressed in the various chapters of this book.

Let me finish this short section with an example of the functioning of the power of judgement in religion from Latour's *Inquiry*:

> The word 'God' cannot designate a substance; it designates, rather, the renewal of a subsistence that is constantly at risk, and even, as it were, the pathway of this reprise, at once word and being, *logos*. It can only be said with fear and trembling, for the expression ought to be given its full weight of realism: these entities have the peculiar feature of being ways of speaking. If you fail to find the right manner of speaking them, of speaking well of them, if you do not express them in the right tone, the right tonality, you strip them of all content. Merely ways of speaking? Doesn't this deprive them of any ontological basis? On the contrary, it is a terrifying requirement that ought to silence hundreds of thousands of sermons, doxologies, and other preachings: if you speak without converting, you say nothing. Worse, you sin against the Spirit.
>
> All the testimony agrees on this point: the appearance of such beings depends on an *interpretation* so delicate that one lives constantly at risk and in fear of lying about them; and, in lying, *mistaking them for another* – for a demon, a sensory illusion, an emotion, a foundation. Fear of committing a category mistake is what keeps the faithful in suspense. Not once, in the Scriptures, do we find traces of someone who was called who could say he was sure, really sure, that the beings of the Word were there and that he had really understood what they wanted of him. Except for the sinners. This is even the criterion of truth, the most decisive shibboleth: the

> faithful tremble at the idea of being mistaken while infidels do not. Exactly the chiasmus that the transmigration of religion into fundamentalism has lost, replacing it by a differentiation – as impossible as it is absolute – between those who believe and those who do not! (Latour [2012] 2013b, 309–10)

Again, similarly to the practice of science, but now in a different mode, the reflective judgements of those who engage in this mode of religion (not a form of ethics for Latour, as it is for Kant) are fully embodied in emotion ('fear and trembling', being kept 'in suspense') and trying to find the right aesthetic form ('the right tonality', 'converting'). Note that for Latour religion is not about rationalisation (which he analyses, both in his *Inquiry* and in *Facing Gaia*, as leading to 'fundamentalism'). In Chapter 4 Latour's mode of religion will be explored more fully.

Conclusion

In this chapter, interpretations of Kant's *Critique of the Power of Judgment* have been used and examples of judgement have been given, with the suggestion that the approach that Kant applied to aesthetics could be generalised to all spheres of culture. I have emphasised the freedom that we have to arrive at judgements involving aesthetics. Connection has been made to James's doctrine of pure experience and Latour's modes of existence work, as well as to Rickert's theory of pro-physics. What still requires more reflection are the *contents* of the *a priori* values in judgement, and classification of the different domains of culture according to those contents. This is the topic of the next chapter.

Notes

1 As I said in Chapter 1, I take 'metaphysics' to be theory about what lies beyond the reach of experience.
2 'Theoretical' and 'practical' are used here in the specific sense that Kant used them. Theoretical knowledge arises from the faculty of understanding, relates to nature and has a sensible substratum; practical knowledge arises from the faculty of reason, relates to freedom and has an intelligible substratum. Note that there can be a 'practical' part of a philosophy of nature.
3 So, while I agree with the thrust of Pihlström's case for revisiting transcendental philosophy through a pragmatist lens – he claims that 'when affirming, in the course of a transcendental argument, that something is a necessary condition for the possibility of something else' one

must abandon 'the assumption that we are speaking about a relation that is "metaphysical and a priori", instead of one that is "merely natural and a posteriori"' (Pihlström 2003, 26) – I do not think that the ontological status of values is best captured by the descriptor '*a posteriori*' or that it is 'metaphysical'.

4 But note that in his book on metaphysics, titled *Some Problems of Philosophy* and published posthumously, in his classification of philosophers as 'rationalist', 'empiricist', or 'mixed' James categorises Kant under 'mixed'. Hegel is categorised under 'rationalist' while James puts himself down as 'empiricist' (James [1911] 1979, 24).

5 Note that some of the diversity in Kant interpretations is a consequence of the fact that his third Critique, on the *a priori* principles of the power of judgement, was not yet conceived at the time that he wrote his earlier Critiques.

6 The label 'Criticism' or 'Critique' is often used for Kantian philosophy; it is also the way in which Latour often refers to (his interpretation of) transcendental philosophy.

7 Please note that references to Kant's works are to the standard German edition, *Kant's Gesammelte Schriften*, edited by the Royal Prussian (later German) Academy of Sciences. The English translations used are taken from the Cambridge Edition, which uses American spelling, hence 'judgment' is used instead of 'judgement'.

8 However, Rickert's works – except for one short work and an abbreviation of his longer work on the distinction between the 'natural' and 'cultural' sciences – were not, and have still not been, translated into English. For an excellent short introduction, the reader is referred to Andrea Staiti ([2013] 2018). Zijderveld (2006) provides a longer introduction, with a focus on the philosophical underpinnings of sociology.

9 The other neo-Kantian school was the Marburg school, emphasising in particular his first Critique. One of the most influential thinkers originating from the Marburg school was Ernst Cassirer (1874–1945).

10 Please note that this was published two years before Arthur Moeller van den Bruck published the book *Das dritte Reich* that influenced the ideology of the Nazi Party. There is no historical or conceptual link between the two uses of the phrase.

11 This will be discussed further in Chapter 4.

12 Of course, one could reinterpret James's doctrine of pure experience transcendentally, by de-emphasising the way he makes a distinction between reality and validity (thus downplaying his claim that this distinction is 'just one of the acts') and emphasising that reality and validity are transcendentally assumed in any act (they are always already 'virtually or potentially' there). But this would misconstrue James's intention.

13 Let me add here that James's interpretation of Kant was a mainstream one at the time (in the Anglo-Saxon world) and also that James, as I showed in Chapter 2, was fully conscious of the difficulties in Kant interpretation.

14 Please note that the English word 'emotion' can be the translation of three different German words in Kant's work: *Gefühl*, *Affekt* and *Rührung*. In the context of this chapter, the word referred to is typically *Gefühl* (cf. Wieland 2001).

15 I would also argue that this element of Kant's thought can be linked to James's notion of 'pure experience' and Rickert's pro-physics. In the case of James: there is not (yet) a dualism between thought and thing at the stage of arriving at a reflecting judgement. In the case of Rickert: the reflective judgement is needed to bridge reality and validity so that meaning can be bestowed in the act of judgement.

16 Note that for Kant, in practical reason, there is always the overarching feeling of respect: the state of mind of a will determined by something is in itself a feeling of pleasure (*Power of Judgment*, 5, 222). I am here exploring another pleasure related to the freedom to decide what the will is to be determined by. Also there is the possibility of a sustained emotion of wonder, as I discussed in Chapter 2.

17 It is important to realise that not all scientific practices strive for unification. There is another central task for scientists to discover differences between phenomena which first looked the same by doing detailed observations (Wartenberg 1992, 240). Thus in Kant's vision there are two kinds of scientists who perform both necessary and complementary tasks within science.

18 Note that Kant did not allow the genesis of a universal to be used in determining its validity.

19 For a fuller discussion on the role of models in dealing with uncertainty, the reader is referred to Chapter 5.

20 As Barth remarks on what Kant's position entails for how the human being relates to God: 'He has to be in a position to measure the God who is, perhaps, proclaimed to him or who, perhaps, even reveals himself to him, against an ideal conception of God which he has set up for himself, in order (it is surely only thus that it is possible!) to recognize the former as God' (Barth [1947] 2001, 268). Thus 'it is the agent of reason, man, that is, who, just as he is the measure of all things, is here thought of and provided for as the measure of religion, too: of its practical and theoretical possibilities, and also, and in particular, as God's measure' (271).

21 Cf. Barth ([1947] 2001, 290).

4
Values

Introduction

For my project, which focuses on the role of uncertainty in the practices of science and religion, and what this means for climate science and politics, a deeper understanding of the values that drive cultural practices is crucial. Only by reflecting on the varying purposes of the array of communal activities that proceed under the labels of 'science', 'religion', 'politics', etc., can the judgements of communities on what is credible, reliable and valuable be evaluated and compared. Therefore the question that is addressed in this chapter is: How do values relate to uncertainty? It must be noted at the outset that besides the uncertainty addressed in the previous chapter, that of how to relate a particular (in reality) to a universal (an unreal value), there is also higher-level uncertainty about what are to be considered the specific values (and there can be several of these) that are taken as the criteria for assessing what counts as good judgement within a particular practice.

In some cases, such as with the phenomenon of 'wonder' in scientific practices described in Chapter 2, a crossing of different types of values may be witnessed. This may occur, for example, when reflection upon scientific findings evokes a religious mystical experience, an intimation of metaphysical transcendence. The emotion of wonder can make one appreciate what is great in science and depends on an aesthetic sense of intellectual beauty. It comes with joy, delight and pleasure. An extreme version of this emotion of scientific wonder can indeed lead to religious wonder: one can think, for instance, of the mystical wonder coming over Werner Heisenberg upon realising the beauty of the laws of quantum mechanics. However, I argue that disentangling the scientific and religious values that simultaneously play their roles here requires a more careful consideration.

As we saw in Chapter 3, the realisation of value in judgement can be analysed as always involving an aesthetic emotion, when one feels freedom in relating a particular to the sphere of the *a priori*. The originator of transcendental philosophy, Kant, focused on the role of *a priori* principles in legitimising aesthetic, theoretical and practical judgements – thus distinguishing only three value domains. For Kant, religion did not have its own underlying value; it rather concerned ultimately moral value expressed in another form. He thus connected religion with practical knowledge and remained sceptical of any other value of religious ritual than moral pedagogy. However, along with Rickert and Latour, I argue that moral and religious values must be disentangled in religious practice.

In this chapter, we delve deeper into the characterisation of the *a priori*, the unreal sphere of values, and put judgement into its wider cultural context. I start with further discussion of the work of Latour and brief examples of his characterisations of the practices of science, religion and politics. I then show the relevance of the work of Rickert to the study of values that underlie cultural practices and that can only be realised in those practices in ways that give rise to perennial, creative and productive uncertainty. Rickert, I argue, provides an important counterpoint to James in the assessment of Latour. The chapter concludes with an overview of Latour's work on values. His philosophy of occasionalist empiricism, in which his work on values is embedded, constitutes, I argue, a version of radical empiricism that is more pluralistic than James's doctrine of pure experience (see Chapter 2). However, even more than James, Latour misses appropriate reflection on the transcendental dimension of philosophy, and he steps outside of transcendental philosophy by moving into metaphysics (which has to be taken on faith and cannot be argued for or against philosophically). This is all recognised from the viewpoint of transcendental naturalism, which I develop further in this chapter.

Latour's empirical approach to values

Bruno Latour who is most famous for his many contributions to science and technology studies originally trained as a philosopher and exegetical theologian and also published a book in religious studies (Latour [2002] 2013a). For three decades he had been working in the background on his metaphysics, his study of 'modes of existence', *An Inquiry into Modes of Existence: An anthropology of the Moderns* (Latour [2012] 2013b). A more complete overview of Latour's philosophy of culture, as I propose to reframe it transcendentally, follows at the end of this chapter. The next section contains brief introductions to Latour's views on scientific, religious and political practices. Here I start with a further description of the philosophical approach taken by Latour, continuing the earlier discussions of his work in Chapters 2 and 3.

In the preface to his *Inquiry*, Latour labels his philosophical method as 'empirical philosophy' (Latour [2012] 2013b, xxi); as commentator Gerard de Vries observes, '[t]o do philosophy, to actually trace the connecting links and to learn to see what we see, Latour got engaged in empirical field studies, in ethnography' (de Vries 2016, 5). While Latour's early philosophical work was in biblical exegesis, the 'empirical philosophy' of Latour subsequently 'took shape and substance in his moves, in ethnographical studies, in the debates he got involved in and in the way he incorporated ideas from a wide variety of sources in his work ... , [as well as in] the many links that [he] ... assembled' (de Vries 2016, 20). Here Latour describes the reason for him developing his philosophy of culture and values:

> It is as though the Moderns (I use the capitalized form to designate this population of variable geometry that is in search of itself) had up to now defined values that they had somehow sheltered in shaky institutions conceived on the fly in response to the demands of the modernization front while continuing to defer the question of how they themselves were going to last. They had a future, but they were not concerned with what was to come – or rather, what was coming. What is coming? What is it that is arriving unexpectedly, something they seem not to have anticipated? 'Gaia', the 'Anthropocene' era, the precise name hardly matters, something in any case that has deprived them forever of the fundamental distinction between Nature and Society by means of which they were establishing their system of coordinates, one step at a time. ...
>
> Is there another system of coordinates that can replace the one we have lost, now that the modernist parenthesis is closing? This is the enterprise that I have been doggedly pursuing, alongside other endeavors, for a quarter of a century, and that I would like to share and extend through this book and its accompanying digital apparatus. (Latour [2012] 2013b, 10)

But how does one obtain the values of modernity?

> In all that follows, I am … going to offer readers a double dissociation: first, I shall try to tease out an experience proper to each value from the account traditionally provided for it; next, I shall take it upon myself to give this experience an entirely provisional alternative formulation that I shall put on the bargaining table and submit to critique. Why proceed this way? Because it seems to me that an experience, provided that it is pursued with care, can be shared, whereas the alternative formulation that I offer of that experience cannot be – in any case, not at the outset. (Latour [2012] 2013b, 11–12)

Latour's approach here is naturalistic (in a non-scientistic form). He starts from empirically observable practices in the world and he does not assume there are credible grounds to conclude that there exist 'supernatural being or beings' or 'power(s)' outside the world, which have causal commerce with it; on the contrary, Latour allows for many beings and powers that – while they may not be explainable by natural science (a criterion held, e.g., in scientistic naturalism) – still belong to *this* world.

Rickert who, as a transcendental philosopher, stipulates that values exist *in* the world and who also does not allow for causal commerce of the supernatural with our world (so is naturalistic too in that sense) would agree with Latour that philosophers do not have special access to the *a priori* values of culture.[1] What is needed in Latour's view, against rationalistic philosophical approaches, is a more 'empirical' approach, which he aims to exemplify in his 'empirical philosophy'. Here is how de Vries captures Latour's approach:

> We need a better diagnosis first – a less confused image of modernity, a more realistic description of the values the Moderns hold dear. Latour suggests that it can be offered by a 'comparative anthropology of the Moderns' that helps contrasting different threads within the modern collective, rather than – what Weber did – by contrasting us, Moderns, with Them, other peoples. To allow this endeavour, a new philosophical vocabulary is required. It is introduced hand in glove with empirical observations. It has resulted in *An Inquiry into Modes of Existence*, a massive book (of almost 500 pages), presented – as one might expect from an empirical philosopher – as a 'provisional report'. (de Vries 2016, 151)

Let me here briefly summarise what Latour means by a 'mode of existence', which is defined by specifying five characteristics:[2]

1. The *hiatus*: 'All continuations of a course of action suppose a discontinuity that must be overcome in order to define a trajectory. It is this discontinuity, and the fact of getting over it, that we call a hiatus, or gap, threshold or break – the actual term is unimportant. This term belongs to the metalanguage of the investigation and allows for a definition of the mini-transcendence required for any definition of the being-as-other [a subsistence view of being].'
2. The *trajectory*: 'This banal term belongs to the investigation's metalanguage and therefore takes on a technical sense in order to specify the type of connection or network that leaves in its wake the beings specific to a given mode. Along with the terms "hiatus", "felicity conditions" and "alteration", it enables us to answer questions about the essence of a mode. Its pedigree is impeccable: "trans jacere", to throw beyond, pass through, journey – all connotations that bring us back to movement and dispatching.'
3. The *felicity/infelicity conditions*: 'The expression is borrowed from speech act theory and allows us to speak of the truth and falsity of a mode without immediately judging it solely according to constatives. We will therefore be able to define each mode's own conditions of veridiction.'
4. The *beings to institute*: 'The term is part of the investigation's metalanguage and designates that to which we respond when we ask about the "essence" of a situation; it is the content of a trajectory, that which is encountered at a particular pass. We pick up here an old definition of the copula "is", in order to highlight the articulation towards the other beings necessary for the continuation or reprise of essence and thus of meaning.'
5. The *alteration*: 'One of the questions that distinguishes one mode from another: what is the form of alteration or otherness particular to this mode, assuming that the being exists as being-as-other [a subsistence view of being] and not as being-as-being [a substance view of being]? It is a question here of the distinction between substance and subsistence. Thus the term has no opposite in the inquiry's metalanguage. It is designed to allow for a passage into all the other alterations that are particular to each mode.'

For example, for science (his mode of reference **[REF]**) Latour captures these five characteristics as follows, in their shortest formulations:

1. *Hiatuses*: Distance and dissemblances of forms.
2. *Trajectory*: Paving with inscriptions.
3. *Conditions of felicity/infelicity*: Bring back/lose information.
4. *Beings to institute*: Constants through transformations.
5. *Alteration*: Reach remote entities.

For religion (his mode of religion **[REL]**) the characteristics are:

1. *Hiatuses*: Break in times.
2. *Trajectory*: Engendering of persons.
3. *Conditions of felicity/infelicity*: Save, bring into presence/lose, take away.
4. *Beings to institute*: Presence-bearers.
5. *Alteration*: Achieve the end times.

And for politics (his mode of politics **[POL]**) Latour lists:

1. *Hiatuses*: Impossibility of being represented or obeyed.
2. *Trajectory*: Circle productive of continuity.
3. *Conditions of felicity/infelicity*: Start over and extend/suspend or reduce the Circle.
4. *Beings to institute*: Groups and figures of assemblies.
5. *Alteration*: Circumscribe and regroup.

In the next section, I will briefly expand on the characteristics of these three modes.

Note that Latour explicitly aligns himself with James, as I have shown in Chapter 2. Commentator de Vries highlights the impact of this alignment on Latour's shifting approach to 'empirical philosophy':

> By endorsing James' concept of experience in *An Inquiry into Modes of Existence*, 'empirical philosophy' gets a different meaning. From now on, an 'empirical philosopher' is not just someone who likes to explore and back-up his philosophical claims by empirical, ethnographical or historical investigations. 'Empirical philosophy' has come to denote a philosophical attitude and a metaphysical position that identifies what is real with what is experienced. (de Vries 2016, 168)

In the overview that he gives of his *Inquiry*, Latour declares that after the first part of the book:

> We shall know how to speak appropriately about a plurality of types of beings by relying on the guiding thread of experience, on empiricism as William James defined it: nothing but experience, yes, but *nothing less* than experience. (Latour [2012] 2013b, xxv)

As I showed in Chapters 2 and 3 Latour, in following James's metaphysics of experience approach (his doctrine of pure experience), subscribes to a philosophy that in Rickert's eyes is distinctly *un*philosophical: Latour's metaphysics of experience (focused on small transcendences), even though it may be inspired by his thinking about, sorting of and working with the materials from experience, must still be taken on faith. What Latour is looking for in each 'mode of existence' is to determine whether there is 'an experience of speaking … that is unique' to each mode (e.g. Latour [2012] 2013b, 340). However, to be able to make such determinations requires, I argue, transcendental assumptions. I will return to this at the end of this chapter when I compare Latour's occasionalist empiricist approach to values with Rickert's transcendental empiricist approach.

Latourian values in scientific, religious and political practices

Values in scientific practices

When Latour characterises the values underlying science, he abstains from the idea that scientific knowledge can be based on an objective and accurate representation of an outside world that can be known. For him, only the study of scientific practices can explain how scientists attribute objectivity, accuracy, reliability and truth to scientific knowledge. The work and maintenance that make up scientific knowledge can be explained by an analysis of networks of human and non-human 'actants', and the ways in which these actants are brought together and change through a process that Latour describes as 'translation'. Translation produces actor networks that are hidden from view in a process identified as 'purification'. This in turn implies that scientific theories are detached from their history, obtain the status of 'objective' representations of nature and are granted the ability to speak on behalf of nature. One can thus say that in his many works Latour has studied scientific practices with the aim of supplanting epistemological assumptions pertaining to objectivity with the articulation of the multiple heterogeneous actants that make up actor networks. However, he also makes clear in his work that one can distinguish an underlying value that drives scientific practice: the value of 'reference'.

Latour's 'mode of reference' dominates scientific practice. Through networks and using technology, scientific laboratory practice institutes constants through transformation, the truth value within this practice being whether information is brought back (as opposed to not bringing back information). Note again that Latour's philosophy is a philosophy of dealing with uncertainty; in the case of scientific practice, the accompanying mode of reference is able to jump over gaps of distance and dissemblances of form.

Latour provides an original identification of the overarching value of 'reference' that drives science – a position that seems at odds with many writings in both the older and the newer philosophy of science.[3] As Larry Laudan describes in his book *Science and Values* (1984), in the philosophy of science of the past 80 years – that is, after neo-Kantianism, to which we will return shortly in the instantiation of Rickert – there was first a period of highlighting consensus in scientific practice (e.g. the logical empiricists and Karl Popper), then subsequently a period of highlighting dissensus (from Thomas Kuhn and Paul Feyerabend onwards). Each period held different views on the role of cognitive values in scientific practice.

Laudan observes that the simple 'hierarchical model of rational consensus formation' (Laudan 1984, 23–41) of the first period, according to which 'disagreements about factual matters are to be resolved at the methodological level' and 'methodological differences are to be ironed out at the axiological level' (Laudan 1984, 26), does not hold. The cognitive values of science are plural (a non-exhaustive list is given by Laudan 1984, 36–7: generality and breadth of scope in our theories; simplicity; coherence; empirical accuracy); they are not necessarily weighted equally – nor held at all by all scientists in the community – and are interpreted differently. However, the 'Leibnizian ideal' of the hierarchical model cannot deal with this plurality, and hence the philosophies of the first period cannot explain dissensus in scientific practice.

Laudan also indicates that the philosophers of the second period, in the footsteps of Thomas Kuhn, cannot explain the transition from 'crisis' to 'normal science'. Kuhn's paradigms understood as worldviews include different underlying values and thus there is no basis to explain (even temporary) closure of scientific debate. Contrary to the philosophies reviewed by Laudan, however, some more recent work by philosophers of science such as Joseph Rouse (discussed in Chapters 2 and 7) does not suffer from this criticism. His practice-oriented reading of Kuhn takes paradigms not as 'primarily agreed-upon theoretical commitments' but as 'exemplary ways of conceptualizing and intervening in particular empirical contexts' (Rouse 1987, 30). Similarly, Latour's philosophy of science takes a practice orientation.

Values in religious practices

In contrast with scientific practices, Latour emphasises for religious practices that their accompanying 'mode of religion' has nothing to do with reference. He also treats religion as a mode of travel – but while in the case of science the interest is in information and representation, in the case of religion the interest is in translation and 'saving'. Instead of focusing on belief in the 'end products' of transformation, which is natural for the mode of reference, Latour focuses in his analyses of the mode of religion on alterations that happen to people when they utter religious speech and engage beings that 'have the peculiar characteristic of bringing persons from remoteness to *proximity*, from death to *life*' (Latour [2012] 2013b, 303).

Latour takes the mode of religion to be aiming to bring the end times into presence (but it may fail and then one loses the connection with 'beings of presence') – *saving* is the value of religion. For Latour, the beings of religion have 'special specifications' – they appear and disappear – and they have particularly discriminating truth values (felicity conditions): 'they define a form of subsistence that is not based on any substance but that is characterized by an alteration peculiar to it: "the time has come" and by its own form of veridiction' (Latour [2012] 2013b, xiii). Again, Latour's philosophy can be seen to be a philosophy of dealing with uncertainty. In the case of religious practice, the accompanying mode of religion is able to jump over the gap of a break in times (now and the end times).

Latour's entry point to discussing both scientific and religious practices – as well as all other practices – is the presence of uncertainty in these practices. Just as when one assesses evidential quality in science one will never reach 100 per cent certainty of reference since one jumps over the inferential gap, when one assesses 'evocational' quality in religion one will never reach 100 per cent certainty of being saved since once jumps over the gap between now and the end times.

Latour's identification of the overarching value of saving – linked to religious truth – that drives religion has strong antecedents in the philosophy of religion. In religious studies a distinction is often made between numinous encounters and mystical experiences (e.g. Barnes

2013, 17). Latour clearly focuses on the former, since he has not identified a mode of existence for the latter. There is a clear difference between Latour's value of religious truth and the value of scientific truth[4] that he identified to drive science, which is also confirmed in religious studies. Note that it is not a difference in the presence or absence of uncertainty *per se*, which some religious scholars erroneously assume.[5] I would argue, on the contrary, that the underlying *a priori* values of the different practices all have their uncertain realisations (it is the values, not the presence of uncertainty, that fundamentally make the different types of practices different) and that how these values are (and should be) interpreted is subject to uncertainty.

The philosophy of religion, as we saw for the philosophy of science, has had a strong orientation towards beliefs and (the possibility or impossibility of) theoretical commitments, and much less towards religious practice. The Jewish philosopher Howard Wettstein has written a penetrating analysis of how in Judaism in the Middle Ages (for instance through Maimonides) doctrinal belief reached the very heart of the religious outlook (Wettstein 2012). Wettstein focuses on the phenomenon of awe and on the role of poetry in religious ritual, arguing 'that religious life is viable in the absence of settled metaphysical beliefs' (Wettstein 2012, 7). It should be clear that Latour, similar to his approach to science, also has a practice orientation in his approach to religion.

Values in political practices

For characterising the values in political practices, I focus here on the political dimension underlying them.[6] For Latour, politics contrasts with the other types of practices that he identifies, in particular scientific and religious practices. Where science is about bringing back information and religion is about saving, politics is about starting over and extending what Latour calls the political 'Circle'. In his analysis of the mode of politics, Latour focuses on alterations that happen when people utter political speech and that pertain to:

> how to connect beings to others so that the collective holds together while respecting a strange condition … : the political has to allow beings to pass through and come back while tracing an envelope that defines, for a time, the 'we', the group in the process of self-production, before it is taken up again by another movement thanks to which the others, called 'they', find themselves fewer in

> number – unless the movement goes in the other direction and they become more and more numerous. (Latour [2012] 2013b, 338)

Politics is not so much about strong leaders or about elites: 'In politics, each of us, at every moment, is in an exceptional situation' (Latour [2012] 2013b, 348). Matters of concern 'oblige the political to curve around it' (Latour [2012] 2013b, 337). The 'bending over backwards' that is thus required in political discourse is very hard to perform:

> Political beings are always accused of lying, whereas they begin *truly* to lie, to lie *politically*, only if they 'go off on a tangent,' as the familiar expression has it, by beginning to proffer straight talk, that is, wanting [to] be 'faithfully' represented or 'faithfully' obeyed. (Latour [2012] 2013b, 344)

Latour takes the mode of politics to be aiming to circumscribe and regroup. However, it may fail, in which case one loses the connection with the beings that have formed groups and 'figures of assemblies'; starting over to form groups (which needs to be done repeatedly) is the value that guides politics. In terms of the uncertainties in the political type of practice, the gap that the mode of politics is able to jump over is the 'impossibility of being represented or obeyed', given that the Circle always breaks down.

Latour's proposal for how to interpret the 'mode of politics' has close affinities with the work of the American pragmatist John Dewey. Dewey, for instance, wrote about the issue of creating publics in his 1927 book *The Public and Its Problems*. A 'public' for Dewey potentially comprises all who are affected by transactions in which they themselves are not engaged: 'When indirect consequences are recognized and there is effort to regulate them, something having the traits of a state comes into existence' (Dewey [1927] 2012, 46). National states have emerged from the wishes of publics that were affected by escalating spirals of violence to have a monopoly of the state on violence. Meanwhile, states have taken on many more public tasks because new publics emerged in response to new problems.

Dewey points to the importance of technological changes for the creation of new indirect consequences and – thus – new publics. First, such publics are rudimentary and unorganised; later they can organise themselves. However, when there are too many too-large changes, too many publics emerge, not all of which have the means to organise themselves. This leads to what Dewey calls the 'eclipse' of publics. It seems clear to me that at present, nearly a century after Dewey published his book, this phenomenon of the eclipse of publics still occurs:

> [The present] age has so enormously expanded, multiplied, intensified and complicated the scope of the indirect consequences [of actions], has formed such immense and consolidated unions in action on an impersonal rather than a community basis, that the resultant public cannot identify and distinguish itself. (Dewey [1927] 2012, 110)

This is also what seems to drive Latour's own efforts in contributing to politics (that is, by finding new ways to create new publics – see, for example, Petersen 2016).

Rickert's philosophy of value

Having briefly highlighted the different types of values that, according to Latour, infuse scientific, religious and political practices and that have their attendant uncertainties in their realisation, the more fundamental question arises about the nature of 'value' and how to thematise its relationship to uncertainty. The best philosophical answer that I have encountered up to now which addresses this question head on is that offered by the neo-Kantian Rickert.[7] In Chapter 3 I offered an initial introduction to Rickert's thought. Admittedly, many neo-Kantians seem to over-rely on epistemology as the entry point into philosophy. But if there is one neo-Kantian philosopher who has written explicitly and extensively about the limits of theoretical knowledge[8] *vis-à-vis* religious truth (and other types of truth) and about the role of judgement in all aspects of culture (science, morality, art, religion, etc.), it is Rickert. I here emphasise again that Rickert is a particularly interesting philosopher to consider when focusing on the role of uncertainty in different cultural practices, and on the links of such practices with different truth values.

Rickert centred his philosophy around an analysis of values. For him, the chief value for scientific practices was the value of (theoretical) 'truth' and for religious practices the value of 'personal sanctity' (when the word 'truth' is used more loosely, that is, not as 'theoretical truth', this can be labelled as 'religious truth', as Rickert sometimes does). While the value of theoretical truth is a prime example of a value in Rickert's philosophy (and in neo-Kantianism more generally), there are also other values that play at least as important a role in our culture, such as religious, moral and political values. Rickert considers values as determining factors of human orientation; theoretical reflection on these values thus gives rise to a philosophy of culture (cf. Krijnen 2015, 111). I argue that uncertainty arises in various cultural practices when value-laden judgements are made under freedom and in context. Since the values that these judgements refer to (in philosophy and more largely in what Rickert denotes as *Wissenschaft* this concerns the value of theoretical truth, and in religious practice the value of religious truth) are *a priori*, there is a productive interaction between the poles of the *a priori* and reality in every cultural practice.

This is not to say that one can have certainty about *a priori* values, however. What I am emphasising here is their separate ontological status from reality. As I showed in Chapter 3, Rickert's realm of 'meaning-bestowed-in-the-act-of-judgement' ontologically sits in between, and is dependent upon, both the realm of the *a priori* and the realm of reality. The philosophical takeaway from Rickert's transcendental philosophy is that values can only be realised in fallible ways in practices.

I here use Rickert's final work, *Fundamental Problems of Philosophy* (1934; German title: *Grundprobleme der Philosophie*), to introduce further and discuss Rickert's philosophy of value. In this book, only 243 pages in length, Rickert offers an overview and typology of all the important philosophical questions pertaining to methodology, ontology and anthropology. He does not extensively elaborate his own answers to these questions (he had already done so in the first volume of his system of philosophy,[9] Rickert 1921), which makes this book both accessible and pertinent today.[10]

After rejecting an ontology that is limited only to the perceptible world (*Sinnenwelt*), which consists of both physical (*körperlich*) and mental (*seelisch*) being, Rickert introduces a distinction between perceptible (*wahrnehmbar*) and intelligible (*verstehbar*) being (Rickert 1934a, 78–82). The latter sort of being is not real (*wirklich*) in the way that the former is. He demonstrates how the values of (theoretical) truth (*Wahrheit*) and falsity (*Falschheit*) constitute a value-pair for scientifically minded people, while 'for people who are minded otherwise, pleasure and pain, good and evil, beautiful and ugly are examples of value-pairs' (Rickert 1934a, 86). In their practices, people typically seek to adhere to positive values and to avoid realising negative values – they do this because they value the positive values (hence the label 'values').

The world of experience (*Erfahrungswelt*) thus comprises both experience of the perceptible world and experience of the world of meaning and value. The latter two worlds are ontologically distinct, which gives rise to the question of how they relate to one another. However, such a question cannot be answered when one stays in the world of experience.

This brings Rickert to distinguish another ontologically distinct world, the 'pro-physical' world (*prophysische Welt*), which I introduced in the previous two chapters.[11] What he describes in the third part of his ontology, on the pro-physical world (pp. 109–34), recapitulates the thoughts on this topic that he had included in his 1921 book, which I described in Chapter 3. The pro-physical world constitutes the linking pin between the world of perception and the world of meaning and value, similar to how Kant's *Critique of the Power of Judgment* constituted the linking pin between 'the concept of nature' and 'the concept of freedom'. Since Rickert reserves the term 'metaphysics' for the fourth part of his ontology, which deals with the 'super-perceptible' (*übersinnlich*) and 'super-intelligible' (*überverstehbar*) world (the 'beyond'), he proposes 'pro-physics' as the theory of

> something that does not lie on the other side but fully on this side, and that is still something fundamentally different from the split object world [of perception and meaning/value], namely something that comes *before* the objectifying cleavage in sensible and intelligible being in the true sense as their 'pre-condition'. (Rickert 1934a, 111)

Following Kant, Rickert emphasises that knowledge of objects in the world of experience presupposes a knowing subject, and that this subject (being different from a mental object) cannot itself become an object of knowledge. Rickert uses the concept of the 'pro-physical subject', his modification of the transcendental Ego, to capture the pre-objective subject that is necessarily implied in all objects (Rickert 1934a, 115).

Now, crucially, the act of knowing an object involves a valuation by a judging subject: the truth value needs to be affirmed. In the natural sciences the approach is to find generalising relationships within delimited domains in the perceptible world:

> The extensive physical being is forever something other than the non-extensive mental being, and also the intelligible being of the entire psychophysical reality is fundamentally different in terms of ontology. First and foremost, the generalising special sciences have an interest to maintain and implement these distinctions. (Rickert 1934a, 108)

Because the value of (theoretical) truth is necessarily assumed in scientific practice, the world of meaning is also implicated in doing science. From the standpoint of Rickert, the true statements (*wahre Sätze*) of science, to which are attached theoretical values such as truth and reality, are empirical cultural goods (to be reproduced in meanings that have a non-empirical component pointing to values).

More generally, in all cultural practices (both theoretical and a-theoretical practices) the power of judgement – a faculty for subsuming under universals and for reflecting to arrive at universals – is necessarily invoked in affirming or negating the values (which are universals) that drive those practices. Note that the subject has the freedom to affirm or negate values.

In his publications in the 1920s and 1930s, Rickert often refers to a 'system of values'. One can get partial access to these values through their deposits in value judgements and cultural goods (e.g. scientific and religious practices). These actual valuations thus studied (e.g. through science studies or religious studies – or, more broadly, 'cultural sciences') are not identical to objective values (see the next section and Chapter 8). Through philosophical analysis the value judgements and cultural goods can be analysed for their deeper meaning, but only to a certain extent and schematically. Rickert (1921) distinguishes six domains of values (see also Table 4.1):

1. Logic (*Logik*) – value: (theoretical) truth (*Wahrheit*).
2. Aesthetics (*Aesthetik*) – value: beauty (*Schönheit*).
3. Mystics (*Mystik*) – value: impersonal sanctity (*unpersönliche Heiligkeit*).
4. Ethics (*Ethik*) – value: morality (*Sittlichtkeit*).
5. Erotics (*Erotik*)[12] – value: happiness (*Glück*).
6. Philosophy of religion (*Religionsphilosophie*) – value: personal sanctity (*persönliche Heiligkeit*).

He makes a distinction between ultimate and instrumental values. The scheme shown in Table 4.1 contains the six dimensions of ultimate values that he distinguishes and included in a fold-out table in his *System of Philosophy* (Rickert 1921) – something that his student Heidegger apparently made fun of in his lectures.[13]

If we look more closely at what Rickert says about science, it is important to note that the cultural good called 'science' (*Wissenschaft*, thus encompassing social science and the humanities), since it concerns a fallible realisation of the value of theoretical truth, is itself historical

Table 4.1 Rickert's scheme of six domains (plus two intermediate domains) of value, originally published as a two-page, fold-out table at the back of Rickert (1921).

Goods: asocial matters (*Sachen*) *Subjective comportment*: monistic contemplation *Form*: encompassing	Stages of completeness	*Goods*: social persons *Subjective comportment*: pluralistic activity *Form*: pervading
Domain of logic (1) *Value*: truth *Good*: science *Subjective comportment*: judgement *Worldview*: intellectualism	FIRST STAGE Un-completable totality Good of the future	**Domain of ethics** (4) *Value*: morality (*Sittlichkeit*) *Good*: community of free people *Subjective comportment*: autonomous action *Worldview*: moralism (*Moralismus*)
Domain of aesthetics (2) *Value*: beauty *Good*: art *Subjective comportment*: intuition (*anschauen*) *Worldview*: aestheticism	SECOND STAGE Fully completed particularity Goods of the present	**Domain of erotics** (5) *Value*: happiness (*Glück*) *Good*: loving community *Subjective comportment*: inclination – devotion (*Hingabe*) *Worldview*: eudaemonism
System of philosophy (8) Comprehensive theory of worldviews	INTERMEDIATE STAGE Immanent syntheses	**Love between male and female identities** (7) *Worldview*: eroticism
Domain of mystics (3) *Value*: impersonal sanctity *Good*: the All-One (world-mystery) *Subjective comportment*: solitude (*Abgeschiedenheit*) (divinisation) *Worldview*: mysticism	THIRD STAGE Fully completed totality Goods of eternity (Transcendent syntheses)	**Domain of the philosopy of religion** (6) *Value:* personal sanctity *Good*: the world of God (*Götterwelt*) *Subjective comportment*: piety *Worldview*: theism – polytheism

Source: Staiti ([2013] 2018, 30), adapted.

and changing. As Rickert notes in his successful book *Kulturwissenschaft und Naturwissenschaft* (Rickert 1926, 133–4),[14] this is as true for the natural sciences as it is for the cultural sciences. In the next section what Rickert has to say about the theoretical value of truth, in debate with James, is examined more closely. This subsequently informs the assessment of Latour's philosophy of value. With respect to religion, it is important to note that within his scheme of ultimate values, Rickert distinguishes between two poles of religious impulse, valuing either impersonal (*unpersönliche*) or personal (*persönliche*) sanctity (*Heiligkeit*). As Benjamin Crowe observes for the impersonal sanctity pole:

> [c]ontemplative mysticism ... illustrates quite clearly the main import of Rickert's system of values. Certain religious phenomena, such as pantheism, theosophy, or mystical experience, can be located at a determinate point in an overarching taxonomy of human cultural activities, goods and values connected with the latter. (Crowe 2010, 629)

He further comments that Rickert's personal sanctity pole offers 'a framework for comprehending and interpreting classically *theistic* religious phenomena' (Crowe 2010, 630).

Interestingly, Rickert dedicated his last book, *Grundprobleme der Philosophie*, to the Theology Faculty of his university, which had offered him an honorary doctorate for his 70th birthday the year before (1933). Like Kant in his *Conflict of the Faculties*, Rickert here limits the reach of philosophy. The fourth part of his ontology starts with a section titled 'The end of philosophy' (*Das Ende der Philosophie*). What makes Rickert decide to include the metaphysical world (*metaphysische Welt*) in his ontology is that:

> [n]othing guarantees that the free act of taking a position with respect to value in the real world will also have *wider influence* beyond what we accomplish as free subjects, and we can see an inescapable demand for unity precisely in the wish to secure a wider influence of values based on our free activity. What meaning would our acts otherwise have in the totality of being? (Rickert 1934a, 136–7)

Further unity has thus to be brought into our life worlds. However, we cannot obtain firm theoretical knowledge about metaphysical being. We have to use images and models, that is, symbols, to bring the desired unity.

In his anthropology, Rickert distinguishes the domain of religion from the domains of science, art, ethics and erotics (love), among others. In the analysis of religion as it is happening 'on this side', religious practices are no different in kind from other cultural practices (hence the similarities in methods from religious studies to other cultural sciences). The experience of the human being's imperfection and incompleteness fuels the search for, and belief in, values which are perfect and complete, incorporated in a super-human being.[15]

But Rickert also states that religious values do stand apart: he claims that there must be a far-reaching intolerance in religious people. Believers cannot put their religious values at the same level as the other values; they must put them at a higher level. According to Rickert (1934a, 200), you can only be a truly religious person if you subsume all other cultural goods to your religion.

So, contrary to Kant, Rickert's analysis of philosophy of religion turns out to have pietistic elements. The value of personal sanctity is affirmed in a-theoretical judgements that endorse experiences resulting from religious participation as a powerful source of personal transformation.

A final observation on Rickert's philosophical approach: given the importance that he attaches, with other neo-Kantians, to theoretical truth and a scientific (*wissenschaftliche*) approach to philosophy, we dare to call his approach 'naturalistic' (even though Rickert fought against scientistic naturalism). Going further, also with other neo-Kantians, Rickert denies a role for metaphysics in philosophy. At the same time, his strictly transcendental approach clearly acknowledges the limitations of science (*Wissenschaft*) in explaining life and peoples' wordviews, and his ontology is pluralistic.

Rickert and James on the value of theoretical truth

In order to prepare the ground for my further discussion of the philosophy of Latour (who aligns himself explicitly with James), it is important first to trace the debate on value, in particular the value of truth, that went on between Rickert and James. In this section I first highlight how James and Rickert talked past each other – instead of reinforcing each other (for which there was a real possibility, I argue) – when they referred to their mutual philosophical contributions, in particular on the subject of the value of theoretical truth (in Rickert's philosophy seen as regulative for scientific practices in general and for philosophy in particular).

Rickert was 21 years younger than James and received his first professorial chair, in philosophy, five years later than James (in

Freiburg in 1894); however, James was the first to refer to the other philosopher's work. For James, Rickert stood as a live example of German rationalist philosophy.[16] In Lecture VI of his *Pragmatism* ([1907] 1975), on 'Pragmatism's conception of truth', he made a reference to Rickert's first major work, *The Object of Knowledge* (1892; German title: *Der Gegenstand der Erkenntnis*),[17] in the following way:

> [J]ust as pragmatism faces forward to the future, so does rationalism ... face backward to a past eternity. True to her inveterate habit, rationalism reverts to 'principles' ... .
>
> When, namely, you ask rationalists, instead of accusing pragmatism of desecrating the notion of truth, to define it themselves by saying exactly what *they* understand by it, the only positive attempts I can think of are these two:
>
> 1. 'Truth is just the system of propositions which have an unconditional claim to be recognized as valid.' [Footnote: A. E. Taylor, *Philosophical Review*, vol. xiv, p. 288.]
> 2. Truth is a name for all those judgments which we find ourselves under obligation to make by a kind of imperative duty. [Footnote: H. Rickert, *Der Gegenstand der Erkenntnis*, chapter on 'Die Urtheilsnothwendigkeit'.]
>
> The first thing that strikes one in such definitions is their unutterable triviality. They are absolutely true, of course, but absolutely insignificant until you handle them pragmatically. (James [1907] 1975, 108–9)

He charges later on in the same chapter that Rickert 'long ago gave up the whole notion of truth being founded on agreement with reality' (113). And in Chapter 13 of *The Meaning of Truth* ([1909b] 1975), on 'Abstractionism and "Relativismus"', he writes that

> absolutists like Rickert freely admit the sterility of the notion [of truth], even in their own hands. Truth is what we *ought* to believe, they say, even tho' no man ever did or shall believe it, and even tho' we have no way of getting at it save by the usual empirical processes of testing our opinions by one another and by facts. (James [1909b] 1975, 143)

James apparently felt the need to criticise Rickert as an exponent of rationalism (and as a representative of those who he took to have 'accus[ed] pragmatism of desecrating the notion of truth', see above).

This was despite the fact that Rickert, in the various later versions of his 1892 chapter on relativism (*Der Relativismus*), had *not* categorised James, nor pragmatist philosophy for that matter, under relativism.

In that chapter Rickert was mainly concerned to point out that even if one accepts that one does not have access to absolute truth, this does not entail absolute scepticism (since there is still the absolute value of truth):

> Everything else that humans know may be uncertain and swaying – yes, perhaps no human being is yet in possession of true judgements; but *one* judgement cannot be false: the judgement that the value of truth is valid absolutely. It is the most certain judgement that we can think of, since it constitutes the condition for *every* judgement. (Rickert, 1892, 75–6)

From the third edition of his book (1915) onwards, Rickert explicitly included a reference to pragmatism and James in his relativism chapter. Rickert claimed, rather disingenuously, that 'James had regarded [Rickert's] text as an attempt to refute pragmatism, even though it was written when not much was known about pragmatism in Germany' (Rickert 1928, 301). Indeed, Rickert himself found the chapter that he had initially written trivial (and worthy of being cut, given that every reader would agree with its point), so he was in fact broadly in agreement with James here.

Rickert *did* attack James in his 1920 book *The Philosophy of Life* [*Die Philosophie des Lebens*, which can also be translated as 'Vitalism']: as mentioned in Chapter 1, he classified James among 'philosophers of life' (*Lebensphilosophen*), together with Friedrich Nietzsche (1844–1900) and Henri Bergson (1859–1941), among others. According to Rickert, the pragmatism elaborated by James functioned as the epistemology of vitalism, but it was not really all that new: the notion that truth is measured not by its theoretical meaning but by its use value in life was already held by Nietzsche and other philosophers before him (Rickert 1920, 25). While Rickert claimed that he valued James as a psychologist, he did not consider him to be a great philosopher:

> [James's] pluralistic metaphysics does not show many original features. The most interesting point in it is that a *uni*verse of vitality does not suffice, and that instead the world must be thought of as a *multi*verse. But the greatest value of this view is perhaps its name. The execution leaves something to be desired. (Rickert 1920, 25)

What made the fashionable currents in vitalism problematic, according to Rickert (1920, 35), was their focus on 'sheer' (*bloßes*) life (the immediate, the perceptible, the intuitive life) in opposition to 'killing' (*tötenden*) concepts (*Begriffe*). As Rickert points out, 'sheer experience of life does not constitute knowledge of real life' (Rickert 1920, 113). I do not believe it is a fair judgement of Rickert's to attribute such a shallow view of life and the associated limited role of knowledge to James, but it does sharply pose the question of what kinds of knowledge can be expected from philosophy and how that knowledge relates to perceptible experience. Here again I think that James and Rickert were actually much closer in spirit than they themselves – or their successors and commentators – have ever wanted to acknowledge.

For example, Rickert did strongly value the philosophers of life (among whom, as I said, he explicitly included James) for offering 'insight into the limits of the knowledge produced by the understanding with respect to abundance and variety [in life], which are originally given and which mock each and every attempt at conceptual mastery' (Rickert 1920, 176). These philosophers – more than 'philosophers of the Enlightenment' (whom Rickert identified as still being present in his time) – tried to get to grips with the 'unreasonable' (*das Unverständige*), and in doing so they offered an outlook on life that included hope. Seen positively, the main task of a philosophy of life is 'to warn us not to *forget* the life that must be "killed"' (Rickert 1920, 180), with the latter part (that life must be 'killed') being a necessary aspect of theoretical reflection and the first part (that one should not forget the living life) being necessary to point out that there is more to life than can be theoretically captured. Note that for someone like James it was attractive to mock neo-Kantian philosophers for paying insufficient attention to other dimensions of life than theory, and vice versa: for someone like Rickert it was attractive to mock philosophers of life for not taking theory seriously. Rickert claimed in particular that a theoretical reflection on values was lacking in the philosophy of life, including James's work. While positively the philosophy of life implies that 'a lively life is always at the same time a valuing life' (Rickert 1920, 185), negatively the philosophy of life cannot undertake a revaluation of all values (*Umwertung aller Werte*, cf. Nietzsche). Rickert criticised philosophers of life for neglecting the distinction between objective values and subjective valuations: the latter are only

> [h]uman valuations *of* and statements *on* values, which should not be confused with the values themselves, [and] can be influenced'. (Rickert 1920, 185)

Even though, according to Rickert, pragmatist philosophy erred in its theoretical interpretation of the value of truth, he still considered that

> it rightly asserts that truth in its essence is valuable, and also that the knowing human being must be understood as a valuing subject. (Rickert 1920, 187)

Putting this (indirect and unproductive) debate between James and Rickert into context, it is worth observing that James's work was 'met with hostility' in the German academy (Nubiola 2014, 21). James's German translator, Wilhelm Jerusalem, who published a German edition of *Pragmatism* in 1908 (only one year after its original publication), wrote to James in 1909:

> the misunderstandings of and the opposition against Pragmatism lies deeper than I thought at first. Science wants a theoretic or static, a timeless truth. (Quoted in Nubiola 2014, 22)

This exchange confirms that Rickert could have reacted (and sometimes did react) more subtly to James's work. Rickert actually understood that judgements are made under uncertainty and only point to timeless values; cultural goods are historical. How does Latour fare *vis-à-vis* this debate between James and Rickert on the value of theoretical truth? I will address this question in the next section, in the context of Latour's philosophy of value.

Latour's philosophy of value further described and assessed

As I wrote in Chapter 2, Latour aligned his philosophy with James's radical empiricism. Like James he loathes dualisms, but rather than a psychological-cum-philosophical outlook he takes an anthropological-cum-philosophical approach. Like James, he analyses gaps in practices. Also like James, he abhors German rationalist philosophy, extreme forms of the Enlightenment that peaked in the nineteenth century. I argue that Latour should not throw out all of Kant – whom he mentions regularly – nor all of Rickert – whom he never mentions – with the rationalist bathwater. My point is that Latour could safely keep elements of Kant's analysis of the power of judgement and its role in the fallible realisation of values in practice. Such elements are well captured in Rickert's transcendental naturalistic approach to the philosophy of culture, again with its emphasis on the fallible realisation of values.

Latour distinguishes 15 ways to 'speak well' (see Table 4.2), each having its own truth value (or 'felicity condition').[18] Like Rickert he presents them in a two-page table at the end of his book. By way of example, I here briefly touch on nine of his modes of existence (the ones that Latour calls 'non-social') and their relevance to the practices of science (which, I argue, is not only described by the mode of reference, even though that is its prime mode). I explicitly make links to the phenomenon of wonder discussed in Chapter 2:

Table 4.2 Latour's scheme of 14 domains (plus one pseudo-domain) of value.

Name	Meaning	Felicity Condition
[REP]RODUCTION	A mode of existence about prolonging existents	Continuation of
[MET]AMORPHOSIS	A mode of existence about mutating existents	Passage from
[HAB]IT	A mode of existence about moving towards courses of action	Attending to
[TEC]HNOLOGY	A mode of existence about inventing unexpected detours	Rearranging
[FIC]TION	A mode of existence about shifting fictionally	Holding up
[REF]ERENCE	A mode of existence about paving with inscriptions	Bringing back information
[POL]ITICS	A mode of existence about acting politically	Starting over and extending the Circle
[LAW]	A mode of existence about linking of cases and actions through legal means	Reconnecting
[REL]IGION	A mode of existence about bringing into presence	Being saved
[ATT]ACHMENT	A mode of existence about having interests in goods and bads	Following interests
[ORG]ANIZATION	A mode of existence about producing and following scripts	Mastering scripts
[MOR]ALITY	A mode of existence about linking of means and ends	Renewing calculations
[NET]WORK	A mode of existence about following heterogeneous connections	Traversing domains
[PRE]POSITION	A mode of existence about detecting crossings of modes of existence	Keeping open all modes of existence
[DC] DOUBLE CLICK	A pseudo-mode of existence about displacing without translating	Speaking literally

- With the overly rationalist – or unreflexive modernist – tradition, Latour associates a mode of existence, or rather not really a viable mode but a pseudo-mode or a 'foil', that he calls *Double Click*. Indisputable Reason reigns and all speech can be taken literally. The existence of any gaps is denied. Wonder cannot be understood and is irrational. There is a horror of hiatuses.
- Latour's instantiation of a limited version of the power of judgement (not reflected on by him to be such) is his mode of *preposition*. This is where judgements are assigned their right category or 'interpretive key' and ontological pluralism is ensured. The truth value of preposition is whether each mode can be expressed. The gaps/uncertainties that this reflexive mode of preposition deals with are risks of category mistakes. Wonder very much relates to this mode of existence – asking oneself what is the right way to express wonder makes one contemplate choosing different modes.
- Many people know Latour for his analysis of the mode of *network*, especially for science in action. The role of judgement is to follow the extension of associations – across heterogeneous networks. The truth value is whether different domains can be traversed. The surprise of associations is an important trigger of wonder. How is it possible that what happens in the laboratory becomes associated with the equations of quantum mechanics, and becomes further associated (for some) with the mind of God? This supposes that such a network holds together at a particular moment: there is no guarantee that such a network comes into place or stays. Links may become severed.
- A very basic mode of existence, that of *reproduction*, is often a cause of, for instance, metaphysical wonder (which Latour does not address). Why do things exist? Why do they keep existing? The mode itself is aimed at prolonging existents through lines of force, lineages or societies.
- A higher-level mode of existence, that of *metamorphosis*, deals with the gaps/uncertainties that psyches can be confronted with – shocks that can change who you are. In some cases wonder can be truly transformational and experiencing the emotion makes one undergo a metamorphosis, coming out of the experience differently.
- The mode of *habit* performs the wondrous miracle of providing continuity in action – and prevents one from reflexively getting stuck in the mode of preposition.
- The mode of *technology* produces wondrous technological set ups that deal with the gap/uncertainty that obstacles and the need for detours bring up in practice.

- The mode of *fiction* may come into play in scientific practice and the experience of wonder when, for instance, poetic expressions are chosen. They have their own truth value: do they make us 'hold up' the emotion of wonder? Do they make others 'believe' in the expressive forms?
- Last but not least in this list of nine non-social modes of existence, let me return to the ostensibly dominant mode in the practice of science which really defines its identity: the mode of *reference* (discussed above). The idea here is that through networks and using technology, laboratory practice institutes constants through transformation, the truth value being whether information is brought back (as opposed to not bringing back information). Wonder can pertain precisely to what this mode is able to do: jump over gaps of distance and dissemblances of form. As I said earlier in Chapter 2, uncertainty remains here – one may be wrong about the insight that triggers the emotion of wonder – but it is the deep realisation of that uncertainty that triggers the emotion.

Latour's remaining six modes of existence are all 'social modes': those of *politics, law, religion, attachment, organisation* and *morality*. I briefly described the modes of religion and politics earlier in this chapter. I will only reiterate one remark on his mode of religion here: since Latour connects this mode with theistic religion focusing on personal sanctity, it becomes apparent that Latour does not have a mode of *mystics* in his scheme.[19]

Let me assess here how Latour's 'modes of reference' and their associated truth values relate to Rickert's 'logic' and its associated 'theoretical truth'. Latour criticises a Kantian metaphysical assumption of 'things-in-themselves' that are taken to stand 'behind' knowledge in Kant's Critiques:

> [T]he notion of 'known thing' does not in fact exhaust what can be said about the world. Not at all because scientists are 'limited' in their knowledge of things that would remain unknowable, since they accede to them quite well and know them admirably, but because the expression 'objective knowledge' (provided that it is materialized) designates a progression, an access route, a movement that will cross paths with other types of movements to which it cannot be reduced and that it cannot reduce, either. This impression that there is always something *more* than what is known in the thing known does not refer at all to the unknowable

(the complaint of Critique is in no way justified) but to the *presence of other modes* whose equal dignity epistemology, despite all its efforts, has never allowed to be recognized. Knowledge can grasp everything, go everywhere, but in its own mode. It is not a domain, whose expansion has to be limited or authorized. It is a network that traces its own particular trajectory, alongside other, differently qualified trajectories, which it never ceases to crisscross. (Latour [2012] 2013b, 85)

So, Latour associates 'objectivity' of knowledge with the progression in building chains of reference, and he adopts effectively a pragmatist notion of truth. Thus Latour runs into the same objection that Rickert made to James (see the previous section): in stating any claim, including about which modes and corresponding values exist, a notion of theoretical truth must be assumed by Latour; this is not reducible to the pragmatist notion of truth but resides in the unreal realm of value and is objective.

This brings me to a final reflection on Latour's philosophy of value and how it can be understood in many respects as a similar attempt at a philosophy of value to Rickert's. Like Rickert, Latour recognises that there is a plurality of truth values. Where Latour emphasises that these truth values have been discovered in history, Rickert notes that even though valuations vary historically, the underlying values that are thus expressed exist outside of time – they are valid, not real (the real valuations about objective truths can be wrong or right – we remain deeply uncertain about the objective truths). Latour, while he is often very critical of Kantian thinking, can be said to rely unreflexively to a large extent on Kant's analysis of the power of judgement, a crucial part of our faculty for thinking that helps us jump gaps. Latour is also willing to systematise, like Rickert. However, he claims to be radically empirical, like James.

What Latour does not acknowledge is that he also implicitly assumes the existence of *a priori* values in the world (he even calls the modes 'categories' too), values to which we can be good and bad 'receptors'. Latour claims that he is afraid of 'bad transcendence' (metaphysical 'substance' thinking), and that what he proposes is 'good transcendence' (what he calls 'subsistence' thinking). I find that Latour's metaphysical choice, following James, of giving primacy to experience alone and implicitly denying the separate ontological status of *a priori* values (including that of theoretical truth) from sense experience causes his philosophy to be unreflexive about the role of transcendental values and their realisation in practices.

Conclusion

This methodological criticism of Latour's project as unreflexively relying on a neo-Kantian element should not detract our attention from the importance of his project. On the contrary: I think that his project can be strengthened with a transcendental naturalistic interpretation.

Latour's project is exciting as it brings a wide-ranging present-day empirical anthropological effort (a cultural science *pur sang*) to bear on the philosophy of value. His project explicitly facilitates diplomatic encounters, both between different societies and, connected to that, between different modes of existence.[20] Also, I claim that significant contributions can be made to the science-and-religion dialogue on the basis of his project, as I aim to demonstrate in Part II, with a focus on his *Facing Gaia*. But first, in the next chapter, I will address the philosophical assessment of the status of models.

Notes

1 With one hopeful exception: the value of theoretical truth. Note that Rickert held that philosophers cannot theoretically determine what the a-theoretical values are. However, he *did* devise a theoretically derived structure encompassing all values (see Table 4.1). And note also that Latour suggests a substructure in his scheme of values (this substructure is not shown in Table 4.2): of the 15 modes shown in the table, the first 12 are clustered into four groups. The second of these he calls 'quasi objects' and the third of these 'quasi subjects' while the fourth of these are a group that 'links quasi objects and quasi subjects' (Latour [2012] 2013b, 443). I would say that Latour unreflectively makes theoretical claims (unreflective in the sense that he cannot account for it philosophically in his so-called 'empirical philosophy').

2 I am providing Latour's explanations of these terms here, taken from the website that accompanies his book, modesofexistence.org.

3 But in Chapter 5 I will argue that there is also an important stream in the history of philosophy of science that emphasises (weak) referential realism. While emphasising different philosophical questions from those addressed by Latour, this is not at odds with his analysis of the importance of the value of reference in scientific practices.

4 I use 'scientific truth' here in the internal sense of Latour's work, that is, as the 'truth of the mode of reference'. Below I consider the difference between this notion of scientific truth and Rickert's.

5 For example, in a recent *Handbook of Education, Religion and Values* one can find the following distinction between different types of practices and where their values come from: 'the reason and deliberation on which agents should base their religious values is not the evidence-based reason of natural or social science, but the practical reason of moral and spiritual life. Since such practical wisdom lies squarely in the realm of freedom of choice, it must be ever open to possibilities of change and development and cannot have the rational or epistemic closure of scientific–technical reasoning' (Carr 2013, 14).

6 In Part II I will address issues in climate policy. It is the mode of politics that ultimately underpins public policy decisions; these can be seen as being political decisions and deriving their legitimacy from politics.

7 While I also think that Latour offers a better empirical investigation into values than Rickert, I am critical of the metaphysical load that comes with his work on the modes of existence and the lack of reflexivity with respect to the ontological status of values, see below.

8 Given my use of the label 'scientific truth' for 'truth of the mode of reference', I here stick to Rickert's use of 'theoretical truth' and 'theoretical knowledge' for the practices that he groups under *Wissenschaft* (which includes natural and social science and the humanities, as well as philosophy). When I refer to 'science' when discussing Rickert's work, I am not assuming Latour's 'mode of reference'.

9 Rickert never finished the other planned volumes.

10 An exception to this enthusiastic endorsement must be made for one paragraph on p. 167 on 'race': Rickert claims that not all cultures can be developed in every race (he is reflecting a particular – superseded – cultural view here). In the Preface, Rickert also notes that the examples he gives of non-scientific worldviews (*außerwissenschaftlichen Weltanschauungen*), particularly in the final part of the book, stem from his contemporary German culture and could be replaced by examples from other cultures (Rickert 1934a, vii). It must be added here, however, that 13 years earlier he strongly objected against mistaking 'race', which is a natural science concept, for a cultural concept: 'Although it may constitute the basis on which the participation in a culture develops more or less easily, it is never sufficient to make a person a member of a people's culture' (Rickert 1921, 323).

11 Note that Rickert uses 'pro-physical' to stand for 'pro-perceptual' (thus this includes both 'pro-physical' in the narrow sense and 'pro-mental'). As I describe below, it is mainly the contrast with 'metaphysical' that drove him to use the term 'pro-physical'.

12 Another word that Rickert uses for 'erotics' is 'love' (*Liebe*), which is taken in a wide sense.

13 It turns out that there is a strong similarity between Latour's system of values and Rickert's also in terms of presentation. Crowe (2010, 629) mentions that in a lecture course in 1923 Heidegger 'lampoons this chart, though without explicitly naming Rickert'.

14 The first edition of this book already dates back to 1899.

15 Cf. Zijderveld (2006, 194).

16 It would have been fairer, I think, for James to have categorised Rickert as 'mixed' (that is, between rationalist and empiricist), as he had categorised Kant in his posthumously published *Some Problems of Philosophy* (see Chapter 3).

17 This work underwent major revision in subsequent editions (in 1904^2, 1915^3, $1921^{4,5}$ and 1928^6). From a brief *Habilitationsschrift* (94 pages) in 1892 with the subtitle 'A contribution to the problem of philosophical transcendence' [*Ein Beitrag zum Problem der philosophischen Transcendenz*], it developed into a fully-fledged book of 252 pages in 1904 with a new subtitle: 'Introduction to transcendental philosophy' [*Einführung in die Tranzendentalphilosophie*]. In 1915 a completely rewritten edition appeared; in its Preface Rickert emphasised that 'the earlier editions should not be used any longer' (Rickert 1928, viii). The final edition has an extent of 484 pages. A historical-critical edition of all six editions appeared in 2018, as the first volume published (*Band 2*, consisting of two sub-volumes) of his complete works, *Heinrich Rickert: Sämtliche Werke*. In *Pragmatism*, James referred to the first edition.

18 One of the modes of existence, *Double Click*, Latour actually judges to be a 'fake' mode, which then leaves 14 ways to speak well.

19 More generally one can observe that, compared with Rickert's scheme, Latour's scheme is more activity-oriented than contemplation-oriented. This again links back to the metaphysical approach of radical empiricism chosen by James and Latour rather than the explicitly transcendental approach chosen by Rickert.

20 See, e.g., Kouw and Petersen (2018) for an analysis of the diplomacy between science and politics in the context of global climate change, which also features in Chapters 7 and 8.

5

Models

Introduction

What shape do cognitive judgements under uncertainty ultimately take in real practices of science and religion, while driven by their respective values? The focus of the previous three chapters has primarily been on reaching individual judgements in practices, and on the wonder, freedom and realisation of values associated with reaching these judgements. In this chapter our focus turns to the resulting 'models' that arise as both cultural products and generative pointers to meaning and action. My interest in this chapter lies primarily in the philosophical status of models, in particular scientific models, in connection with the uncertainty that remains attached to them, and in analysing their philosophical status using a transcendental naturalistic approach. In claiming that models are central cultural 'artefacts' in all cultural practices, I argue that it is important to complete the argument for transcendental naturalism with a philosophical consideration of models.

Let me begin with some examples. In *Facing Gaia* Latour assigns a large role to the models developed in the practices of climate science to underpin important facts about climate change, such as attributing the recently observed warming to human influences:

> [T]he scientific disciplines that have come together to develop these facts that have become so sturdy do not come from the prestigious sciences such as particle physics or mathematics; they come from a multitude of earth sciences whose certainties have been achieved not by some earth-shaking, fool-proof demonstration but by the weaving together of thousands of tiny facts, reworked through

> modelling into a tissue of proofs that draw their robustness from the multiplicity of data, each piece of which remains obviously fragile. Between a tissue of proofs and a tissue of lies, we understand that people who know nothing about the practice of science are quick to confuse the two – especially if it's really in their interest that the data prove false. (Latour 2015 [2017], 31)

Scientific models also feature in the opening 'scene' of *An Inquiry into Modes of Existence*. In 2010, after a French climate scientist has been publicly challenged about uncertainty in attributing climate change to human influences, he responds:

> 'If people don't *trust the institution of science*, we're in serious trouble.' And he begins to lay out before his audience the large number of researchers involved in climate analysis, the complex system for verifying data, the articles and reports, the principle of peer evaluation, the vast network of weather stations, floating weather buoys, satellites, and computers that ensure the flow of information – and then, standing at the blackboard, he starts to explain the pitfalls of the models that are needed to correct the data as well as the series of doubts that have had to be addressed on each of these points. 'And, in the other camp', he adds, 'what do we find? No competent researcher in the field who has the appropriate equipment.' (Latour [2012] 2013b, 3)

Scientific models are part of larger networks. Through these networks 'chains of reference' are built up, with the aim of bringing back information, for instance about the human influence on climate change, via 'inscriptions'. Uncertainty remains attached to scientific models (see Petersen [2006] 2012 and Chapter 7 of this book for discussions on the thin line between climate models as part of a 'tissue of proofs' or a 'tissue of lies').

Latour also makes use of different models of God or the Transcendent in *Facing Gaia*, when naming the 'supreme authority' that makes a people a collective (for a summary table see Latour [2015] 2017, 181). For example, for the 'people of Nature' (see Chapter 6) he announces that he will specify a model for their supreme authority:

> I am going to try to define the people associated with this supreme authority whose features we are going to attempt to specify. What name shall we give to the authority? To avoid the word 'God',

> which would be too disrespectful, too provocative, in this context, I propose 'Out-of-Which-We-Are-All-Born', 'OWWAAB'. (Latour [2015] 2017, 159)

In qualifying the properties of this 'deity' model, he uses labels such as 'laws of nature' and 'deanimated'.[1] The 'people of Creation' use another – as Latour argues, correlated – model, with the deity being an 'ordering God' who is 'overanimated'. Latour proposes two alternative models for 'terrestrialized' peoples who aim to live in the face of 'Gaia' (that is, to live appropriately in the 'Anthropocene', in the 'new climatic regime')[2] and whose deities are labelled, respectively, 'multiverse' (animated) and 'God of ends/ends of God' (animated). In Part II of this book I further analyse in the context of climate change the meanings and consequences of these different religious models discussed by Latour.

Latour's philosophy, as we saw, is a philosophy of how practices get reproduced by jumping over different types of gaps, that is, by dealing with different types of uncertainty. He exemplifies the value of reference in scientific practice in the context of a philosophical discussion on the status of models. And he, like transcendental naturalism, does reject any form of scientific realism that defines truth in terms of a correspondence between a theory or a model and reality. He explains, as we saw in Chapter 2:

> The lines traced by these chains will now allow us to unsettle the ordinary notion of correspondence. In fact, what are usually called the 'knowing mind' and the 'known object' are not the two extremes to which the chain would be attached; rather, they are *both* products arising from the lengthening and strengthening of the chain. A knowing mind and a known thing are not at all what would be linked through a mysterious viaduct by the activity of knowledge; they are the progressive result of the extension of chains of reference. (Latour [2012] 2013b, 80)

In the previous chapters we have dealt with the metaphysical load that is present here. While some similarity exists at a methodological level between Latour's philosophical description of the operation of the mode of reference and both James's description of 'pure experience' and Rickert's description of 'pro-physics' (see the previous three chapters), there are also important differences. The main similarity is between James and Latour: where for James the doctrine of pure experience held that all sensible events are made of the same neutral stuff and whether they qualify as mental or physical depends on the way in which the events are seen in a sequence (with thus mind and object being different products of activity, different aspects of events that are unfolding), Latour's modes of existence are similarly the result of activity and viewing different aspects of the events that are unfolding from the perspective of a value (such as the value of the mode of reference).[3] However, the main difference sits between James and Latour, on the one hand, and Rickert, on the other. In transcendental naturalism, adopting Rickert's philosophy of pro-physics, the transcendental assumptions that come *logically* before the objectivising split into perceptible and intelligible being are *not the result of activity*. Rather they are, ontologically speaking, *a priori* assumptions that mingle with experienced reality from the start. Relatedly, we found in Chapter 4 that Latour lacks an explicit notion of objective theoretical truth.

However, there is also an important commonality between James's, Latour's and Rickert's assessment of epistemology which is relevant for the present chapter, namely that *epistemology should not come in a strong form of realism*. James and Latour have been picking fights with problematic forms of realism, as too has Rickert.[4] My claim is that this leads to an appropriate openness to models and the associated uncertainty in a variety of practices. Over his career Latour has been very much dismissive of philosophy of science as a whole.[5] However, I will emphasise in this chapter that there have been more than a few philosophers of science who have been reflecting on the use of models in practice and who have developed weak versions of referential realism that are in line with transcendental naturalism.

The broad question at issue here (of which this chapter tackles only a part) is: how are models of nature (including human nature and society) and models of God or metaphysical transcendence used in their respective practices, and how do they reflect uncertainty so that they can function as grounds for creativity and openness in these practices? In short: how do models relate to uncertainty and what does this imply for their philosophical status?

Now here is why this question is too large to tackle in its entirety in this book. Models have very different properties and functions in the different modes of existence, in connection with the different values underlying these practices (see Chapter 4). Even if we use the same term 'model' to refer to, for instance, the scientific model of nature as built up from atoms (mode of reference), the public policy model of 'ecological modernisation' (Hajer 1995) for dealing with environmental problems (mode of politics)[6] or the religious model of

God as father (mode of religion), the meanings of the word 'model' differ in several respects. Still, I would argue that all these uses of the term 'model' involve *viewing something in terms of something else*. Intrinsically a model has uncertainty attached to it: *there remains a gap between the model and the 'truth'* (scientific, religious, etc.) with respect to actual reality (in past, present or future, depending on the matter of interest). The manifold flux of experience thus cannot be fully pinned down in models.

In science, there are limitations to models in referring to distant entities, which can partly be expressed statistically but which often involve a recognition of ignorance (fundamental limitations in knowing about nature). In politics, models may not be able to keep citizens grouped through the narrative for policy action that is attached to them (fundamental limitations in knowing – and influencing – the peoples' political frames). And in religion there is the ineptness of models to evoke, for instance, the end times in the present, which can partly be attributed to the inaccuracy of metaphorical language but again involves a recognition of ignorance (fundamental limitations in knowing[7] God or in intimating metaphysical transcendence).

While most of this chapter is devoted to an in-depth exploration of this tension in scientific practices (with 'models' taken as a 'catch-all' term that also encompasses other conceptual content in scientific practices such as theories, see below), I start by discussing similarities and differences between models in scientific and religious practices. This is followed by an exposition of early twentieth-century philosophy of science debates on models, highlighting the views on realism and 'instrumentalism'[8] of contemporaries of James and Rickert. The position of physicist, historian and philosopher Pierre Duhem is shown to be a particularly rich resource with which to demonstrate some of the philosophical issues that concern my argument. These include comparing the status of models in science with that of models in religion: against positivists who wished to distinguish between epistemic certainty in science, on the one hand, and epistemic uncertainty in religion, on the other, Duhem went out of his way to demonstrate that *both* science *and* religion were deeply uncertain affairs (Martin 1991). In the subsequent section I investigate contemporary views in philosophy of science on the topic of models and scientific realism.[9] Finally, in the conclusion, I highlight the position of transcendental naturalism on models.

Similarities and differences between models in science and religion

In this section I discuss work by Ian Barbour, Sallie McFague, Janet Soskice and Ernan McMullin on similarities and differences between models in the practices of science and religion before I briefly rehearse Latour's views on this.

The American scholar (physicist and theologian) Ian Barbour (1923–2013), who played a significant role from the 1960s in creating the field of 'science and religion', published an accessible book *Myths, Models and Paradigms* in 1974, which is very relevant for the present study. Barbour refers to the philosophical school of linguistic analysis to argue for each 'field' (science, religion, etc.) to have its own type of language and 'logic'. He delves more closely into the fields of science and religion and claims that these both feature models, where Barbour defines a model as 'a symbolic representation of selected aspects of the behaviour of a complex system for particular purposes' (Barbour 1974, 6). There are many similarities in the use of models in religion as compared with science:

> Models in religion are also analogical. They are organizing images used to order and interpret patterns of experience in human life. Like scientific models, they are neither literal pictures of reality nor useful fictions. One of the main functions of religious models is the interpretation of distinctive types of experience: awe and reverence, moral obligation, reorientation and reconciliation, interpersonal relationships, key historical events, and order and creativity in the world. (Barbour 1974, 7)

The main difference, according to Barbour, is that several of the functions of religious models do not have a parallel in science, especially emotive and valuational functions (the experiences of wonder in scientific practices that I described in Chapter 2 do not receive their proper due in Barbour's book). Here it is worthwhile to note Barbour's anti-instrumentalism (models should *not* be considered 'useful fictions').

Even though the non-cognitive functions of models in religion are distinctive, Barbour maintains that this does not imply that religious models do not have cognitive functions: they influence perception and interpretation (also poetry has cognitive functions, he adds). The felicity condition for religious (or poetic) language is 'its faithfulness to concrete human experience' (Barbour 1974, 14). He considers models as more elaborated than metaphors and symbols:

> Metaphors are employed only momentarily and symbols only in a limited range of contexts, but models are more fully elaborated and serve as wider interpretive schemes in many contexts. We are asked, in the biblical case, to construe the world through the model of a father's love and purpose. Other religious traditions have used dominant models which are impersonal in character. (Barbour 1974, 16)

Interpretations of history and human experience are influenced by such religious models.

Barbour pays attention in his book to both numinous encounters and mystical experiences, and to the different types of religious models associated with these practices:

> *Numinous encounter* is characterized by awe, reverence, mystery and wonder. There is a sense of being grasped and laid hold of, and a conviction that one's response is evoked. ... This pattern, we saw, is typically associated with worship and with personal models of the divine. *Mystical union*, on the other hand, is characterized by joy, serenity and peace. The mystic speaks of the unity of all things and the loss of individual identity. He practices meditation and tends to use impersonal models. (Barbour 1974, 121)

Different religious traditions compare differently on these two poles within religion, for instance 'Theravada Buddhism is remarkable for its simplicity, but perhaps at the price of comprehensiveness, since numinous experience and worship are less strongly represented than in other religions', such as Christianity, which includes 'a richer interweaving of many strands, but at the price of simplicity' (Barbour 1974, 143–4). Near the end of his book (pp. 155–65), Barbour discusses four models of God (monarchical, deistic, dialogic and agent) and adds a fifth (process).

In the 1980s several authors took their cue from Ian Barbour (and Arthur Peacocke and John Polkinghorne) in discussing the similarities and differences between models in science and religion. Here I briefly feature the works of Sallie McFague (1982), Janet Soskice (1985) and Ernan McMullin (1985). In terms of similarities, McFague sees models as 'systems [that] are constructed that provide intelligibility, not just to this or that phenomena, but to reality as a whole' (1982, 102). They are always partial, 'necessitating both alternative and complementary models as well as eternal vigilance against their literalization, *against the loss of the metaphorical tension*' (McFague 1982, 102).

According to McFague (1982, 103–8), the differences between scientific and theological models are large and fundamental. Religion (of the Judeo-Christian kind) has an original model or root-metaphor of 'a cosmic, metaphysical drama of relationships, of action and response, which includes everything that exists' (McFague 1982, 104); science does not remain science but becomes metaphysics when it tries to move beyond the interrelations among scientific laws to overarching root-metaphors. In addition, 'scientific models refer to the quantitative dimension of the world while theological models refer to the qualitative dimension' (McFague 1982, 106).

In her discussion of the use of models in creeds, McFague asks the question: 'Is credal language open-ended, relative, tensive, iconoclastic, and indirect or is it absolutistic, possessive, static, literalistic, and idolatrous?' (McFague 1982, 113). She notes that two of the major images – 'Father' and 'Son' – are 'concrete, detailed models which simplify in an intelligible way what are otherwise impregnable mysteries, that is, God and Jesus of Nazareth' (McFague 1982, 113). However, she pleads for a metaphorical theology that is able to balance the hegemony of the paternal model.

Soskice (1985) finds it important to distinguish 'model' from 'metaphor': 'an object or state of affairs is said to be a *model* when it is viewed in terms of some other object or state of affairs. A model need not be a metaphor, for a model need not be linguistic at all' (Soskice 1985, 55). She criticises Barbour for conflating the two, for regarding their difference as only a matter of degree and for associating them both with analogy (Soskice 1985, 101). She criticises the following two putative differences between models in science and religion: (1) the models of science are exploratory and those of religion affective (but, as Soskice claims, 'in practice Christians tend to regard their models as both exploratory and reality depicting', Soskice 1985, 112) and (2) the models of science are dispensable whereas those of religion are not (but, in both practices, they are indispensable: 'On any satisfactory account of scientific practice, it seems we cannot easily separate the model from the theory', Soskice 1985, 115).

According to Soskice (1985), naïve realism with respect to God should be left behind but similarly, as for scientific realism, a case can be made for theological realism: 'we do not claim to describe God but to point through His effects, and beyond His effects, to Him' (Soskice 1985, 140). Theological realism, like scientific realism when both are interpreted as forms of referential realism, 'emphasizes, in a way that neither an empiricist nor an idealist position does, the importance to Christian belief of experience, community, and an interpretive tradition' (Soskice 1985, 149).

Ernan McMullin is critical about the carrying over of scientific realism to theological realism:

> In short, the reason why the language of theology is held to be analogical ('metaphorical' in the extended contemporary usage) lies not in its procedures but in the character of its object which is said to transcend all human modes of expression. In science, the emphasis on metaphor comes from a different quarter. ... Much metaphor in science does *not* rely on analogy; it is not as though the extension of our imagination into the unknown is always accomplished by means of analogies with what we already know. (McMullin 1985, 47)

Paul Allen, in comparing the different versions of 'critical realism' of Ian Barbour, Arthur Peacocke and John Polkinghorne, on the basis of their Gifford Lectures, finds Polkinghorne to be the most emphatic about the differences in the way science and religion deploy models (Allen 2006, 35). Still, there is a desire for a unified worldview among science and religion scholars, and '[c]ritical realism integrates the act of knowing with the known in the affirmation of a unified worldview' (Allen 2006, 34). While McMullin is very careful in extrapolating scientific realism to theological realism, his 'preferred notion for describing the science–theology relationship is "consonance". It appears to have been coined by McMullin to claim a principle of interdisciplinary non-contradiction' (Allen 2006, 159). Allen interprets McMullin's consonance as a form of critical realism, 'in which knowledge is cognitively discovered and verified in both disciplines' (Allen 2006, 160).

Let me now, at the end of this short overview of discussions on the similarities and differences between models in scientific and religious practices, return here to Latour, who in 2002 published his book *Jubiler* in French (translated in 2013 as *Rejoicing*), a study of the mode of religion (in contrast with the mode of reference that characterises science) already introduced in Chapter 4. For Latour, models in religious practices also 'refer', but in a different way.[10] This is what he writes about reference in religion:

> [W]hat we call religious speech *has no reference* – any more than amorous exchanges do. Of course, it has a server, in the old-fashioned sense of the term of one serving at mass; it does indeed register something essential; uttered judiciously, it is neither empty nor vain. It very definitely has some referent, then, in the ordinary sense of the term. But it doesn't have a referent in the precise sense of the term that the study of the sciences has allowed us to define: it does not distil information through a chain of graduated documents, each of which serves as material for formatting the next one. (Latour [2002] 2013a, 28)

The models that are used in religion do not have a similar role as they have in science, that is, to inform and represent; instead, the models used in religion are there to translate and 'save'. While there are no chains of reference built up in religion, persons are brought from remoteness to proximity, from death to life: religious language does refer to that reality.

Early twentieth-century discussion on models in science and instrumentalism

As James makes clear in his *Some Problems of Philosophy*, '[t]he intellectual life of man consists almost wholly in his substituting a conceptual order for the perceptual order in which his experience originally comes' (James [1911] 1979, 33). Where James emphasises the percept pole, Rickert stresses the role of values in shaping concepts. He acknowledges the historicity of concepts in the different practices due to uncertainty, but he also identifies the 'value-ladenness' of models. First and foremost they are laden with values that are seen historically to determine a cultural domain. For natural science, Rickert, for example, highlights:

> For the natural scientist, that on which he himself works exists as reality only in the real thoughts of individual persons who have either formed or understood the concepts of natural science. From a situation in which no one pursued natural scientific reflections, a natural scientific investigation of the world has gradually developed as a result of the work of many individuals. This unique developmental sequence must be represented with scientific necessity in such a way that its individuality is related to the cultural value of natural science. But it is precisely the advocate of [scientistic] naturalism who must acknowledge this cultural value, which

> governs concept formation, as unconditionally valid. And since the historical development of natural science cannot be isolated but, rather, stands in a historical-causal connection with the total cultural development of humanity – indeed, the distinctiveness of this total development must also have had an essential influence on the distinctiveness of the development of natural science – the objective historical value is necessarily transposed onto the total development of human culture. (Rickert [1929] 1986, 224)

We are thus confronted with both the historicity of models – which have uncertainty associated with them – and the transcendental values that underpin their performative role in the cultural practices where these models are being shaped and evaluated on the basis of such values.[11]

Indeed, the category of 'model' has itself historically evolved. In science as we know it since the scientific revolution in the seventeenth century, it has been customary to distinguish between 'experiment' and 'theory'. The precise relationship between these two elements characterising the natural sciences – both how they relate in fact and how they should relate – has been the subject of much debate over the past centuries. Since the end of the nineteenth century often a third element, the 'model', has been drawn into these discussions – but ambiguously so. This has led to a wider appreciation of the role of uncertainty in scientific practice. Let us study this period in the history and philosophy of science more closely here, especially to understand better the value-ladenness of models.

English physicists such as Lord Kelvin used all kinds of mechanical models in their theories. French physicist and philosopher Pierre Duhem (1861–1916) has portrayed this use of models as follows:

> Understanding a physical phenomenon is … for the physicists of the English school, the same thing as designing a model imitating the phenomenon; whence the nature of material things is to be understood by imagining a mechanism whose performance will represent and simulate the properties of bodies. (Duhem [1914] 1954, 72)

Duhem was certainly not positive about the use of models in science. His vision of theories and models is discussed below.

In the late nineteenth and early twentieth centuries, many physicists and philosophers, including Pierre Duhem but also prominently the German physicist and philosopher Ernst Mach (1838–1916) – and more broadly the neo-Kantians – railed against dogmatic metaphysics and against linking model use in scientific practice to metaphysical interpretation (see also Chapter 3). According to them, it is futile to offer science metaphysical foundations from a fixed metaphysical system because science cannot be completely derived from such foundations. As we shall see, later in his career Duhem was convinced – in contrast to Mach – that science could lead at least to a tentative metaphysics. The most elaborate philosophical position of these two philosophers can be found in Duhem's book *La théorie physique: Son objet, sa structure* (1906, 1914^2), which I take here as an interesting proxy into the practices and thoughts of a set of prominent turn of the century scientists.[12]

But first let me clarify some terminology. It has become common practice in discussions of models to distinguish between scale models, analogical models and theoretical models. Scale models involve an enlargement or reduction of the geometric shape of the study object (e.g. a scale model of the double helix of DNA). Analogical models depict the structure of the study object by means of the structure of other – generally more familiar – objects (the aforementioned mechanical models are examples of this). The third type of model, the theoretical model, is a set of assumptions and mathematical equations that are supposed to summarise the main characteristics of the study object. An example of a theoretical model is the billiard-ball model of kinetic gases.

The distinctions introduced between the three types of models are not absolute. For instance, the billiard-ball model of kinetic gases can, in principle, be categorised as an analogical model, in which the emphasis then is on the possibility of using real billiard balls (or to imagine actual billiard balls) in order to simulate a kinetic gas structure and behaviour. The billiard-ball model can also be realised as a scale model. However, I argue, following Mary Hesse's *Models and Analogies in Science* (1963), that the billiard-ball model should in the first place be understood as a theoretical model that includes certain positive analogies, excludes certain negative analogies and initially left some neutral analogies aside, e.g., to consider molecules as spherical balls.[13]

A theoretical model is not merely comprised of mathematical equations. The interpretation of the equations is also a part of the theoretical model. An interpretation that refers to billiard balls, for example, makes it possible to work out neutral analogies using new or reworked mathematical equations. At this point the question arises as to what distinguishes theoretical models from theories. Duhem thought that models should not be part of physical theories, but he acknowledged that *de facto* they often are. And Norman Campbell, in *Physics: The elements* (1920), referred like Duhem to mechanical *theories*.[14]

The above characterisation of the differences between models and theories is consistent with the description by Duhem. However, Duhem draws the conclusion that the use of models is barren, a view that after his death (he died in 1916) was belied by the development of Bohr's atomic model into the fully-fledged theory of quantum mechanics.[15] Duhem defines a physical theory as 'a system of mathematical propositions, deduced from a small number of principles, which aim to represent as simply, as completely, and as exactly as possible a set of experimental laws' (Duhem [1914] 1954, 19). Such a conception of theories as sets of propositions is called a 'statement view' in the philosophy of science.[16] Ideally, all the principles that form the basis of a theory (Duhem calls these principles 'hypotheses') are symbolic translations of experimental laws. However, this ideal is not fully achieved in physics, nor can it be achieved.

In general, assumptions must be constructed from experimental results by means of correction, generalisation or analogy. In principle, hypotheses can take any position on the range from experimental laws to purely speculative assumptions. The fact that the ideal of experimental laws is not achieved in practice leads to an intrinsic limitation of the theory: the uncertainty in the hypotheses translates into inaccuracies in the consequences of a theory. When a theory shows discrepancies with experiments, for instance in a new domain of application, the conclusion is not necessarily that the theory is bad: a theory is in fact always constructed with a view to the application in a particular, limited domain. It is expected, though, that the closer the hypotheses are to the ideal, the longer the theory that rests upon them will be able to stand.

It is included in Duhem's definition of a theory that theories must represent experimental laws 'as exactly as possible'. For cases where in terms of their consequences theories are not distinct from one another, so where all theories match experimental laws within the required accuracy, Duhem offers four criteria that enable scientists to determine an order of plausibilities – which can be seen as his proposal for the driving values of scientific practices. A first drastic culling takes place via the criterion of logical consistency (scientists search for a 'system of propositions'). The following three criteria can then help in choosing a theory: the domain of theory ('as completely as possible'), the number of hypotheses ('a small number of principles') and the nature of the hypotheses ('as simply as possible'). Duhem explains the latter criterion as follows:

> The hypotheses on which the theories rest can be simpler, and more natural or can translate experimental results more immediately than can those on which the other theory rests. (Duhem [1892] 1996a, 23)

Duhem thus proffers a set of values for scientific practices that emphasises consistency, completeness, conciseness and simplicity.

Mach and the early Duhem are generally considered 'instrumentalists', as they are called in present-day philosophy of science: their notion of theoretical truth does not involve realism.[17] Take a statement such as:

> a true theory is not a theory which gives an explanation of physical appearances in conformity with reality; it is a theory which represents in a satisfactory manner a group of experimental laws. … *Agreement with experiment is the sole criterion of truth for a physical theory*. (Duhem [1914] 1954, 21)

According to Mach and the early Duhem, the function of science is to 'replace' experience in some way (cf. James's statement on substituting a conceptual order for the perceptual order, quoted at the beginning of this section). The comparison with experience is the criterion for assessing the validity of a law.[18] Often, however, scientists posit laws without having been able to test all the consequences. Making predictions is thus accompanied by the *pretence* of the validity of a law. In such cases, recourse is made to instinctive knowledge. However, this is only experimental knowledge and 'as such is liable … to prove itself utterly insufficient and powerless, when some new region of experience is suddenly opened up' (Mach [1933] 1960, 94). Theory formation therefore does not specifically focus on the discovery of new laws. The discovery of laws by purely theoretical work happens only rarely, according to both Mach and Duhem.

Where Mach can rightly be called an instrumentalist, I would argue that Duhem ultimately takes a slightly different position. According to Duhem, science not only revolves around Mach's 'intellectual economy', which aims for the smallest number of hypotheses replacing a large number of laws. A theory is also a *classification* of experimental laws. And when a theory achieves a high degree of perfection (in terms of the definition given earlier), we can find in it even a *natural* classification. Duhem's position appears to be a kind of 'referential realism' (versus instrumentalism),[19] and he puts it as follows:

> Without claiming to explain the reality hiding under the phenomena whose laws we group, we feel that the groupings established by our

> theory correspond to real affinities among the things themselves. (Duhem [1914] 1954, 26)

However, Duhem did not reach this position before *Théorie physique*.

A normative consequence of Duhem's (late) view on the desirability of theoretical perfection is that the use of models in science is really out of the question. In earlier writings, he resisted the use of mechanical models just as Mach did, but did not dismiss them categorically.[20] In a mechanical model all physical quantities are composed by geometrical and mechanical elements of a fictive system. The hypotheses of mechanical models are thus not mere generalisations of experimental laws. The major drawback of mechanical models, according to Duhem, is that the restriction of the number of elements that may be used in the theoretical representation of a group of laws leads to the construction of very complicated combinations of these elements. The early Duhem had already asked the following rhetorical question:

> Who assures us that all physical concepts and experimental laws may be symbolized by even a very complicated combination of purely mechanical concepts? (Duhem [1892] 1996a, 13)

He then still admits that mechanical theories have yielded fruitful results. Such fertility must and can, however, be taken over by 'purely physical theories'. One of the reasons given by Duhem is that up to that point (1892) he had not seen a satisfactory mechanical theory for the Carnot Principle.[21]

Like the early Duhem, Mach too does not reject models in their entirety. In a lecture in 1882, he states:

> In natural science one should not see *realities* behind the phenomena captured in self-created, variable economic means: the molecules and atoms. ... The atom may still remain a means of presenting phenomena, like mathematical functions. ... *[Natural science] recognises the most economical, simplest conceptual expression of the facts as its goal.* (Mach [1896] 1910, 237–8)

Here Mach expresses his appreciation for the mathematical possibilities offered by the atomic hypothesis.

During his lifetime Duhem became more negative about mechanical models, but more positive about the fertility of seeking unification in physics. In *Théorie physique* he envisaged abstract theories and mechanical models as diametrically opposed to one another and he linked these opposites to some other opposites, that is, continental versus English, narrow versus broad minded, strong versus weak minded and unity versus diversity.[22] The fertility of models is often greatly exaggerated, according to Duhem. In many cases there was already a theory for a particular phenomenon before a model was created. Models then only serve to be able to imagine previously discovered phenomena.

However, Duhem does appreciate the use of analogies in science, especially in those cases where there is applicability of the same mathematical formulas in different domains. On that basis one could expect Duhem to be positive about the use of theoretical models. Yet on theoretical models (he gives the example of Maxwell's equations) he is even more negative than on analogical models (such as Lord Kelvin's mechanical models). Duhem formulates his objection to the way in which Maxwell (and continental physicists influenced by him) deal with mathematics:

> Whereas the French or German physicist intends the algebraic part of a theory to replace just the series of syllogisms used to develop this theory, the English physicist regards the algebra as playing the part of a *model*. (Duhem [1914] 1954, 79)

According to Duhem, models appeal to the imagination rather than to reason. When using models, the attention of scientists for the grounds on which they adopt the model disappears. He therefore criticises those who had used the Maxwell equations uncritically:

> [Maxwell's] equations were accepted just as they stood without discussion of any kind, without examination of the definitions and hypotheses from which they are derivable. They were treated as self-sufficient without submitting the consequences obtained to experimental test. (Duhem [1914] 1954, 90)

Summarising, Duhem's opposition to the use of models boils down to his concern that models are separated too far from experimental results and thus are too uncertain. Now Duhem is well aware that one always has to work with hypotheses in science. However, he is not willing to not give up the pursuit of unity, and since that unity implies simplicity for Duhem, the use of different, complicated models leads science astray.

The English physicist Norman Robert Campbell responded in 1920 to the position of Mach and Duhem in his book *Physics: The elements*.[23]

Campbell makes a distinction between mechanical and mathematical theories, and he classifies Mach among (physics-oriented) 'mathematicians' who, according to him, have elevated the development of mathematical theories to their supreme goal – in contrast to the (experimental) 'physicists', among whom Campbell counts himself.

Campbell defines a theory as follows:

> A theory is a set of propositions which are divided into two groups. One group [the 'hypothesis'] consists of statements about some collection of ideas which are characteristic of the theory; the other group [the 'dictionary'] consists of statements of the relation between these ideas and some other ideas of a different nature. (Campbell [1920] 1957, 122)

Both mechanical and mathematical theories fall under this definition. Both types of theories use mathematical formulas in their propositions. However, the main difference is that in mathematical theories

> every hypothetical idea is related directly by means of the dictionary to a corresponding concept; it is the ideas themselves and not functions of them which are mentioned in the dictionary. (Campbell [1920] 1957, 141)

Campbell's 'mathematical theories' thus come close to Duhem's ideal: all hypotheses must be based directly on experimental laws.

Unlike Mach, Campbell interprets theories in a realist manner. He believes it is the intention of a theory to *explain* experimental laws. When evaluating a theory, besides giving a *formal* derivation of these laws, what the theory *means* also plays a role. Precisely that element in theories which cannot be expressed in formal terms is what allows meaningful distinction between theories. Different types of scientists may be using different criteria. Proponents of mechanical theories rely on the criterion of familiarity, while proponents of mathematical theories give priority to the criterion of simplicity. Campbell makes no choice between the two alternative kinds of theory. However, he, like Duhem, has his reservations about the vastly increased complicatedness of mechanical theories, remarking: 'It is possible that in the future we shall have to choose between the advantages of simplicity and those of familiarity' (Campbell [1920] 1957, 157). He thus does not feel called to defend the English scientists from the continental attack (incidentally he does draw the same national boundaries as Duhem). However, Campbell indicates that as well as simplicity, familiarity is an important and valid criterion for scientific theories.

For Duhem, there is a parallelism in terms of openness to uncertainty in science and religion. Duhem's position on this openness in scientific practice can be summarised as follows:

> like religious belief *both* the experimental method in physics *and* its practice by physicists rested on assumptions incapable of proof: common sense or, perhaps, even metaphysics, was needed to justify the demand for coherent physical theories. (Martin 1991, 32)

For Duhem, following Blaise Pascal, judgement involves both *géométrie* and *finesse*: deductive reason and intuitive judgement respectively. This is not to say that common sense (*bon sens*) can be used directly to derive hypotheses via intuitive judgement; it is rather a meta-principle, to be used in evaluations of scientific practice (Martin 1991, 81).[24]

Contemporary philosophy of science on models

I now jump from early twentieth-century philosophy of science to late twentieth- and early twenty-first-century philosophy of science – not because nothing interesting or relevant happened around the middle of the century, but mainly because the attention paid to models in science has really taken off since the 1980s.[25] Also the discussions on the philosophical realism of scientific practices, which had increasingly come to be seen as using models, took off around the same time.[26] I highlight the work on models by Nancy Cartwright (1983), Ernan McMullin (1984), Ronald Giere (1988), Margaret Morrison and Mary Morgan (1999) and Henk de Regt (2015, 2017), and reflect on what their work means *vis-à-vis* Latour.

Cartwright's causal account and referential realism

Nancy Cartwright works out the theme already mentioned above about the tension between diversity and unity in *How the Laws of Physics Lie* (1983). She thinks it unlikely that nature would be a unity, while our knowledge of nature shows such a diverse picture and is so 'compartmentalised'. The main thesis of her book is that the fundamental laws of nature, although they certainly create unity in the natural sciences, are all *false*. Because Cartwright uses different notions of truth in her book, her argument gains in clarity when we split it into two parts: (1) the fundamental laws of nature themselves do not give precise descriptions of the most concrete phenomena; and (2) although fundamental laws of nature can create unity in phenomenological laws, they are therefore not true in a realist sense.[27]

These two claims are related and they are intertwined in Cartwright's book. She pays most attention to the falsity of fundamental laws in the sense of the first claim. As for the second claim, she shows that scientific realism is based on a metaphysical assumption. Cartwright herself starts from another metaphysical assumption, namely that nature ultimately shows no unity and cannot – even in principle – be explained by unified laws of nature.[28] She tries to make this metaphysical assumption plausible by pointing to the compartmentalisation of science, which in turn is due to the inadequacy of fundamental laws for the description of concrete phenomena (her first claim).[29] Cartwright's position in the realism debate can be characterised as 'entity realism' (which, I argue, can be considered a version of 'referential realism', introduced below): although the laws of nature can best be understood instrumentally, a role is played in causal explanations by theoretical entities that can best be interpreted realistically. The discussions on causality and on the 'lying' of the fundamental laws of nature are relatively unrelated in *How the Laws of Physics Lie*. Let me go into more depth here on those elements of her book which concern the relationship between models and theories (related to Cartwright's first claim).

Cartwright shows that the 'covering-law' model of explanation, dating back to the tradition of logical positivism, cannot adequately describe how scientists explain phenomena. The fundamental laws cover only *ceteris paribus*, and this means that the scope of what they explain is necessarily limited. Cartwright demonstrates the limitations of the deductive-nomological model of explanation (which is representative of the covering-law model of explanation) on the basis of cases in which there are joint causes:

> Most real life cases involve some combination of causes; and general laws that describe what happens in these complex cases are not always available. (Cartwright 1983, 51)

There are usually no general laws that indicate what is the composite effect of different fundamental laws. The interaction of causes often provides an open research question; this cannot be answered by purely theoretical work, but also requires experimental work (see Cartwright 1983, 67).

Cartwright points out the importance of phenomenological laws in scientific practice and contrasts this with the minor importance that philosophers often assign to them. 'Phenomenological' laws are typically seen by physicists as explanations of observed phenomena by means of mathematical equations that should not be understood as 'fundamental'. In addition, Cartwright uses the opposition fundamental–phenomenological and defines the term 'phenomenological' negatively (that is, as 'non-fundamental'). Furthermore, the concepts of 'fundamental' and 'phenomenological' hang together with the respective concepts of 'unity' and 'diversity'. However, they do not run parallel completely, mainly because there is a diversity of fundamental laws (there is no 'theory of everything' yet). Cartwright clearly has theoretical physics in mind when she talks about fundamental laws. In more applied fields, such as fluid dynamics, she says that often 'old-fashioned phenomenological laws' are used (Cartwright 1983, 63).

Cartwright does not make a distinction between theories and models. The role of models is – despite the undeducibility of phenomological laws – still to use fundamental laws in giving a theoretical explanation. Models therefore connect more fundamental theory with more phenomenological theory and are themselves part of the theoretical explanation. The multiplicity of theoretical explanations is linked to the multiplicity of models:

> For different purposes, different models with different incompatible laws are best, and there is no single model which just suits the circumstances. The facts of the situation do not pick out one right model to use. (Cartwright 1983, 104)[30]

Models thus constitute the bridge between fundamental theory and phenomenological laws and can bring about this mediation in different ways. To emphasise that models should be interpreted in an anti-realist manner, Cartwright calls models 'simulacra'. A simulacrum is defined as 'something having merely the form or appearance of a certain thing, without possessing its substance or proper qualities' (Cartwright 1983, 152–3).[31] In models some properties of objects do find a representation, but others do not. In addition, it is possible to introduce 'properties of convenience' in models. These do not correspond to actual properties, but are necessary in order to make a theoretical treatment of a particular system possible.

I would argue that the distinction between 'fundamental' and 'phenomenological' laws is arbitrary, and also that the 'levels' between which models mediate may shift. Furthermore, the equations on which models are based are true of the modelled objects by construction (without saying that they are true of the actual objects). As Cartwright writes:

> In general, nature does not prepare situations to fit the kinds of mathematical theories we hanker for. We construct both the theories and the objects to which they apply, then match them piecemeal onto real situations, deriving – sometimes with great precision – a bit of what happens, but generally not getting all the facts straight at once. The fundamental laws do not govern reality. What they govern has only the appearance of reality and the appearance is far tidier and more readily regimented than reality itself. (Cartwright 1983, 162)

In forming theories about certain processes, we usually work with models that necessarily do not give a fully adequate representation of reality. For each model one must therefore determine where it can be used (and where it cannot).

McMullin's fertility account and referential realism

Ernan McMullin, in his seminal publication on scientific realism (McMullin 1984), like Cartwright, also argues for 'referential realism', but of a different kind, less focused on *entities* and more on *structure*. He first analyses the variety of sources for anti-realism – in scientific practice, the history of science and the philosophy of science – and argues against these for a basic claim of scientific realism, namely that 'the theoretical terms of successful theories refer' (McMullin 1984, 26). Models play an essential role in his reading of the history of successful theories:

> in many parts of natural science there has been, over the last two centuries, a progressive discovery of *structure*. Scientists construct theories which explain the observed features of the physical world by postulating models of the hidden structure of the entities being studied. This structure is taken to account causally for the observable phenomena, and the theoretical model provides an approximation of the phenomena from which the explanatory power of the model derives. (McMullin 1984, 26–7)

It must be clear that McMullin's take on 'approximation' here is different from that of Cartwright (she cannot put any realistic weight on approximation, since it is impossible to determine whether there is approximation in the first place). Cartwright in essence has a more instrumentalist reading of models than McMullin. However, McMullin's realism stands far from traditional realism. There is no quick route from scientific explanation to realist truth: science is an ongoing activity, full of uncertainty.

For McMullin it is especially the fertility of models that underpins his plea for scientific realism:

> [i]f an anomaly is encountered or if the theory is unable to predict one way or the other in a domain where it seems it *should* be able to do so, the model itself may serve to suggest possible modifications or extensions. These are *suggested*, not implied. Therefore, a creative move on the part of the scientist is required. (McMullin 1984, 31)

McMullin adds that models in science function like metaphors in ordinary language, as used for instance by poets. Metaphors 'can lead the mind in ways that literal language cannot' (McMullin 1984, 31).[32]

Giere's semantic view

In *Explaining Science: A cognitive approach* (1988), Ronald N. Giere takes the presentation of scientific knowledge in textbooks as a basis for the clarification of the relationship between models and theories; in particular, he analyses textbooks on classical mechanics. Analogous to Cartwright, Giere shows that the laws of classical mechanics do not operate as well-confirmed empirical generalisations. Idealisations and approximations play a central role in the application of the fundamental laws. Also Giere calls the idealised systems 'models'. However, a key difference with Cartwright is that Giere, similar to McMullin, does not distinguish between fundamental and phenomenological laws: Giere counts fundamental laws among the models.[33]

In the discussion of correspondence rules (which in the logical positivist model of science coupled terms in a formal language to previously understood terms), Giere points out that although the logical positivist model is obsolete, the problem of 'correspondence' does play a role in scientific practice. The mathematical symbols used in scientific theories should be interpreted, on the one hand, and identified with (aspects of) certain objects, on the other. Giere thus opts for a 'semantic view' instead of a 'statement view' of theories. Where Cartwright still loosely notes that the equations forming the basis of the model are true for the modelled object (but where she does not hold a 'semantic view'), Giere views the model equations as more central

> The interpreted equations are *true* of the corresponding model. But truth here has no *epistemological* significance. The equations truly describe the model because the model is defined as something that exactly satisfies the equations. … The particular linguistic resources used to characterize those models are of at most secondary interest. (Giere 1988, 79)

The semantic view of theories stems from logic.[34] Where for a logician the existence of a 'model' guarantees the consistency of a formal system, so scientific models can be conceived as satisfying the axioms of a theory expressed in formal language.

Morrison and Morgan's models as mediating instruments

Morrison and Morgan (1999) and Morrison (1999) treat models as 'mediating instruments' and 'autonomous agents'. Since models are partially independent of both theories and the world, they have an autonomous component and therefore can be used as instruments for exploring both theories and the world. Models are only partly dependent on theory and experiment and partly independent of them: precisely because of this partial independence they can fulfil a bridge function between theory and experiment. The elements that determine the construction of models are heterogeneous.

The instrumentality of models is described by Morrison and Morgan as relating to the three different functions that a model can have: (1) for the construction and exploration of theories, (2) for the performance of measurements and (3) a design and intervention function. Examples of models with a construction function are the chemical formulae that changed the manner of theory development in chemistry at the beginning of the nineteenth century. An example of the use of models to perform measurements is the determination of the temperature in the upper atmosphere from measurements of infrared radiation by satellites. And an example of the third function of models, the design and intervention function, is the use of optical models in the design of lenses. Morrison and Morgan emphasise that you can learn from manipulating and playing with models, and that models can thus be regarded as 'technologies for investigation' (1999, 32).

de Regt's philosophy of scientific understanding

Finally, in this brief overview of contemporary philosophy of science on models, I include Henk de Regt's work on scientific understanding (de Regt 2015, 2017). On the basis of his earlier work (e.g. de Regt et al. 2009), de Regt argues against 'the realist thesis that science can provide understanding of the world only if its theories and models are (at least approximately) true descriptions of reality' (de Regt 2015, 3794). How models are actually used plays a pivotal role in de Regt's reasoning:

> The practice and history of science reveals that understanding can be – and is in fact often – achieved through models that are unrealistic, highly idealized representations of the target system, or on the basis of theories that are strictly speaking false, for example because they have been superseded by theories with radically different ontological assumptions. Accordingly, the traditional view of scientific understanding should be replaced by an alternative interpretation that allows for understanding without truth. I have offered such an alternative by characterizing understanding as a skill rather than as a kind of knowledge. (de Regt 2015, 3794–5)

He thus treats intelligibility as a pragmatic value that depends on the context.

The thesis of de Regt that understanding is essentially a skill does not entail that truth is completely irrelevant:

> On the contrary, there are several ways in which truth – if interpreted differently – can be conducive, or is even essential, to understanding. First and foremost, at the level of the empirical phenomena of interest the models should provide descriptions or predictions that are true in the sense that they agree with the observations in relevant aspects and to a sufficient degree. If interpreted as fit between the model and relevant parts of the observable world, truth is essential for understanding – but the desired degrees of fit and the relevance relations are determined by the context, and a higher degree of fit does not necessarily imply a higher degree of understanding. (de Regt 2015, 3795)

Still, rejecting the realist thesis regarding understanding does not imply rejecting scientific realism itself. Understanding can be achieved independently of whether one interprets scientific theories and models realistically. According to de Regt, various weaker forms of scientific realism can be compatible with his analysis of understanding.

Latour on uncertainty in models

A common thread among the above-mentioned positions on models in contemporary philosophy of science is a positive evaluation of the ubiquitousness in scientific practice of building models and tinkering with them, and the openness towards different philosophical assessments of their status (realist or instrumentalist). Latour, in his work on scientific practice, does not engage with these philosophers of science or their claims. He thus misses important distinctions in the analysis of, for instance, computer-simulation uncertainties and their role in climate science and policy advice (Petersen [2006] 2012), which cannot be captured through one generic 'mode of reference' that guides all scientific practices. I would say that Latour underplays climate-simulation uncertainty in *Facing Gaia*, although at the end of the book he writes:

> Our knowledge about the ecological mutation is based on long-term measuring campaigns but also on models, which offer the only way to approach phenomena whose complexity outstrips our capacities for analysis. As for the loops that are beginning to be added to our existence, one after another, making us more aware every day of the reciprocal feedback among agents of the terrestrial world, we need to make models of them – fictions – long before they can be verified in reality. (Latour [2015] 2017, 257)

For a further discussion of Latour on models in the context of climate change, the reader is referred to Chapter 7.

Conclusion

The philosophy of science approaches highlighted in this chapter all give a central role to the uncertainty that remains attached to models, while offering different interpretations of realism. The question of realism has often arisen in twentieth- and twenty-first-century debates on the use of models in science and religion. Some of the pragmatically inclined philosophers of science discussed in this chapter, including Duhem, Cartwright and McMullin, who from the epistemological point of view can be considered 'idealists' (the objects are not able to become knowledge without thought), often end up with a sort of realism that has been called 'referential realism' in this chapter.[35] The known objects are indeed as 'real' as they can get, in being independent from the knowing mind, and the operations that have been performed on them flow via real networks, which also include concrete concepts in individual minds. This realism can be included in a non-metaphysical re-interpretation of Latour's mode of reference as it works in science, and also of the crossing between the mode of reference and the mode of religion. While the latter is largely a-theoretical, when one asks the epistemological question about realism with reference to God, or metaphysical transcendence, the least one can say, as was shown in Chapter 2, is that experience can feature intimations of God, or metaphysical transcendence.

For transcendental naturalism, a position of weak 'referential realism' is defensible. This entails the basic acknowledgement that there is a world independent of the human mind. I would argue that Latour's modes of existence philosophy could be reinterpreted transcendentally and could then be seen to be in line with weak referential realism. To philosophise in addition that it is the real characteristics of this world that determine how we theorise about it brings us into metaphysics (either in the form of strong versions of scientific realism or Latour's occasionalist empiricism) – a step that transcendental naturalism aims to refrain from taking.

This concludes Part I. Part II will apply transcendental naturalism to philosophy in the context of climate change by addressing some themes that are connected with problems caused by scientistic forms of naturalism and that also play important roles in Latour's *Facing Gaia*.

Notes

1 While Latour does not analyse actual practices of 'religious naturalism', I suspect that some religious naturalists would find his description of their 'deity' model to conform to what inspires them religiously; see also Chapter 6.

2 '[T]he name of this geohistorical period [Anthropocene] may become the most pertinent philosophical, religious, anthropological, and – as we shall soon see – political concept for beginning to turn away for good from the notions of "Modern" and "modernity"' (Latour [2015] 2017, 116).

3 An interesting difference, addressed in Chapters 3 and 4, is the large number of modes for which Latour upholds that a similar mechanism operates.

4 In his *Pragmatism* James, for instance, mocks philosophers who put over and against a pragmatist notion of truth a notion of 'objective truth' which 'must be an absolute correspondence of our thoughts with an equally absolute reality' (James [1907] 1975, 38). In his *Inquiry*, Latour notes that the crux of the matter is finding the right way to address the question of 'correspondence': 'Everything hinges on the question of the correspondence between the world and statements about the world. Some will say that if there is any subject

that ethnology ought to avoid like the plague, it is this famous *adequatio rei et intellectus*, at best good enough to serve as a crutch for an elementary philosophy exam. Unfortunately, we cannot sidestep this question; it has to be faced at the start. Everything else depends on it: what we can expect of the world and what we can anticipate from language. We need it in order to define the means of expression as well as the type of realism that this inquiry has to have at its disposal. By way of this apparently insoluble question, nothing less is at stake than the division between reality and truth. The opacity peculiar to the Moderns comes from the inability we all manifest – analysts, critics, practitioners, researchers in all disciplines – to reach agreement on the condition of that correspondence. We shall never be able to define the other modes if we give up on this one at the outset' (Latour [2012] 2013b, 71). And Rickert has throughout his career rejected what he calls the copy-theory or pictorial theory (*Abbildtheorie*) of knowledge; he writes, e.g., that this theory incorrectly holds that 'the act of knowing has to depict (*abbilden*) a reality independent from its activity of representing (*vorstellen*)' (Rickert 1921, 119). Note that Rickert labels his own position in the end as 'epistemological idealism' (see Rickert 1934a, 47–53).

5 Recently, in *Facing Gaia* (Latour [2015] 2017), he wrote: '[I]n the face of [climate] emergency, ordinary philosophy of science doesn't carry much weight' (26); 'We can grasp the full perversity of the appeals [by climate sceptics] to the "state of the natural world" when we note that the counter-attack has been able to work only because the default position, that of ordinary philosophy of science, continued to look like common sense to everyone' (27); 'The climate skeptics have thus been clever enough to turn ordinary philosophy of science against their adversaries' (27); 'Although the official philosophy of science takes the second movement of deanimation as the only important and rational one, the opposite is true: animation is the essential phenomenon; and deanimation is the superficial, auxiliary, polemical, and often defensive phenomenon' (70). Note that Latour contrasts 'ordinary' or 'the official' 'philosophy of science' with 'the philosophy of science of Isabelle Stengers' (49).

6 There are important areas of crossover between science and politics, where for instance models of the future of a delta (physical and socio-economic, with water, people and more) are used in a policy to 'manage' the delta; see Chapter 8.

7 'Knowing' in different cultural practices has different connotations. For instance, while in all cultural practices there is a cognitive element ('knowing about'), in religion there is a particularly strong emotive element involved in meeting the Other, or being One. But note that, as we saw in Chapter 2, the phenomenon of wonder in science can sometimes involve a more mystical experience too, having emotive connotations relating to intimations of metaphysical transcendence.

8 'Instrumentalism' is a pragmatist philosophy of science championed by, e.g., John Dewey (who besides James was another American pragmatist thinker who significantly influenced Latour).

9 My rendering of recent philosophy of science in this chapter does not aim to be comprehensive. For recent book-length philosophy of science contributions on the role of modelling and simulation in natural science, see Petersen ([2006] 2012) and Weisberg (2013). Joseph Rouse's most recent contribution to naturalistic philosophy of science (Rouse 2015) is extensively discussed in Chapter 7.

10 So I do need to qualify my statement in Chapter 4 that, according to Latour, religious practices have nothing to do with reference.

11 Note that within practices there are usually several different values providing guidance, which can also be inconsistent and competing. An example in science is, on the one hand, values of simplicity and unity versus, on the other, values of comprehensiveness, complexity and diversity, a topic that is addressed below.

12 In the remainder of this section I explicitly signal at which important points earlier writings by Mach and Duhem differ from *Théorie physique*.

13 Hesse distinguishes between 'model$_1$' and 'model$_2$' (in the terminology used here model$_2$ pertains to analogical models and model$_1$ to theoretical models). With negative analogies, the analogical relation consists in a certain characteristic belonging to the one but not to the other object (for example, the colour of a billiard ball has no analogue at the molecular level). Hesse (1963, 9–10) also distinguishes positive and neutral analogies. Movement and momentum are examples of positive analogies for the kinetic billiard-ball model of gases, as these are properties of billiard balls attributed to the molecules. The remainder category of

neutral analogies (where it is still unknown whether the analogies are positive or negative) is the most interesting for a theoretical model, according to Hesse, because that makes it possible to make new predictions. The spatial extent of billiard balls can, for example, serve as a model for the spatial extent of molecules, resulting via mathematical calculation in an adjustment of the ideal gas law.

14 Today the difference between 'theory' and 'model' is often made gradually: theories have to meet more constraints than models. Examples of differences are: models are not dependent on the existence of an underlying theory, the principles used may be *ad hoc*, and models, when they are embedded in false theories, remain relatively independent of the fate of those theories (Weinert 1999, 320–1). Specific constraints for theories are: logical consistency, certain mathematical conditions (such as continuity and renormalisability), methodological standards (e.g. simplicity and avoiding *ad hoc* changes) and coherence (theoretical consistency) (Weinert 1999, 310). Models do not have to meet these conditions.

15 In the transition from models to theories, the structure of the constraints changes too. Bohr's atomic model of 1913 is an example of a model that was embedded in a false theory (it was known that at the atomic level application of classical mechanics resulted in all sorts of problems). In the development of the theory of quantum mechanics, the model was no longer maintained in its original form.

16 Below, in a discussion of various twentieth-century philosophical views on scientific theories, another conception (the 'semantic view') is discussed. Here I limit my discussion in the first instance to the 'statement view'.

17 Martin (1991) argues that Duhem ultimately maintains a realism pertaining to a truth behind the appearances, but that the tensions and inconsistencies in his *Théorie physique* had let his interpreters consider the later Duhem as still an instrumentalist.

18 Duhem ([1903] 1996b, 115) adds that finding a law differs from verifying a law. He introduces a distinction between two contexts (which he calls 'process of invention' and 'process of demonstration').

19 I would like to suggest here that in transcendental naturalism a combination is possible between a form of referential realism (weaker than Duhem's) and a truncated form of Latour's modes of existence philosophy (see the conclusion to this chapter).

20 Duhem calls 'mechanical models' and also 'mechanical theories'; because of the (gradual) distinction introduced above between models and theories I use both terms interchangeably.

21 The statistical-mechanical derivation of the second law of thermodynamics – from which the Carnot Principle also follows – had been completed 15 years earlier by Boltzmann (in 1877), but was not accepted by Duhem.

22 Duhem introduced these opposites earlier in an article of 1893. Then his final verdict on the English mind was slightly less negative; e.g., in that article the section on the lack of proof for the fertility of mechanical models was not yet included. The opposites of unity and diversity walk in parallel with the difference between two kinds of scientists (attributed to Kant in Chapter 3, note 17): those who strive for unification and those who look for differences between phenomena.

23 Campbell refers explicitly only to Mach and not to Duhem. However, he treats a position that is shared by Mach and Duhem.

24 In Chapter 3 we saw that for Kant a meta-principle with similar import – the assumption of nature's systematicity when we strive for unification of empirical laws – was assumed as an *a priori* principle of the power of judgement.

25 With Mary Hesse's (1963) book, cited above, being one of the few exceptions.

26 Again Hesse (1974) provided an early contribution. In that paper entitled 'In defence of objectivity', she uses the pragmatist hermeneutic approach of Jürgen Habermas to argue for the importance of 'hermeneutics' in the interpretation of the practice of natural science. This approach is more subtle than instrumentalism, which holds that '[i]f the aim of science is essentially to enable man to learn his way about in his environment, then the only necessary condition for its success is efficiency of learning' (1974, 291). As Hesse indicates, 'we have no idea what is the most efficient method of learning even in [a certain kind of stable] environment, for the problem of finding theories in terms of which we can learn never has a unique solution' (1974, 291). The objectivity of natural science is in the end analysed by Hesse via objectivity of the hermeneutic method (a human science).

27 The distinction between fundamental and phenomenological laws is discussed below.

28 She fills in this assumption as follows: 'I imagine that natural objects are much like people in societies. Their behaviour is constrained by some specific laws and by a handful of general principles, but is not determined in detail, even statistically' (Cartwright 1983, 49).

29 She writes about the status of metaphysical assumptions: '*A priori* intuitions and abstract arguments are not good enough. We best see what nature is like when we look at our knowledge of it' (Cartwright 1983, 13). I do not take this to mean that Cartwright claims that *a priori* values play no role.

30 From the example given by Cartwright of the different models used by Perrin to determine Avogadro's number, we can conclude that even for a single objective different models can be used (some of which may be better than others, without us necessarily having the possibility to identify the best model).

31 Cartwright takes this definition from the *Oxford English Dictionary*.

32 Still, as I show below, for McMullin the role of metaphor in religion is different to what it is in science.

33 Thus the gradual distinction between models and theories, as described for Cartwright (and see also note 14 above), is non-existent for Giere.

34 A particularly influential semantic view on the role of models in science is that of van Fraassen (1980). For him science consists in the 'construction of models that must be adequate to the phenomena' (van Fraassen 1980, 5). He summarises his semantic conception of theories (and their relationship to models) as follows: a model is '[a]ny structure which satisfies the axioms of a theory' (van Fraassen 1980, 43).

35 Cf. Hans Radder ([1984] 2012).

Part II

Themes in science and religion, applied to climate science and politics

6
Poetics and climate: modern myth and disenchantment

Introduction

In Part II of this study, the transcendental naturalistic analyses of wonder, judgement, values and models of Part I are further developed and applied to specific themes in 'science-and-religion' which, I argue, underlie Latour's analysis in *Facing Gaia* ([2015] 2017) of science, religion and politics in the context of climate change. These themes are connected with three problems that are associated with scientistic naturalism and are addressed by Latour in his book: the religious disenchantment of nature, the scientific disbelief in a plurality of value-laden perspectives and the disregard for non-modern worldviews in politics. I argue that transcendental naturalism does not lead to these problems, and that the philosophical contribution to their 'solution' is therefore to be found in a naturalistic acknowledgement of uncertainty without giving up the separate ontological status of transcendental values – thus avoiding both the risks of scientism and unreflexive incorporation of metaphysics (as Latour does) into one's philosophical methodology. First, one has to realise that poetics are available to read meaning, including religious meaning, in the world via judgement under uncertainty (this chapter). Second, one has to recognise a plurality of cognitive authorities in any practice, including that of science, so that arriving at expert judgement under uncertainty becomes a value-laden exercise (Chapter 7). And third, one has to keep futures really open in politics under uncertainty by breaking through the mutual disregard by, on the one hand, modern planning and science, and, on the other, non-modern worldviews (Chapter 8). In summary: Part II makes the case that poetics and plural authorities have a crucial role to play in making decisions that impact the future of our planet.

In this part I address the mentioned themes that surface in Latour's *Facing Gaia* by engaging with late nineteenth- and early twentieth-century scholars (mainly William James and Heinrich Rickert, but also George Santayana), as well as contemporary scholars (Fernand Hallyn, Alister McGrath, Lisa Sideris, Joseph Rouse, Philippe Descola, Richard Jones, Kevin Schilbrack and Koo van der Wal), and by analysing case studies of (climate) science and climate politics. The discussions in Part II will also shed further interpretive light on Latour's work.

With respect to the first theme, addressed in this chapter, Latour observes that a narrative of the 'disenchantment of nature' is presently dominant: 'Many people still hold the rather naïve belief in a supposedly deanimated "material world"' (Latour [2015] 2017, 40). Counter to this, he argues that there is no need to add a separate spirit to nature, since science has not disenchanted nature:

> I am saying not that science has 'disenchanted' the world by making us lose any connection with the 'lived world', but that science has always *sung a quite different song* and has always *lived fully enmeshed in the world*. Perhaps it might be of some use to offer, at last, a view of materiality that is no longer so directly and awkwardly politico-religious and that offers a pathetically inexact vision of the sciences. We could then get away from any and every 'religion of nature'. We would have a conception of materiality that is finally worldly, secular – yes, non-religious, or, better still, earthbound. (Latour [2015] 2017, 72)

Latour here draws on his argument that 'matter' is only an idea (stemming from the seventeenth century), linked to both science *and* religion: the scientific worldview 'is also a certain religious view of the nature of causes' (Latour [2015] 2017, 71). In his plea for succeeding *old* views of 'nature' and 'religion' (both being forms of what he calls 'natural religions') with *new* views of 'nature' and 'religion'[1] (both being forms of what he calls 'terrestrialization'), he correlates the assumed disenchantment of nature with an assumed 'overanimation' of God. As will be shown in this chapter, it is hard for modern myth and poetics to enchant a scientistic naturalism that adheres to Latour's 'nature one' (the old view). Latour's 'nature two' (the new view), with its openness to networks and its acknowledgement of the 'multiverse', is in line with an anthropological reading of science and does not end up in conflict with 'religion two', Latour's anthropological reading of what he considers real religion, with a God of ends, multiple and embodied. According to Latour, both nature and God are 'animated'.

This all connects for Latour with how one should treat the Nature/Culture distinction:

> The distinction between humans and nonhumans and the difference between culture and nature have to be treated the same way: to be sure that we are not using them as resources but rather as objects of study, we have to go a level deeper, to the common concept that distributes the figures into separate parts. To believe that these terms describe anything at all about the real world amounts to taking an abstraction for a description. (Latour [2015] 2017, 58)

A consequence of clinging to the old Nature/Culture distinction is that a moralising normativity inconsistent with the disenchantment view gets attached to the findings of science. This happens, for instance, in the context of climate change and the wider ecological crisis:

> If ecology drives us crazy, it's because it obliges us to plunge head first into the confusion created by reference to a 'natural world' that is said to be at once fully endowed and not at all endowed with a normative dimension. 'Not at all', since it describes only an order; 'fully', since there is no order more sovereign than the order to obey that order. (Latour [2015] 2017, 34)

This makes the proposal for 'religiopoiesis' by Goodenough (2000) and others – which wishes to build a new religious myth on the basis of the 'scientific worldview' – thoroughly problematic. I argue that a non-scientistic notion of wonder based in transcendental naturalism can better underpin ecological action philosophically by, for instance, circumscribing in a transcendental naturalistic way the 'intrinsic value' of non-human life forms (that is, relating these back to cultural values understood in a non-modern way and involving poetic expression).

This chapter takes up as a first theme the supposed process of 'disenchantment' of the world and the role science has been claimed to play in this process *vis-à-vis* religion. It also considers what this implies for motivating people for climate policy, or ecological conservation more generally, on the basis of science. It is a central present-day question in the field of science-and-religion (see, for example, Sideris 2017) whether a science-compatible modern myth can be construed – atheistic, agnostic or theistic in kind – that replaces or amends classical religious myths and can 're-enchant' the world. In dealing with this theme I will focus on 'poetics', a term that encompasses but has a wider sense than 'poetry' and refers to the coming together and effects of textual elements. In Part I, the importance of poetics for experiencing what James calls the 'more' – not to be equated, according to James, with the absolute or God, both of which are rationalist constructions (cf. Carrette 2013) – has been mentioned. The overarching question here is: how do poetics relate to uncertainty?

In this chapter, I first engage with the perspectives of William James and his Harvard colleague and former student George Santayana on poetics in connection with science-and-religion, in dialogue with Latour. This then informs my subsequent analysis of poetics in the context of contemporary science-and-religion and ecology discussions.

James, Latour and Santayana on poetics and science-and-religion

In his 1895 lecture 'Is life worth living?', William James makes use of the poetic imagination to address the question of the worth of human life, by 'search[ing] the lonely depths ... and see[ing] what answers in the last folds and recesses of things our question may find' (James [1897] 1979, 34).[2] In the lecture he distinguishes two 'classes' of mind, which can both be 'intensely religious': those who are 'naturally' very free in the 'exercise of religious trust and fancy' (*enchanted*, one could say) and those who are 'tied to their senses, restricted to their natural experience' and are often 'shocked by the easy excursions into the unseen that other people make at the bare call of sentiment' (*disenchanted*, one could say). The second class is susceptible to 'pessimism' (or even to becoming suicidal), which James diagnoses as being a 'religious disease' that may be cured in some sufferers:

> The nightmare view of life has plenty of organic sources; but its great reflective source has at all times been the contradiction between the phenomena of nature and the craving of the heart to believe that behind nature there is a spirit whose expression nature is. What philosophers call 'natural theology' has been one way of appeasing this craving; that poetry of nature in which our English literature is so rich has been another way. Now suppose a mind of the latter of our two classes, whose imagination is pent in consequently, and who takes its facts 'hard'; suppose it, moreover, to feel strongly the craving for communion, and yet to realize how desperately difficult it is to construe the scientific order of nature

> either theologically or poetically – and what result *can* there be but inner discord and contradiction? Now, this inner discord (merely as discord) can be relieved in either of two ways. The longing to read the facts religiously may cease, and leave the bare facts by themselves; or, supplementary facts may be discovered or believed-in, which permit the religious reading to go on. (James [1897] 1979, 40–1)

Not all people hold a religious attitude in James's sense, that is, an attitude of apprehending themselves in relation to whatever they may consider the divine.[3] For James, a sure way to lose an enchanted view of the world is via natural religion, which 'naïvely and simply taken' leads to its 'inevitable bankruptcy', since visible nature with both its good and its evil constitutes a 'moral multiverse', not a 'moral universe' (James [1897] 1979, 43). James concludes:

> I cannot help, therefore, accounting it on the whole a gain (though it may seem for certain poetic constitutions a very sad loss) that the [scientistic] naturalistic superstition, the worship of the God of nature, simply taken as such, should have begun to loosen its hold upon the educated mind. In fact, if I am to express my personal opinion unreservedly, I should say (in spite of its sounding blasphemous at first to certain ears) that the initial step towards getting into healthy ultimate relations with the universe is the act of rebellion against the idea that such a God exists. (James [1897] 1979, 43)

Instead, without explicitly endorsing theism, James maintains that a sensible alternative is to follow 'all the higher religions' in assuming that 'what we call visible nature, or *this* world, must be but a veil and surface-show whose full meaning resides in a supplementary unseen or *other* world' (James [1897] 1979, 43).

Latour, who alludes to James in his use of the term 'multiverse' to characterise his worldview (invoking a new concept of 'nature', that is, 'world'), also eschews theism and warns against the use of old concepts of 'nature' and 'God', since for the 'people of Nature' (Latour's term) these lead to the 'pessimism' described by James:

> The strangest thing of all, what has most surprised all the other peoples, is that *it believes that it is alone in finally inhabiting this material world, the true inanimate world here below*, whereas it

> comes from elsewhere and still resides in the lovely global space of nowhere! Here is the proof that it contains in itself something ferocious, dangerous, unstable, and – why not say it – profoundly unhappy. Yes, the people of Nature are wandering souls who never stop complaining about the irrationality of the rest of the world. (Latour [2015] 2017, 166)

Carrying through his analysis, Latour lands on a fundamentally altered view of the link between science and religion. He sees the enchantment that is offered to a scientistic naturalist worldview by those favouring a religious argument from design as assuming an *over*animated designer God. And the supposed disenchantment associated with a worldview that only has chance in it as a cause is assuming a *de*animated Nature – a 'nothing more than' dead matter that constitutes the 'mystique of reductionism'; a 'sad triumph on the part of our clever naturalist' (Latour [2015] 2017, 170, 172). Latour adds that in the old sense of 'Nature', 'no one has ever … lived "*in* Nature"' (Latour [2015] 2017, 124). Given the evolved amalgam of 'natural religion', he instructs that the separation of science and religion that needs to be carried out has to be done very carefully by first rethinking them. Without yet standing in the shadow of Gaia, I claim that James has already offered some basic building blocks for such rethinking.

In order to get cured from pessimism, James thinks that it may be enough to be freed from the model of a scientistic naturalistic God (monism) – that is, to have no scientistic naturalistic religious reading of the facts and to not consider oneself damned for taking this liberty, that is, reaching such a judgement under freedom. James describes this step as acting upon healthy natural instincts (James [1897] 1979, 43–5). The additional step to the next stage of holding religious beliefs that are outside of scientistic naturalism is risky but may well be worth it, and it definitely represents a genuine value (even though all realisations in the form of models of God or the Transcendent are fallible). James argues:

> that we have a right to believe the physical order to be only a partial order; that we have a right to supplement it by an unseen spiritual order which we assume on trust, if only thereby life may seem to us better worth living again. But as such a trust will seem to some of you sadly mystical and execrably unscientific, I must first say a word or two to weaken the veto which you may consider that science opposes to our act. (James [1897] 1979, 49)

Thus on the one hand James argues for the validity of religious values on the basis of his radical empiricist position that they can be observed to be at work in practice (they actually do have the effect of making life worth living – and this can be studied by the social sciences grouped under 'religious studies'); on the other hand, he claims that opposition to this analysis on the basis of scientific values will be significantly weakened upon further scrutiny. The latter point is connected to the role of uncertainty in practice (both scientific and religious practices).

James makes much of human freedom under uncertainty, for both the practices of science and those of religion. He does not opt for an absolute 'unknowable', but instead keeps an openness in specifying the limitations of thought (Carrette 2013, 156–81). With respect to science, which had just begun in its Modern form a few centuries before, he asks:

> Is it credible that such a mushroom knowledge, such a growth overnight as this, *can* represent more than the minutest glimpse of what the universe will really prove to be when adequately understood? No! our science is a drop, our ignorance a sea. Whatever else be certain, this at least is certain – that the world of our present natural knowledge *is* enveloped in a larger world of *some* sort of whose residual properties we at present can frame no positive idea. (James [1897] 1979, 50)

Important to note here is his reference to 'present' knowledge. As Carrette shows, James had incorporated the French philosopher Charles Renouvier's (1815–1903) post-Kantian sense of the limits of knowledge into his own philosophy. This means that the 'unknown' is not unknowable as such but 'rather that our knowledge is partial, incomplete and in process' (Carrette 2013, 173). Fundamentally, for James:

> the 'scientific' life itself has much to do with maybes, and human life at large has everything to do with them. … [N]ot a deed of faithfulness or courage is done, except upon a maybe; … [n]ot a scientific exploration or experiment or text-book, that may not be a mistake. It is only by risking our persons from one hour to another that we live at all. And often enough our faith beforehand in an uncertified result *is the only thing that makes the result come true*. … [T]he part of wisdom as well as of courage is to *believe what is in the line of your needs,* for only by such belief is the need fulfilled. Refuse to believe, and you shall indeed be right, for you shall irretrievably perish. But believe, and again you shall be right, for you shall save yourself. You make

> one or the other of two possible universes true by your trust or mistrust – both universes having been only *maybes*, in this particular, before you contributed your act. (James [1897] 1979, 53–4)

I argue in this chapter that it is the poetic dimension that both in the case of science and (more so) in the case of religion assists us in jumping over gaps/uncertainties.[4]

Primarily James fights against dogmatic thinking, both in science and in religion. He opposes Herbert Spencer's 'unknowable' that was offered in the nineteenth century as a solution to the science-and-religion debate (that is, that religion concerns the 'unknowable' of which science cannot say anything): such an approach closes the mind. As Carrette summarises this:

> The universe is not so much 'unknowable' as overwhelming. … Where Spencer wishes to contain, James perceives a universe that is unending in discovery and new relations – there is always 'more'. (Carrette 2013, 159, 162)

As was alluded to in Chapter 2, 'relations' play a central role in James's radical empiricism; they are themselves part of experience. Carrette connects this emphasis on relations to James's concept of the 'more': 'The relational metaphysic grounds James's entire thinking and specifically positions his idea of the "more" in his thinking about "religion"'(Carrette 2013, 162). Carrette argues that James's 'more' is a pluralistic concept, and that it deserves greater attention in scholarship on James.

In the context of the present study, I think that we can safely conclude that according to James uncertainty is not to be taken as negative and absolute; it should rather be analysed as having a positive role in scientific and religious practices since it prevents dogmatism and evokes wonder. There is always more to know and experience, in a never-ending history. What is crucial about this 'more' is that it alludes to a metaphysics of relations, to perception and to emotion, and that James hence resorts to expressing non-theoretical truths (poetic and therapeutic) rather than just limiting himself to theoretical philosophy (cf. Carrette 2013, 164).

Carrette has analysed the genealogy and vagueness of James's concept of the 'more' in the context of religion and observes:

> the analytical imprecision of the 'more' reflects a particular response to modernity and religion in the nineteenth century by

> revealing the poetic imagination behind the concept. … [P]oetry is important to James's thinking about religion and how the poetry is itself part of the 'more', another dimension of reality. (Carrette 2013, 170)

Poetry plays an essential role in the affirmation of life. It assists in evoking acts of affirmation. James emphasises that one is, of course, free to maintain an agnostic positivist attitude and not allow ourselves to suppose anything about the unseen. However, philosophical neutrality cannot really be maintained in practice. From psychology we learn that 'belief and doubt are living attitudes, and involve conduct on our part' (James [1897] 1979, 50). This means that '[o]ur only way, for example, of doubting, or refusing to believe, that a certain thing *is*, is continuing to act as if it were *not*' (James [1897] 1979, 50). While, according to James, the emergence of science has responded to our inner need for uniform laws of causation, he asks why the emergence of religion should not analogously be allowed to be a valid response to 'the inner need of believing that this world of nature is a sign of something more spiritual and eternal than itself' (James [1897] 1979, 51). Religion works on a different plane and science, according to James, does not have 'authority to debar us from trusting our religious demands … , for she can only say what is, not what is not; and the agnostic "thou shalt not believe without coercive sensible evidence" is simply an expression (free to any one to make) of private personal appetite for evidence of a certain peculiar kind' (James [1897] 1979, 51). Religion, in order to function and make life worth living, does not have to involve dogma or definition:

> The bare assurance that this natural order is not ultimate but a mere sign or vision, the external staging of a many-storied universe, in which spiritual forces have the last word and are eternal – this bare assurance is to such men enough to make life seem worth living in spite of every contrary presumption suggested by its circumstances on the natural plane. (James [1897] 1979, 52)

As Carrette argues, the idea of the 'more' relates to the faculty of intuition that is at work in the poetic – it 'carries a feeling of plurality and affectivity of logic' – and 'religion' (taken in a wide sense) 'does not need to defend itself against facts and truths, because it – like poetry – is sustaining human life at the affective level rather than the logical and positivistic level' (Carrette 2013, 175–6). On the link between poetry and religion in James's thought, Carrette concludes:

> The poet articulates the feeling from which we then think through the logical and rational sense of things. Religion begins with feeling for James, and it thus rests upon the poetic and literary form. (Carrette 2013, 178)

Much of James's thinking on the role of poetry in the science-and-religion discussion remains somewhat hidden in his writing, while Carrette's James interpretation draws out the poetic dimension more clearly. I now aim to situate and corroborate the role for poetry identified here in the work of a thinker who is closely related to James and who published a whole book about poetry and religion (*Interpretations of Poetry and Religion*) in 1900, which was read and commented on by James: George Santayana. In discussions of James and Santayana their differences are often emphasised (e.g. Porte 1990; Carrette 2013, 180): for example, James's realism versus Santayana's anti-realism (idealism) and James's liberal Protestantism versus Santayana's (remnants of) orthodox Catholicism. However, despite the fact that James indeed qualified Santayana's book in a letter as the 'perfection of rottenness' (see Perry 1935, 252; Porte 1990, xiv; Carrette 2013, 180), I maintain that with respect to some crucial elements of their analyses of the role of poetry in the science-and-religion discussion, James and Santayana are actually much in agreement with each other.[5]

James was Santayana's mentor and subsequently his colleague in philosophy at Harvard.[6] Santayana was informed, just as James was, by the Enlightenment and the post-Darwinian world. The influence of James's thinking on Santayana was large:

> Primarily, Santayana credited James, among other both positive and negative influences, for giving him a sensitivity for 'the immediate; for the unadulterated, unexplained, instant fact of experience'. (Lovely 2012, 85)

James, in a letter to a colleague in 1900, called reading Santayana's *Interpretations* a 'great event' in his life; he claimed to have 'literally squealed with delight at the imperturbable perfection with which the position is laid down on page after page' (quoted in Perry 1935, 319; Porte 1990, xiii–xiv). James and Santayana shared a crusade against (scientific) dogmatism:

> Santayana, just as James does, flies in the face of analytic philosophy and scientific materialism in the study of religion, despite his own

> *disillusion* in regard to the supernatural. Hence, we understand better his contempt for the liberal Protestant reduction of myths and symbols in the spirit of science and modernistic compliance. (Lovely 2012, 93)

Carrette characterises the difference between James and Santayana as follows: 'Poetry and religion for James were about achieving a sense of moral support from the reality of the "unseen" to give strength to live actively in the world. They were not for retreating from life' (2013, 180). I argue, however, that Santayana actually gives poetry the same religiously moral import *vis-à-vis* science's amoral stance as James, even though their specific religious affinities were different.

According to Santayana, '[p]oetry is called religion when it intervenes in life, and religion, when it merely supervenes upon life, is seen to be nothing but poetry' ([1900] 1990, 3). Religious value is to be distinguished from scientific value:

> For the dignity of religion, like that of poetry, lies precisely in its ideal adequacy, in its fit rendering of the meanings and values of life, in its anticipation of perfection; so that the excellence of religion is due to an idealisation of experience which, while making religion noble if treated as poetry, makes it necessarily false if treated as science. Its function is rather to draw from reality materials for an image of that ideal to which reality ought to conform, and to make us citizens, by anticipation, in the world we crave. (Santayana [1900] 1990, 3)

Santayana had written his doctoral thesis on the early neo-Kantian philosopher Hermann Lotze and subscribed to a philosophy of value (which he saw many around him not adhere to):

> The expedient of recognising facts as facts and accepting ideals as ideals, – and this is all we propose, – although apparently simple enough, seems to elude the normal human power of discrimination. (Santayana [1900] 1990, 4)

The fundamental problem that Santayana has with liberal Protestantism is that it 'attempts to fortify religion by minimising its expression, both theoretic and devotional … ; it subtracts from faith that imagination by which faith becomes an interpretation and idealisation of human life'. He goes on to warn that '[m]ythology cannot become science by being reduced in bulk, but it may cease, as a mythology, to be worth having' (Santayana [1900] 1990, 4). To the disenchanted – those 'who have a sense for reality, but no ideals' and who belong to 'the positivistic school of criticism' – he attributes an 'apathetic naturalism', in comparison to which

> all the errors and follies of religion are worthy of indulgent sympathy, since they represent an effort, however misguided, to interpret and to use the materials of experience for moral ends, and to measure the value of reality by its relation to the ideal. (Santayana [1900] 1990, 4–5)

In the first essay in the book, 'Understanding, imagination, and mysticism', Santayana highlights the role of the faculty of the imagination, which functions differently in science as compared with religion: 'understanding ... is an imagination prophetic of experience, a spontaneity of thought by which the science of perception is turned into the art of life'. Here science is taken by Santayana to be characterised by the ideal of verification; in a Latourian reading this could be taken as the ideal of establishing chains of reference. By contrast, the 'absence of verification distinguishes revelation from science; for when the prophecies of faith are verified, the function of faith is gone' (Santayana [1900] 1990, 10). In a similar way to James, Santayana appeals to the moral effect of the religious imagination:

> Faith and the higher reason of the metaphysicians are therefore forms of imagination believed to be avenues to truth, as dreams or oracles may sometimes be truthful, not because their necessary correspondence to truth can be demonstrated, for then they would be portions of science, but because a man dwelling on those intuitions is conscious of a certain moral transformation, of a certain warmth and energy of life. (Santayana [1900] 1990, 10–11)

There is also instrumental value in poetry that stirs the religious imagination:

> Without poetry and religion the history of mankind would have been darker than it is. Not only would emotional life have been poorer, but the public conscience, the national and family spirit, so useful for moral organisation and discipline, would hardly have become articulate. (Santayana [1900] 1990, 11)

It becomes especially clear here that for Santayana poetry and religion are related to actively living in the world, not for retreating from life.

In mysticism, which does offer a way to retreat from life, Santayana sees an approach that takes uncertainty in imagination to the (logically contradictory) extreme:

> It consists in the surrender of a category of thought on account of the discovery of its relativity. If I saw or reasoned or judged by such a category, I should be seeing, reasoning, or judging in a specific manner, in a manner conditioned by my finite nature. But the specific and the finite, I feel, are odious; let me therefore aspire to see, reason and judge in no specific or finite manner – that is, not to see, reason or judge at all. So I shall be like the Infinite, nay I shall become one with the Infinite and (marvellous thought!) one with the One. (Santayana [1900] 1990, 14)

According to Santayana:

> mysticism, although a principle of dissolution, carries with it the safeguard that it can never be consistently applied. We reach it only in exceptional moments of intuition, from which we descend to our pots and pans with habits and instincts virtually unimpaired. … And although mysticism, left free to express itself, can have no other goal than Nirvana, yet moderately indulged in and duly inhibited by a residuum of conventional sanity, it serves to give a touch of strangeness and elevation to the character and to suggest superhuman gifts. It is not, however, in the least superhuman. (Santayana [1900] 1990, 15–16)

Santayana emphasises that a contemplative mind easily drops its practical occupations. It is human to like to lose oneself in, for instance, the music of the spheres: '[t]he better side of mysticism is an aesthetic interest in large unities and cosmic laws' (Santayana [1900] 1990, 16). Such an indulgence

> serves to keep alive the conviction, which a confused experience might obscure, that perfection is essentially possible; it reminds us, like music, that there are worlds far removed from the actual which are yet living and very near to the heart. (Santayana [1900] 1990, 17)

So, there is value for Santayana in mysticism, practised in moderation.

There is a risk of religion losing its value if it loses its poetry. In his essay 'The poetry of Christian dogma', Santayana concludes that Christianity has fallen prone to the 'natural but hopeless misunderstanding of imagining that poetry in order to be religion, in order to be the inspiration of life, must first deny that it is poetry and deceive us about the facts with which we have to deal' (Santayana [1900] 1990, 71–2). He asks:

> Can Christianity escape these perils? Can it reform its claims, or can it overwhelm all opposition and take the human heart once more by storm? The future alone can decide. The greatest calamity, however, would be that which seems, alas! not unlikely to befall our immediate posterity, namely, that while Christianity should be discredited no other religion, more disillusioned and not less inspired, should come to take its place. Until the imagination should have time to recover and to reassert its legitimate and kindly power, the European races would then be reduced to confessing that while they had mastered the mechanical forces of Nature, both by science and by the arts, they had become incapable of mastering or understanding themselves, and that, bewildered like the beast by the revolutions of heavens and by their own irrational passions, they could find no way of uttering the ideal meaning of their life. (Santayana [1900] 1990, 72)

While the concern here is formulated in a way that is centred on Christianity, the impetus is more general: whenever a conflation of the modes of religion and science occurs – and religion no longer feels free to resort to the use of poetry – something essential is lost.

In the final essay of his book, entitled 'The elements and function of poetry', Santayana arrives at the heart of what poetry is and how it relates to science and religion. First of all, poetry is a means to deal with experience. Santayana writes:

> The great function of poetry is precisely this: to repair to the material of experience, seizing hold of the reality of sensation and fancy beneath the surface of conventional ideas, and then out of that living but indefinite material to build new structures, richer, finer, fitter to the primary tendencies of our nature, truer to the ultimate possibilities of the soul. (Santayana [1900] 1990, 161)

Now both science and religion are means to grapple with experience; poetry has an analytical role in both types of practices:

> Science and common sense are themselves in their way poets of no mean order, since they take the material of experience and make out of it a clear, symmetrical, and beautiful world; the very propriety of this art, however, has made it common. Its figures have become mere rhetoric and its metaphors prose. Yet, even as it is, a scientific and mathematical vision has a higher beauty than the irrational poetry of sensation and impulse, which merely tickles the brain, like liquor, and plays upon our random, imaginative lusts. The imagination of a great poet, on the contrary, is as orderly as that of an astronomer, and as large; he has the naturalist's patience, the naturalist's love of detail and eye trained to fine gradations and essential lines; he knows no hurry; he has no pose, no sense of originality; he finds his effects in his subject, and his subject in his inevitable world. (Santayana [1900] 1990, 161)

Often we will find poetry turned into prose in science; it is then important to remember the poetic or aesthetic quality of mathematically formulated hypotheses (see the section below).

While in science the original experiences that mathematical equations relate to may often be quite remote, in religion the experiences that religious expressions refer to must remain near. Poetry assists us in making sense of experiences that we have had in terms of religious value:

> The highest ideality is the comprehension of the real. Poetry is not at its best when it depicts a further possible experience, but when it initiates us, by feigning something which as an experience is impossible, into the meaning of the experience which we have actually had.
>
> The highest example of this kind of poetry is religion; and although disfigured and misunderstood by the simplicity of men who believe in it without being capable of that imaginative interpretation of life in which its truth consists, yet this religion is even then often beneficent, because it colours life harmoniously with the ideal. (Santayana [1900] 1990, 168–9)

Of course, not all poetry is embedded in religious practice and vice versa: not all religious practice contains poetry. Santayana summarises:

> Religion is poetry become the guide of life, poetry substituted for science or supervening upon it as an approach to the highest reality. Poetry is religion allowed to drift, left without points of application

> in conduct and without an expression in worship and dogma; it is religion without practical efficacy and without metaphysical illusion. (Santayana [1900] 1990, 171)

I return later in this chapter to Santayana's phrase that 'religion is poetry substituted for science or supervening upon it'. Obviously there is some reduction involved in such an expression. What is missing in poetry when it is not actually embedded in religious practice are 'points of application in conduct' and 'expression in worship and dogma' (Santayana [1900] 1990, 172). The fully coming together of poetry and religion is described by Santayana as follows:

> Poetry raised to its highest power is ... identical with religion grasped in its utmost truth; at their point of union both reach their utmost purity and beneficence, for then poetry loses its frivolity and ceases to demoralise, while religion surrenders its illusions and ceases to deceive. (Santayana [1900] 1990, 172)

Again, this is clearly not framed as aiming for a retreat from life.

This concludes my review of James and Santayana regarding poetics and science-and-religion. In the next section, I will engage with contemporary authors on this topic.

Contemporary reflections on poetics and science-and-religion

Poetics play a fundamental but varied role in the practices of science and religion. Poetics can trigger the experience of wonder. In science, which started to come into being as a practice in the seventeenth century, this poetic dimension has been relegated to the sidelines in most modern scientific practices from the nineteenth century onwards. Religious practices are still visibly full of poetry, both new and old.[7] Through poetics, judgements can be arrived at that correspond to a fullness of thought to which no linguistic expression on its own is fully adequate: poetics expand the mind by setting the imagination free.[8] The affirmation of particular values (e.g. scientific or religious) assumes a subject that cannot be considered an object, which is what Rickert denotes as the 'pro-physical subject'.[9] Values can only be realised in practice in fallible ways; poetry offers a means for fallible expressions of a-theoretical truths. Such truths may lie 'on the other side', then being expressions of metaphysical truths, for example pertaining to metaphysical correlates of wonder in scientific or religious practices. However, philosophical reflection on the role of poetry in linking the world of perception and the world of value starts 'on this side' (pro-physics) as an analysis of experience (cf. James).

Different values are at stake in the disenchantment–re-enchantment discussion, and poetry offers a viable means, connecting to experience, for relating different values to each other. Models thrive on poetic expression (using metaphors), albeit differently in science as compared with religion. In science, models appeal to the imagination and are necessary for making progress in scientific research, even though they should not be taken literally and do not necessarily build on analogies with what we already know in daily life. In religion, poetically expressed models similarly appeal to the imagination and are necessary for evoking religious responses. However, they build on communal religious experience and are both exploratory and affective (the latter being less the case for science – but with regard to the former, it is important also to recognise that poetry in religion has cognitive functions). In any case, poetry must remain faithful to concrete human experience in order to fulfil its role. This latter observation is relevant for assessing re-enchantment: models that rely solely on science and that do not allow for peoples' individual experiences will find difficulty in providing meaning and motivating action.

The role of poetics in scientific practices is acknowledged but undertheorised by Latour. He describes how Newton arrived at his idea of a gravitational force:

> Through several hundred pages of angelology, Newton gradually managed to trim their wings and transform this new agent into a 'force'. A 'purely objective' force? Of course, because it had answered the objections, but it was still charged, upstream, by millennia of meditations on an 'angelic system of instant messaging'. As we know quite well, purity would sterilize the sciences: behind the force, the wings of angels are always beating invisibly. (Latour [2015] 2017, 66)

So Newton has 'drawn out of his own culture a set of features for the new agent that later imposed itself as "universal attraction"' (Latour [2015] 2017, 65). However, Latour does not want to associate this process with poetics: 'We mustn't see this bond between gravity and law as a matter of poetic licence' (Latour [2015] 2017, 65). But why should we not analyse this example as an instance of the poetics of science? As happens more often in *Facing Gaia*, Latour offers a more subtle position in the subsequent lecture, where he makes clear that science cannot be separated from poetics, or myth:

> Myth and science, as we well know, speak languages that are only apparently distinct; as soon as we approach the metamorphic zone that we have learned to identify, they begin to exchange their features, so that they can manage to express, to extend, what they want to say. 'There is no pure myth other than [that of] science purified of any myth', as Serres put it. (Latour [2015] 2017, 85–6)

Having identified some hesitation on the part of Latour to link science and poetics, it must be noted more generally that the intersection between poetics and science-and-religion appears quite understudied nowadays. Neither *The Oxford Handbook of Religion and Science* (Clayton 2006) nor *The Cambridge Companion to Science and Religion* (Harrison 2010) – together comprising over 1,350 pages – make any reference to this topic. It looks as if James's 'class of mind' of the disenchanted are dominating the discussion. Where did the richness of (the analysis of) both scientific and religious practices go?

If we follow Peter Harrison's (2015) argument about the origins of the terms 'religion' and 'science', we might conclude that both science and religion have undergone a sort of disenchantment over the past few centuries, in the sense of an increased analytical emphasis on outward institutionalisation at the expense of inward virtues. In the seventeenth century virtues and powers in nature were removed and replaced by external laws; at the same time, analogously, human virtues became subordinate to divinely imposed laws, for instance, moral laws (Harrison 2015, 15–16). So in order to study poetics and science-and-religion, it makes sense to return briefly to the sixteenth century (through a contemporary lens).

But first let me highlight how one can understand poetry to impinge constructively on scientific practice, using Latour as a guide.[10] In Chapter 4 Latour's philosophy was characterised as a philosophy of uncertainty and a philosophy of value. In the case of scientific practice, the dominant mode is that of 'reference', which has the ability to jump over gaps of distance and dissemblances of form. Scientific knowledge is neither by definition nor as result of the application of a 'scientific method' a certain and accurate representation of an outside world that can be known. Instead, in practice only on the (uncertain) basis of scientists' success in translating human and non-human actants' interests and incorporating them into the networks that underpin their claims can non-absolute attributions be made of objectivity, accuracy, reliability and truth. Note that the heterogeneity of actants can be large. While Latour himself, especially in his early work of the 1970s and 1980s (e.g. Latour 1987), has mainly focused on tangible connections to society in the form of entities and artefacts, and has been critical of a realist attitude towards society, there is nothing fundamental that prevents us from analysing the mobilisation of non-tangible cultural resources in scientific practice. One of Latour's suppositions is that networks can become stabilised, especially when enrolling tangible entities; in this view, network linkages to cultural resources such as texts are much easier to destabilise. I argue, however, that it is important and rewarding for the analysis of scientific practice to include non-tangibles, as long as one keeps in mind that one should not reify culture. Instead we should view cultural goods, with Rickert, as the fallible realisations of different types of values.

Philologist Fernand Hallyn (1945–2009) is one of very few recent authors who has studied the 'poetics' of science, in connection with religion (Hallyn [1987] 1990). Hallyn considers in particular the way in which hypotheses are established (cf. Latour's 'science in the making' versus 'ready-made science'; Latour 1987). Many heterogeneous elements come together in the establishment of a new hypothesis; given the uncertainty in the situation – besides, for instance, the observation of new phenomena and the development of new techniques – there is considerable room for emotion, imagination and poetry, and through those elements for the mobilisation of a large variety of cultural resources. Science in the making involves modern myth making:

> A new hypothesis, as long as it is not sufficiently validated and accepted, is formally similar to a *mythos* [cf. Aristotle's *Poetics*], to the intrigue or plot of a tragedy ... [, which] is nothing other than ... 'the organization of the events'. Now the goal of a hypothesis is precisely to organize 'events' systematically. (Hallyn [1987] 1990, 13–14)

According to Hallyn in his book *The Poetic Structure of the World: Copernicus and Kepler* (1990, original French edition 1987), attending to the poetics of science entails a close study of the commonplaces that scientists deal with, of the scientists' insertion in other cultural domains and of the 'tropes' (e.g., metaphors and models) that scientists use (Hallyn [1987] 1990, 15–29). For the Copernican revolution Hallyn analyses how Copernicus made use of 'organicism' (demand for symmetry) and 'formism' (preference for circular form), how he was tightly linked to the intertextual field of the Renaissance and how he associated the solar centre with the conception of the divine (Hallyn [1987] 1990, 281–4). With regard to Kepler's poetics, Hallyn ([1987] 1990, 284–6) shows how Kepler examined the poetic presuppositions of Copernicus and realised some new potentialities: he added harmonic requirements from music to the mix (bringing in the elliptical form), he followed 'Mannerism' in emphasising the ellipse and building an aesthetics on the basis of a theory of ideas (resulting in Kepler's universe looking like a *Wunderkammer* or *Kunstkammer*) and he grafted a multiplicity of metaphors and models onto the global order (e.g. Copernicus's theme of the solar centre leads in Kepler to the allegory of centre, radius and surface as a figure for the Trinity).

Copernicus's poetics involved irony and paradox, which is visible for instance from the relationship between the epistle that precedes his work *De revolutionibus* (1543) and the main body of the work. While the epistle presents the Copernican system as a fiction to be judged solely for its effectiveness and not its theoretical truth, many passages in the main body express Copernicus's conviction to speak the truth. Hallyn argues that this textual behaviour was occurring more widely in the sixteenth century ([1987] 1990, 49–52). The trope does flag uncertainty, makes readers more aware of the role of judgement (for Copernicus and for themselves) and nudges readers to be charmed by the beauty of the new theory.

However, Copernicus was no relativist, nor at the same time did he wish to defer to authority. There are 'codes' that can be mastered and that provide more or less reliable interpretations of the world. Like the philologists required to interpret Scripture, astronomists – with their mastery of mathematics – are needed to read the 'book of the world'. Furthermore, it is questionable whether in terms of obtaining more accurate results, the Copernican system could be considered more effective. It is rather at the poetic level, in the move from the 'monstrosity' of the Ptolemean system to the 'symmetry' of the Copernican system, that the (emotional) effectiveness of the new theory should be located.

Symmetry plays a central role in the Copernican system. It has poetic connotations, which also feature in Copernicus's lyrical praise of the centrality of the sun in the universe:

> At rest, however, in the middle of everything is the sun. For in this most beautiful temple, who would place this lamp in another or better position than that from which it can light up the whole thing at the same time? For the sun is not inappropriately called by some people the lantern of the universe, its mind by others, and

> its ruler by still others. ... Thus indeed, as though seated on a royal throne, the sun governs the family of planets revolving around it. (Copernicus [1543] 1978, 22)

Hallyn opposes some interpretations of this passage as 'purely literary', that is, as exterior to the scientific hypothesis: 'Rather than consider such passages as "literary", why not recognize in their coherence and insistence a specific constituent element in the comprehensiveness and unity of the Copernican enterprise?' ([1987] 1990, 129). Hallyn subsequently shows how Copernicus, by appropriating traditional metaphors, established a new symbolic perspective on the organisation of the universe.[11]

Kepler, in his first book (*Mysterium cosmographicum*, published in 1597), moved beyond Copernicus's symmetry to add what can be called 'eurythmy' (having harmonious proportions) as a principal consideration (Hallyn [1987] 1990, 183–7). Kepler's starting point for finding an explanation of the universe was the assumption that the work of the Creator should be of the greatest beauty. Actually, the other part of the book's title (*de admirabili proportione orbium*/'on the remarkable proportions of the spheres') stood out visibly on the title page of the original edition, which confirms the centrality of proportions. According to Kepler, nothing is superfluous – neither the magnitude of the intervals between the planetary orbits nor the number of planets. He gave the five regular polyhedrons a structural role in the cosmos; in doing so he operated in the artistic context of his time, where the study of the five solids also played a central role in the development of the pictorial perspective (Hallyn [1987] 1990, 196–9). Despite being charged with 'poetic conceit' (in later years, e.g., by Galileo) – the question was asked: Does it really add anything to astronomy to fill the voids in Creation by embedding polyhedrons in spheres? – Kepler never completely gave up on giving a role to the polyhedrons.

In his later work *Harmonices mundis* (published in 1619), which he considered the crowning achievement of his life, Kepler provided an aesthetic justification of the ellipse. As Hallyn summarises it:

> The ellipse gives birth to the superior beauty of harmony. Elliptical motion is a geometric imperfection that assures musical perfection. ([1987] 1990, 218)

His preoccupation with celestial harmony also returned full force. Kepler transformed the earlier Pythagorean music of the spheres by linking the problem of harmony to the relation between the circle and polygons:

> So Kepler succeeded in constructing a complete musical theory, while rigorously checking his deductions against empirical data. (Hallyn [1987] 1990, 236)

Where he had failed to show perfect agreement between the cosmological hypothesis and the astronomical facts in *Mysterium cosmographicum*, Kepler had now succeeded.

In *Facing Gaia*, Latour describes the post-Copernican shock of climate change:

> This time, we humans are not shocked to learn that the Earth no longer occupies the center and that it spins aimlessly around the Sun; no, if we are so profoundly shocked, it is on the contrary because we find ourselves at the center of its little universe, and because we are imprisoned in its minuscule local atmosphere. (Latour [2015] 2017, 80)

The latest shock has major worldview implications, including feeling exposed and being forced to become inventive in our new ways of being on Earth, which according to Latour is reminiscent of the sixteenth century (Latour [2015] 2017, 190). New poetics, encapsulating a new myth, are needed to address Gaia. But the new myth must be 'wholly secular' (Latour [2015] 2017, 82) or 'worldly' (87). Latour does not highlight this, but there is definitely poetics – albeit at the risk of being Faustian – in his exclamation: 'the Earth is becoming sensitive to our actions and we humans are becoming, to some extent, geology!' (Latour [2015] 2017, 113).

For Latour, the world is enchanted and we can leave behind the dichotomy between a disenchanted 'Nature' and an overanimated 'God'. How does he then address the poetics of religion in *Facing Gaia*? Latour highlights the presence of contradiction in religion, which cannot be overcome:

> That the world has an end does not mean that it has a goal in the sense of having being 'created with a goal', but that it is possible to experience it as having achieved the end – which can be translated by a whole host of formulas, strange ones for many of our contemporaries, all of which have the same meaning: to be 'saved', to be 'children of a God who cares for us', to be 'God's chosen people', to 'find ourselves in the Presence', 'to have been created', and so on. These are all provisional, awkward formulas that are immediately

> attacked as insufficient, deceitful, or impious by other versions of these same counter-religions. (Latour [2015] 2017, 174)

The role of religious poetics is to 'read'/experience the world, for which a dedicated kind of poetics is needed, the difficulty being in particular 'that the end times have come, *but that time is lasting*! ... The end has been reached, and it is unreachable' (Latour [2015] 2017, 174). One may keep a reference to 'God' in such poetry, but one should realise that Latour's view of religion implies also 'the *end* of all the gods and divinities, and even in a sense the *end of God*, in the well-known sense of the death of God' (Latour [2015] 2017, 176).

In Chapter 4 I showed how in his earlier work on religion Latour contrasted religion with science as involving translation and 'saving' instead of information and representation. One can thus characterise the difference between religion and science as that between poetry that saves and prose that refers.[12] However, for poetry in religion to be able to perform its saving role, Latour wants *new* poetry:

> Sympathize with me now in my misery: to articulate the first language game, the one involving the consoling 'God', the faithful have at their disposal six thousand years of poets, preachers, inspired psalmists; to articulate the second, the game involving non-control of words, I have nothing, no breviary, no psalter, no song book, not the smallest image, nothing but myself, I who am nothing – not even a believer. And yet, the old term has indeed become unutterable, unsituatable, unjustifiable – except inside the narrow fold, among those in the habit of praying among themselves. Now, what I really need is something new. ... It's not the object of prayer that has died out, it's the prayer form itself that has become outmoded. (Latour [2002] 2013a, 13–14)

Methodist minister Neville Ward, who wrote a penetrating analysis of the practice of praying three and a half decades before Latour, could sympathise with him, but only to an extent. Like James, Ward distinguishes between religious people (in his example, Christians) with different temperaments:

> Many Christian people think of prayer as something that religious people are supposed to do. It would be difficult to find a more unfortunate approach. It is impossible to explore the world of prayer with interest and hope of discovery if you feel guilty because

> you do not pray or when you do not pray. The subject never comes alive to guilt, but it does to curiosity and interest. It is worth while admitting that it is quite possible to get along without prayer if 'getting along' means living life with a reasonable amount of happiness and without excessive regret. Many people must do just this, and many Christians among them. (Ward 1967, 11–12)

Praying comes more naturally for the enchanted. Wonder is evoked in them by both traditional and new poetic texts that are prayed:

> Much of God's will has been done by people who never found themselves able to pray in the traditional forms. However, some of the radical criticism of traditional Christian prayer overlooks the fact that there is an extensive literature written by people who have liked prayer, believed in it and studied it deeply. Everyone should look at some of this and see if he does not feel the stirring of some desire for that unvisited, or lost, domain of religious life in which so many admirable and interesting people have lived so importantly. (Ward 1967, 12)

Of course, Latour is not alone in his struggle with the church. As we saw in Chapter 2, James was frustrated with his contemporary church and its theism:

> An external creator and his institutions may still be verbally confessed at church in formulas that linger by their mere inertia, but the life is out of them, we avoid dwelling on them, the sincere heart of us is elsewhere. (James [1909a] 1977,18)

James's concern is with individual saving experiences and intimacy with God versus a theistic view of humans being outsiders and mere subjects to God. Ward, in his analysis of prayer, contextualises such individualism by indicating that '[i]f we pray at all it is because we have been brought into a praying community' (Ward 1967, 13). In Christianity, the church has developed a desire to pray, has shaped a poetic liturgy of prayer with the Eucharist as its pinnacle – beginning with thanking and offering – and gives individual people 'participation in that desire whatever the condition of [their] faith at any particular time' (Ward 1967, 13). From this perspective, private prayer is a secondary thing, important but derivative. What Latour's *Facing Gaia* shows us is that with climate change and the ecological crisis, as analysed by science and evoking the frightening poetics of Gaia, formulating new religious poetry while responsibly re-appropriating past traditions constitutes a prime challenge for the world's cultures.

Modern myth and ecology

While the companion and handbook on science-and-religion mentioned in the previous section do not explicitly address poetics as such, the closest they come to this is in their treatments of natural theology and religious naturalism respectively. On natural theology, Jonathan Topham notes that its historic role was typically 'to offer exemplifications of divine design in illustration or confirmation of revealed theology' (2010, 60). These exemplifications often took poetic form, as was alluded to by James in his lecture 'Is life worth living?' (see above). Topham explains that:

> the rise of natural theology in seventeenth-century England was prompted not only by a desire to legitimate the new [mechanical] philosophy and defend it from imputations of an irreligious tendency, but by a range of religious motivations, including the desire to foster Christian belief in both sceptics and believers, to sanctify the practice of natural philosophy and natural history and to explore the theological consequences of new scientific findings. (Topham 2010, 63–4)

In terms of the desire to provide meaning on the basis of science, it seems not a large step from natural theology to a religious form of naturalism (atheistic, agnostic or theistic). For instance, Willem Drees indicates that we:

> ought to accept a naturalistic view, since it is the position that is most respectful of the epistemic success of the natural sciences, and thus cognitively preferable. It is also morally preferable, as it incites us to work with our knowledge. For those who accept theistic considerations, naturalism should be the preferred view of reality as God's creation, since it does not locate God's role in our ignorance or limitations, but in what we know and what we are able to do. (Drees 2006, 108)

My interest in this final section lies in how naturalism would 'incite' us, in particular to climate and wider ecological action. What is the role of poetics? Does it lie in providing, for instance, an evolutionary epic? Drees himself has offered 'a justified creation story' (Drees 2002, 2). He acknowledges that coming up with such a story involves 'a quest for new images' for which poets are best qualified (Drees 2002, 2). But is it possible for poetry fed largely by science to bring re-enchantment of nature and motivate action against the ecological crisis?

Let me explore this question first from a theistic perspective. Theologian Alister McGrath starts his book *The Reenchantment of Nature: The denial of religion and the ecological crisis* (2002)[13] from the assumptions that 'Christianity offers an explanation of the world and our place within it' and that the natural sciences and Christianity share a 'fundamental conviction that the world is characterized by regularity and intelligibility' (McGrath 2002, 11). According to McGrath, a deeper meaning can be discerned in nature that neither follows from nor is precluded by science. Aesthetics, beauty, wonder and poetry all feature in McGrath's book, on the basis of a fundamental alignment between nature and God (as should be expected in a theistic position):

> It is as if there is a congruence or fundamental resonance between our sense of beauty and the beauty that is actually embodied in the natural world – almost as if we have been programmed or hardwired to recognize and respond to the beauty of the world.
>
> The Christian doctrine of creation suggests that this fundamental resonance is no accident, but is grounded in the structures of creation itself. Our sense of wonder at the beauty of nature is thus an *indirect* appreciation of the beauty of God. Rightly perceived, nature points beyond itself. (McGrath 2002, 17)

McGrath mobilises Christianity's rich history, including its poetic history, to provide a healthy antidote against the human-centred assumptions of the Enlightenment (and the New Atheists), which entail that only science can liberate and that we need to get rid of religion and poetry – it is this assumption that leads to disenchantment, not science *per se*. McGrath flags the need for an ontology of nature that identifies it as significant independently of whether humans think so or not: 'Reenchantment depends upon the reaffirmation that nature is special and clarification of how this "special" character is to be understood' (McGrath 2002, 74). He sees the risks of the 'Faustian pact' where humans want power over nature and sell their soul to the devil in order to obtain it via technology. Obtaining power over nature in a careless way, with disregard for all sorts of negative consequences, including the ecological crisis, is not sanctioned by God, according to McGrath. Using scientific models, such as that of mechanism, we have not only come to see nature that way, but also have started intensively to treat it like that (McGrath 2002, 110).

McGrath has two problems with this. Firstly, nature is more complex than any one model can capture and science always retains deep uncertainty – thus highlighting that the mechanical model downplays other possible models (McGrath 2002, 116). Secondly, '[w]e must *encounter* nature, not simply *experience* it' – we need to treat nature as a 'Thou' and acknowledge that it possesses mystical qualities that underpin our perception of its intrinsic value (McGrath 2002, 125–6).

At the core of a poetic imagination, a re-enchantment of nature, the beginnings of dealing with the ecological crisis, McGrath places the phenomenon of 'wonder', as he outlines in a section titled 'The wonder of nature and intimations of glory' (McGrath 2002, 138–43). He lists three aspects that theology attaches to humans' wonder at Creation: (1) an immediate sense of awe, not mediated through any understanding; (2) an enhanced sense of appreciation, resulting from understanding; and (3) a blessed sense of ignorance,[14] based on realising that nature points beyond itself to the glory of God, the Other, the Unknown. Like we saw in James, given the importance McGrath attaches to knowledge, the uncertainty or recognised ignorance here should not be taken as absolute and has a positive connotation: there is always more to know and encounter, in a never-ending history. Where Santayana wrote that 'religion is poetry substituted for science or supervening upon it', McGrath has a clear narrative for religion as poetry supervening upon science: there is no need to disregard the beauty discovered in science.

How could one construe an analogous argumentation against disenchantment and falling into a scientistic trap without taking a theistic position? In her recent contribution to religious studies, *Consecrating Science: Wonder, knowledge, and the natural world* (2017), Lisa Sideris takes up the same challenge as McGrath (also entering into debate with New Atheists), but without adopting a theistic perspective. Sideris criticises the suitability of science to deliver the ingredients for a poetics that can help us deal with the ecological crisis. She detects impoverished notions of 'wonder' and 'ignorance' in attempts such as the *Epic of Evolution* or the *New Cosmology* to instil an ecology-saving attitude in the recipients of these poetic expressions of scientific insights. She actually considers them as hindrances in dealing with the ecological crisis.

According to Sideris, 'mythopoeticised science' is a form of scientism, in which science is made sacred. It involves knowledge-based wonder:

> The new cosmology calls on us to respond with awe and wonder to what is deemed most authentically real. Scientific information – if presented in sufficiently rich poetic and mythological language – is seen to fulfill many of the functions of a religious cosmology, while also orienting us toward deeper connection with and concern for the natural world. (Sideris 2017, 6)

The projects that Sideris criticises lack 'an ability to dwell in doubt, mystery, and ambiguity and to resist the categorization of all phenomena and experience into a system of knowledge' (Sideris 2017, 11). She emphasises that wonder should not be (primarily) seen as a function of uncertainty, associated with a consecutive series of reductions of ignorance. She notes that the 'age of wonder' (a period from roughly the middle of the seventeenth to the middle of the eighteenth century) ran in parallel with the age of disenchantment. Instead of seeing wonder as a function of reducing ignorance, 'wonder may provide the conditions for novel forms of knowledge to emerge, even as wonder is not exhausted by new knowledge' (Sideris 2017, 26). Like McGrath when he describes encountering nature, Sideris brings to the fore that encountering something in wonder is like an I–Thou encounter. But unlike McGrath, she does not emphasise the enhanced sense of appreciation of Creation that can result from science.

Latour's analysis of science-and-religion, as portrayed in *Facing Gaia*, poses a challenge for both McGrath and Sideris (as well as many others) whose image of science still comes closest to Latour's 'religion of Nature':

> The chimera that interests me involves imagining groups of people who would not remain insensitive to the features of [the terrestrialized conceptions of science and religion]. It would no longer be a question of natural religions, since the shared feature would be that of no longer having an ordering principle. There would certainly be a supreme authority, but this would lie no longer in unity – capable of designing a universe – but in connection or composition. More precisely, every time any entity whatsoever has to extend itself, it has to pay the full price of its extension. Which is another way of saying that it has a history. In other words, the members of these peoples would no longer feel that they are living under a Globe, but in the middle of relations that they have to compose one by one without any means of escaping historicity. To accentuate the contrast, I propose to say that such population groups would share

> the same feeling of *earthboundedness*. If there's no such word, it's precisely because we have yet to bring into existence the thing that it designates! Such groups would share the need to protect each other against the temptation of unifying too quickly the world that they are exploring step by step. Both groups, indeed, find themselves on a ground whose materiality and fragility they are discovering more and more every day. Neither of the two believes itself to be located outside of the time that is passing. (Latour [2015] 2017, 181–2)

Since a 'durably secularized collective' cannot exist, according to Latour, there is always a supreme authority (with name and properties) 'in whose name they gather' (Latour [2015] 2017, 153) – and always poetics involved in the gathering. Latour finds the use of the word 'God' for the supreme authority for people of Nature – 'Out-of-Which-We-Are-All-Born' – 'too disrespectful' (Latour [2015] 2017, 159). There is a role for poetics in the 'tragedy' that we are in: Gaia needs to have appearance of threat to make us sensitive to 'mortality, finitude, "existential negation" – to the simple difficulty of being of this Earth' (Latour [2015] 2017, 244).

We need new ritual, new language and new poetics to deal with Gaia. As Latour reports about a group simulation:

> While Nature could reign over humans as a religious power to which a paradoxical cult, civic and secular, had to be devoted, Gaia only requires that power be shared *as secular and not religious powers*. … Even though, up to now, there has been no civic cult for such an outlining of the 'planetary borders' that a political body would impose on itself, what we did in the simulation was offer a glimpse of such a ritual. (Latour [2015] 2017, 281)

Note that climate scientists invoking 'nature' does not bring peace. Science has now moved beyond its earlier claims of descriptive neutrality and we are impelled to action through climate scientists' utterances. With respect to normative utterances, Latour rightfully flags (with respect to climate change) that 'this type of utterance now comes not only from poets, lovers, politicians, and prophets, but also from geochemists, naturalists, modelers, and geologists' (Latour [2015] 2017, 49). I contend that we should also start to think about the poetics involved with Gaia.

Where does this all leave us for dealing with the ecological crisis, for 'sharing the planet'? A non-scientistic notion of wonder can perhaps indeed underpin the intrinsic value of non-human life forms.

There seems to be no alternative route to argue for intrinsic value; as physicist Johan van Klinken and zoologist Jan van Hooff argue, it is not possible 'to offer a compelling scientific argumentation' for non-anthropocentric values (van Klinken and van Hooff 2003, 102). I argue that new poetic expression should be sought for such 'intrinsic value' linked to a transcendental naturalistic understanding of Gaia in a multitude of cultural backgrounds. Also, in response to the scientistic naturalistic approaches to ecological conservation observed by Sideris, I agree with Jane Goodall. She realised that alternative approaches are needed when, in her educational conservation projects, she let young people experience wonder in hands-on projects focused on real people and real animals in real environments (Goodall 2003). Abstract knowledge may not do the trick: we may also need individual experiences – and to make poetic reference to them – in order to find meaning and motivate action.

Conclusion

In this chapter I have addressed the question of how judgements under uncertainty in science-and-religion are facilitated by poetics and put this question in the context of Latour's *Facing Gaia*. While different values are assumed in the practices of science and religion, poetry can play a driving role in transcendental judgements. The narrative at the end of the nineteenth century was that of poetry versus science. Both James and Santayana defended poetry against scientism, but they also realised that there is a creative connection between science and poetry; a connection that was much more evident in scientific works in the sixteenth century. A central present-day question in science-and-religion is whether a science-compatible modern myth can be construed – whether theistic, agnostic, or atheistic in kind – that replaces or amends classical religious myths and can 're-enchant' the world.

After considering the roles of poetics in science and religion, I discussed the challenge of present attempts to address the ecological crisis through modern myths based on science (and the arguments that have been made against such a scientistic naturalistic approach in environmental politics, including with respect to climate change). I identified some problems that are connected with aiming for ecological conservation based on a religious interpretation of science, and I flagged that Latour is interested in poetics and rituals associated with Gaia, though he did not really develop this aspect. In the next chapter, we delve deeper into the question where the cognitive authority of judgements, including those involving poetics, derives from.

Notes

1 I denote Latour's 'counter-religion' (Latour [2015] 2017) with 'religion' here, as he does for the new view of religion – called 'counter-religion two' in Latour ([2015] 2017) – in Latour ([2012] 2013b). Here is how he introduces the terms 'religion' and 'counter-religion' in *Facing Gaia*: '[T]he word "religion" does no more than designate that to which one clings, what one protects carefully, what one thus is careful not to neglect' (Latour [2015] 2017, 152). '[T]here is no such thing as a durably *secularized* collective; there are only collectives that have modified the name and the properties of the supreme authority in whose name they gather' (Latour [2015] 2017, 153). 'Translating the name of the one into the name of the Other became not only unfeasible but scandalous and even impious. "True" divinity became untranslatable by any other name; no cult but its own could be tolerated, on pain of idolatry. It is as if the real God had fulminated: "You shall not make my cult *commensurable* with any other, under any circumstances." The old sense of the word "religion" was no longer comprehensible: quite to the contrary, the new injunction required neglecting that to which the others clung! This is why Assmann proposes, for this new association between religion and truth, the apparently counter-intuitive term *counter-religion*' (Latour [2015] 2017, 156).

2 The lecture was published in 1897 as an essay in *The Will to Believe*.

3 In 'Is life worth living?' James states that he uses 'religion' in 'the supernaturalist sense, as declaring that the so-called order of nature, which constitutes this world's experience, is only one portion of the total universe, and that there stretches beyond this visible world an unseen world of which we now know nothing positive, but in its relation to which the true significance of our present mundane life consists' (James [1897] 1979, 48). In *The Varieties*, he ('arbitrarily') defines 'religion' as: 'the feelings, acts, and experiences of individual men in their solitude, so far as they apprehend themselves to stand in relation to whatever they may consider the divine' (James [1902] 1985, 34).

4 In Chapter 4 I analysed Latour's modes of existence and compared his thought with both Rickert's and James's. For instance, for the different modes Latour emphasises that they all have to jump different gaps/uncertainties in their respective practices. It is the power of judgement that sets the imagination free and makes such jumps possible: in science there are gaps of 'distance and dissemblances of form' (scientific value: bringing back information, reaching remote entities) and in religion there are gaps of a 'break in times' (religious value: bringing beings into presence, achieving the end times).

5 As Santayana himself also observes in a letter to James of Easter 1900 (in response to James's comments on *Interpretations of Poetry and Religion* that had been shared with him): '[A]part from temperament, I am nearer to you than you now believe. What you say, for instance, about the value of the good lying in its *existence*, and about the continuity of the world of values with that of fact, is not different from what I should admit' (Perry 1935, 320). I am not making a statement on the similarity of James's and Santayana's entire philosophies here, and I focus mainly on Santayana's 1900 book. But it is worth noting that a similar pattern of criticism from James and accommodating response from Santayana happened in 1905 upon the publication of Santayana's next book, *The Life of Reason*. James wrote: 'It has no *rational* foundation, being merely one man's way of viewing things. … And his naturalism, materialism, Platonism, and atheism form a combination of which the centre of gravity is, I think, very deep. But there is something profoundly alienating in his unsympathetic tone, his "preciousness" and superciliousness' (Perry 1935, 399). And Santayana responded: 'You are very generous; I feel that you want to give me credit for everything good that can possibly be found in my book. But you don't yet see my philosophy, nor my temper from the inside; your praise, like your blame, touches only the periphery, accidental aspects presented to this or that preconceived and disparate interest' (Perry 1935, 401).

6 In 1891 Santayana had published an 'admirably penetrating review of the *Principles*' (Perry 1935, 111) in the *Atlantic Monthly*. In this he ultimately judged the book to be 'rich and living,

in which a generous nature breaks out at every point, and the perennial problems of the human mind are discussed so modestly, so solidly, with such a deep and pathetic sincerety' (quoted in Perry 1935, 111). James, in a letter to Harvard's President Eliot in 1898, urged for a promotion for Santayana: 'I wish to say that I am distinctly in favor of it. … Whatever shortcomings may go with the type of mind of which he is a representative, I think it must be admitted to be a rare and precious type, of which Harvard University may well keep a specimen to enrich her concert withal. We shall always have "hustlers" enough – but we shall not often have a chance at a Santayana, with his style, his subtlely of perception, and his cool-blooded truthfulness' (Perry 1935, 270).

7 For James and Latour there are limits to poetically aroused emotions using poetry that is hundreds to thousands of years old (such as the example that I gave of the expression of religious wonder in Psalm 139, in the sixteenth-century translation used in the Book of Common Prayer): in their view, new poetic expressions – for instance in form of new hymns – will continually be needed as well.

8 At the end of this chapter I will address attempts at re-enchantment in the context of climate change and the ecological crisis. It is then crucial to evaluate which types of poetics can really evoke *those* emotions and set the imagination free on *those* paths which lead to both the world regaining deeper meaning in the context of present-day science and people being motivated to act for 'sharing the planet' (cf. van der Zwaan and Petersen 2003).

9 Rickert's notion of the 'pro-physical' has been described in Chapters 3 and 4. Let me add here again that he actually means pro-*perceptual*, which includes the pro-physical – in the narrow sense of 'before perception of physical being' – and the pro-mental – in the sense of 'before perception of mental being'.

10 Or rather, forcing him into this role.

11 If we compare Hallyn's emphasis on Copernicus's poetics with how Harrison speaks of the Copernican world – 'The new Copernican world was far removed from the cozy, medieval, Ptolemaic world in which moral meanings were inscribed on the cosmos. … The vast expansion of the cosmos, the idea of empty space, the evacuation from nature of transcendental meanings, all presaged a mute universe that seemed to offer no moral guidance to those who studied it' (Harrison 2015, 136) – one cannot help but note that the poetic element is missing in Harrison's characterisation.

12 This is notwithstanding my earlier comments on the possibility of a Latourian approach to the poetics of science.

13 The UK edition of his book has another subtitle, which we will see is relevant to our discussion: 'Science, religion and the human sense of wonder'.

14 McGrath does not use the phrase 'blessed sense of ignorance'; this is my characterisation of the third aspect that he describes (crafted here for its symmetry, in terms of phrasing, with the first two aspects). McGrath refers to '"liminality" – a sense of standing on the border of some unknown territory' (McGrath 2002, 140).

7
Authorities and climate: modern rationality and disbelief

Introduction

The next step in showing that transcendental naturalism is not confronted with the problems that scientistic naturalism evokes is to go beyond the results of the previous chapter on ways to read meaning under uncertainty via poetics and to address the issue of cognitive authority under uncertainty head on. In *Facing Gaia* Latour criticises various forms of disbelief across different domains (science, religion, politics), in particular modern disbelief in the authority of practices that are anthropologically shown to be networks dealing with uncertainty. In science, for instance, certainties from top-down modelling (or their refutation) should not have the authority they seem to be awarded – the picture should rather be of authority resting 'on a very strange system of election and proofs' involving a 'network of instruments, the Vast Machine that the climatologists have built' (Latour [2015] 2017, 33). Interestingly, Latour traces (the ideal of) scientific certainty to religious certainty:

> Whatever we may think of the Moderns, however non-believing they deem themselves to be, however free of any divinity they may imagine themselves, they are indeed the direct heirs of th[e] 'Mosaic division', since they continue to connect supreme authority with truth, with one nuance: the division henceforth passes *between, on the one hand, believing in any religion at all and, on the other, knowing the truth about nature*. (Latour [2015] 2017, 156–7)

Now also religion, according to Latour, should not be about beliefs that have certainty attached to them. As we saw in the previous chapter, poetics and more tentative theological imagery are more suitable means of expressing the cognitive content of religious practices. With respect to politics, Latour points out that one must question the 'notion of humans prematurely unified' (Latour [2015] 2017, 247) – especially for a problem such as climate change, it becomes clear that the authority to speak in the name of nation-states (which may aim to reach a political consensus) is questioned by those who claim authority to represent many new agents involved in the climate system. As Latour writes, 'Gaia ... is ... the name proposed for all the intermingled and unpredictable consequences of the agents, each of which is pursuing its own interest by manipulating its own environment' (Latour [2015] 2017, 142), and '[n]o business-as-usual anthropomorphic character can participate in the Anthropocene' (Latour [2015] 2017, 121).

'Anthropogenic climate change' is a problematic term, according to Latour: 'Who can claim to speak for the human in general without arousing a thousand protests at once?' (Latour [2015] 2017, 121). He mentions as example protestors: 'Indian nations in the Amazonian forest', 'poor residents in Bombay's shantytowns' or 'worker[s] forced to travel long distances ... [un]able to find affordable housing near' (Latour [2015] 2017, 121–2). Who and which statements hold authority in the various practices is clearly a precarious matter.

Latour importantly points out that political quarrels about climate change do not go away because of progress in climate science. He observes that 'we have entered into a *postnatural* period' (Latour [2015] 2017, 142) in which both climate scientists and 'the public at large' have been thrust 'outside of nature' (Latour [2015] 2017, 143), with 'nature' used here in the scientistic naturalistic sense. Uncertainty remains within science and about what 'the driving forces that agitate humans or the goals of politics' may be (Latour [2015] 2017, 150). Matters of fact – that need networks doing work in practices to maintain their indisputability – have become what Latour calls 'matters of concern' (Latour [2015] 2017, 164). Climate scientists will thus have to learn to work wisely and diplomatically with what Latour considers to be their real authority:

> Naturalist scientists – those who proudly assert that they are 'of Nature' – are unfortunate figures, bound to disappear, disembodied, behind their Knowledge, or to have souls, voices, and places, but at the risk of losing their authority. In contrast, earthbound scientists are embodied creatures. They form a people. They have enemies. They belong to the territory outlined by their instruments. Their knowledge extends as far as their

> ability to finance, to control, to maintain the sensors that make the consequences of their actions visible. They have no scruples about acknowledging the existential drama in which they are engaged. They dare to say how afraid they are, and from their viewpoint such fear *increases* the quality of their science rather than *diminishing* it. They appear clearly as a new form of *non-national power that is explicitly participating as such in geopolitical conflicts*. If their territory knows no national boundaries, this is not because they have access to the universal, but because they keep on bringing in new agents to be full participants in the subsistence of the other agents. Their authority is fully political, because they represent agents who have no other voice and who intervene in the lives of many other agents. They do not hesitate to outline the shape of the world, the *nomos*, the cosmos in which they prefer to live. (Latour [2015] 2017, 242–53)

This is no small ask for climate scientists. In this chapter we will see how difficult climate scientists find it to be reflexive about the networks and uncertainties of their practices – particularly when they think that they must hold up a modern image of science *vis-à-vis* nation-state politics within the context of the Intergovernmental Panel on Climate Change (IPCC). I argue that such reflexivity can be underpinned philosophically by a move from scientistic naturalism to transcendental naturalism.

The theme of this chapter is the role of 'authority' or 'authorities' in the practices of science and religion, applied to climate science and politics. Another way to frame this theme is in terms of 'rationality' or 'rationalities'. Why should one believe what one believes? Should belief in science lead to disbelief in religion or politics, or vice versa? How do authorities who have been groomed with modern rationality deal with belief and disbelief across different types of practices? For instance, how do scientists reflect different types of values (epistemic and non-epistemic) in their 'expert judgements' when they provide science advice to politics under uncertainty? The overarching question here is: how do authorities relate to uncertainty?

In his 1896 lecture 'The will to believe', William James refers to 'authority' as 'all those influences, born of the intellectual climate, that make hypotheses possible or impossible for us, alive or dead'; this includes 'all such factors of belief as fear and hope, prejudice and passion, imitation and partisanship, the circumpressure of our caste and set' (James [1897] 1979, 18). Likewise, I do not assume that humans acting in their practices are absolute subjects who are free to evaluate and choose their hypotheses according to an innate, infallible rationality (the so-called 'modern rationality'), which then provides for authority.

In this chapter I first address the perspectives of William James and Heinrich Rickert on authorities in connection with science-and-religion, in dialogue with Bruno Latour. This then informs my subsequent analysis of authorities in the context of contemporary science-and-religion and science advice discussions.

James, Latour and Rickert on authorities and science-and-religion

In his lecture 'The will to believe' James focuses on how belief formation works in practices, both in science and in religion, and on the philosophical import of his conclusion that the authority of beliefs derives largely from passions. He deals with belief in hypotheses, which in their turn rely on concepts, including complex concepts such as models. People are typically not aware where the authority in their use of concepts and models comes from; we just come to believe in the hypotheses that contain them. James notices: 'As a matter of fact we find ourselves believing, we hardly know how or why' (James [1897] 1979, 18). Rationalists may find it best to deal with uncertainty concerning error in a hypothesis by abstaining from belief. Situations in which humans can adopt such a pure judgemental stance, involving a full exercise of their freedom, do indeed exist according to James:

> Wherever the option between losing truth and gaining it is not momentous, we can throw the chance of *gaining truth* away, and at any rate save ourselves from any chance of *believing falsehood*, by not making up our minds at all till objective evidence has come. In scientific questions, this is almost always the case; and even in human affairs in general, the need of acting is seldom so urgent that a false belief to act on is better than no belief at all. (James [1897] 1979, 25–6)

However, in situations where a decision between two hypotheses must be made (called an 'option' by James) and the option is 'genuine' – meaning live instead of dead, forced instead of avoidable and momentous instead of trivial (James [1897] 1979, 14) – the 'authority' of modern rationality turns out not to be of much use.

James provides examples from the practices of science and of religion in his lecture. For science, he claims that discovery is actually dependent on not always 'weighing reasons *pro et contra* with an indifferent hand'. He continues:

> For purposes of discovery such indifference is to be less highly recommended, and science would be far less advanced than she is if the passionate desires of individuals to get their own faiths confirmed had been kept out of the game. (James [1897] 1979, 26)

On the same subject, scientist and inventor James Lovelock provides for Latour a beautiful example of such creativity: Lovelock's Gaia theory signifies a move against holism and for uncertainty and it resonates with Latour's occasionalist metaphysics. Gaia theory, in the form that Latour considers, portrays 'a version of the Earth that comes entirely from *here below*. Let's say that, to study the Earth, one has to come back down to Earth' (Latour [2015] 2017, 87).

Of course, there will be subsequent trials of strength (Latour's terminology) and a weeding out of hypotheses. Here is how James captures that process:

> The most useful investigator, because the most sensitive observer, is always he whose eager interest in one side of the question is balanced by an equally keen nervousness lest he become deceived. Science has organized this nervousness into a regular *technique*, her so-called method of verification; and she has fallen so deeply in love with the method that one may even say she has ceased to care for truth by itself at all. It is only truth as technically verified that interests her. (James [1897] 1979, 26–7)

In Latourian terms, if one focuses on what the 'technique' of verification does, it is verifying chains of reference in a heterogeneous practice.[1] For James, how the practices of science develop is very much an open affair, since both the context of discovery and the context of justification are deeply uncertain. Even while scientists find themselves within a sea of ignorance (see Chapter 6), they may sometimes feel that they are basing themselves on 'objective evidence' whenever they uncritically abandon themselves:

> Of some things we feel that we are certain: we know, and we know that we do know. There is something that gives a click inside of

> us, a bell that strikes twelve, when the hands of our mental clock have swept the dial and meet over the meridian hour. The greatest empiricists among us are only empiricists on reflection: when left to their instincts, they dogmatize like infallible popes. (James [1897] 1979, 21)

This shows for James that authority deep down is embodied (the 'click inside of us') and is not following an abstract modern rationality.

Similarly for religious people: they may also feel that they are basing themselves on 'objective evidence', leading to a 'pre-existing tendency', for instance for Christians to believe in God. James demonstrates what he means by this in a discussion of Pascal's wager – a passage in which Pascal uses a rational argument to force us into Christianity by reasoning as if our concern with the truth of God's existence resembled our concern with the stakes in a game of chance. But is it really possible to obtain religious belief through such rational thought? James thinks not:

> Surely Pascal's own personal belief in masses and holy water had far other springs; and this celebrated page of his is but an argument for others, a last desperate snatch at a weapon against the hardness of the unbelieving heart. We feel that a faith in masses and holy water adopted wilfully after such a mechanical calculation would lack the inner soul of faith's reality; and if we were ourselves in the place of the Deity, we should probably take particular pleasure in cutting off believers of this pattern from their infinite reward. It is evident that unless there be some pre-existing tendency to believe in masses and holy water, the option offered to the will by Pascal is not a living option. (James [1897] 1979, 16)

Our 'willing nature' is not entirely free to choose what to believe; instead it follows the authority of 'all those influences, born of the intellectual climate, that make hypotheses possible or impossible for us, alive or dead' (James [1897] 1979, 18). This is true for both science and religion.

In his posthumously published *Some Problems of Philosophy* (in the Appendix entitled 'Faith and the right to believe'), James characterises faith as 'one of the inalienable birthrights of our mind' (James [1911] 1979, 113). We will have to act on probabilities (even if we cannot calculate them):

> Of course it must remain a practical, and not a dogmatic attitude. It must go with toleration of other faiths, with the search for the most

> probable, and with the full consciousness of responsibilities and risks. (James [1911] 1979, 113)

One example of such 'toleration' can for instance be witnessed in James's attitude towards mysticism (discussed more fully in Chapter 8). As Carrette observes:

> In *Some Problems of Philosophy,* in a rare moment of philosophical closure, James limits discussion of mysticism, perhaps frustrated that it challenged one of his central claims to plurality. In his concern with the 'One and the Many', he discusses mystical monism in the Hindu and Islamic tradition, only to dismiss these monistic challenges to his pluralistic thinking as reflection of an 'ineffable' order and thus 'not strictly philosophical', which is seen as 'essentially talkative and explicit'. ... It was for the same reasons that James disconnected mysticism as a reliable form of authority in *The Varieties*. ... Mysticism may be on the boundary of philosophy and hold no specific authority for religious knowledge, but perhaps all knowledge-experience is not captured by philosophy. (Carrette 2013, 68–9)

For James, in the end authority is thus still dependent on philosophical appraisal – not in a rationalist vein, of course, but preferably through a radical empiricist lens.

James's argument also pertains to philosophy, for instance its notion of (theoretical) truth. As I discussed in Chapter 4, there was quite some disagreement between James and Rickert concerning this notion. Where James accused Rickert, taking him as representative of neo-Kantianism and of having a sterile notion of truth (only being a transcendental value), Rickert accused James of having given up on the notion of truth by making it wholly dependent (like other philosophers of life had done) on its use value in life. Both accusations are not entirely without merit, but they do divert attention away from the importance of both their notions and from the common ground that can also be found between James and Rickert, which underpins my proposal for a transcendental naturalism: their focus on uncertainty.

Let us look more closely here at some of the statements these thinkers made about truth. As I already showed in Chapter 4, Rickert maintained in his 1892 *Habilitationsschrift*:

> Everything else that humans know may be uncertain and swaying – yes, perhaps no human being is yet in possession of true judgements;

> but *one* judgement cannot be false: the judgement that the value of truth is valid absolutely. It is the most certain judgement that we can think of, since it constitutes the condition for *every* judgement. (Rickert 1892, 75–6)

He later said about pragmatist philosophy that while it errs in its theoretical interpretation of the value of truth, 'it rightly asserts that truth in its essence is valuable, and also that the knowing human being must be understood as a valuing subject' (Rickert 1920, 187). In his 1896 lecture, James has the following to say about the relationship between the will to believe and the notion of theoretical truth:

> Our faith is faith in some one else's faith, and in the greatest matters this is most the case. Our belief in truth itself, for instance, that there is a truth, and that our minds and it are made for each other – what is it but a passionate affirmation of desire, in which our social system backs us up? We want to have a truth; we want to believe that our experiments and studies and discussions must put us in a continually better and better position towards it; and on this line we agree to fight out our thinking lives. But if a pyrrhonistic sceptic asks us *how we know* all this, can our logic find a reply? No! Certainly it cannot. It is just one volition against another – we willing to go in for life upon a trust or assumption which he, for his part, does not care to make. (James [1897] 1979, 19)

Philosophical styles are thus also taken up by our willing nature on authority of our passions, according to James. This is definitely not a position Rickert was willing to entertain, at least not with respect to the validity of transcendental philosophy nor, particularly, with its notion of theoretical truth.

Note that Latour sides with James in this dispute; he sees no useful philosophical role for the transcendental notion of truth and attacks scientistic naturalism for its naïve notions of truth and certainty. In the context of climate change this leads to the idea that Science can act as a political arbiter, with the established Truth having simply to be 'policed':

> If you carry out your ecological conflicts as though they are taking place under the aegis of an impartial arbiter, is it not self-evident that they will be reduced to simple policing operations, without bringing into play the friend/enemy distinction in any form? We will be dealing only with rational beings seeking to bring irrational

> people *back* to reason or to *indisputable knowledge* of deanimated objects. Here we have the source of the depoliticization of ecological questions: the [scientistic] naturalists have no enemy, since, in the proper sense, *the case has been made and won*, in legal as well as scientific terms. (Latour [2015] 2017, 237)

If we assume a transcendental notion of (theoretical) truth, however, I maintain that this allows for philosophical discussion – for instance, on making distinctions between value domains – to be meaningful, as I pointed out using Rickert in Chapter 4, without the risk of falling into the scientistic naturalistic trap identified by Latour.

It is also relevant here to reflect further on the authority of the value of theoretical truth within Rickert's six domains of ultimate value (see Chapter 4). Rickert's 'system of values' contains values that can only partially be accessed through their deposits in value judgements and cultural goods (e.g. scientific and religious practices). He distinguished the following six domains of (ultimate) values (see also Table 4.1):

1. Logic (*Logik*) – value: (theoretical) truth (*Wahrheit*).
2. Aesthetics (*Aesthetik*) – value: beauty (*Schönheit*).
3. Mystics (*Mystik*) – value: impersonal sanctity (*unpersönliche Heiligkeit*).
4. Ethics (*Ethik*) – value: morality (*Sittlichtkeit*).
5. Erotics/love (*Erotik/Liebe*) – value: happiness (*Glück*).
6. Philosophy of religion (*Religionsphilosophie*) – value: personal sanctity (*persönliche Heiligkeit*).

The goods that are associated with the first and last domains, logic and philosophy of religion, for instance, are respectively 'science' (*Wissenschaft* – in the widest possible sense, including natural and social science and the humanities, and focused in particular on their theoretical claims) and 'the world of God' (*die Götterwelt*). However, it should be noted that the actual practices of science and religion, on the one hand, are not purified modes of reference or religion (Latour's terms), nor, on the other, do they primarily aim for theoretical (read: philosophical) truth. This is where Latour downplays and transcendental naturalism highlights that besides analysing the different modes and their crossings, there always remains the possibility of reflecting philosophically on theoretical truth.[2]

Rickert's own philosophy of value can be read in Latourian terms as a crossing of the domain of logic with the other five domains.

Now Rickert is very much aware of the limitations of philosophy, which is why he begins his *Grundprobleme der Philosophie* with a section on 'Worldviews and philosophy as science' (*Weltanschauung und Philosophie als Wissenschaft*). He explains the meaning of the term 'worldview' (*Weltanschauung*) as he wishes to use it as being that of 'conception of life' (*Lebensauffassung*), in which a human being's attitude towards life is expressed (Rickert 1934a, 2). He also explains that the extent to which a worldview can be assessed philosophically is only limited:

> although scientific philosophy is not in a position to impart to the human being a substantively determined worldview with which he is able to lead his full life as a whole human being, it certainly need not proceed without offering him *theoretical clarity* in worldview questions of an extra-theoretical nature and thereby gaining influence on his practical life. (Rickert 1934a, 10)

So, at a theoretical level, worldviews can be studied and probed, without there being the possibility of grounding them theoretically.

One of the crucial theoretical distinctions in Rickert's philosophy (not fundamentally differing from the philosophies of Kant or fellow neo-Kantians, but more developed) is that of the difference between the 'noetics of validity' (*Geltungsnoetik*) and the 'noematics of validity' (*Geltungsnoematik*),[3] which are two distinct ways to analyse acts of value judgement, Rickert's two 'paths of epistemology' (*Wege der Erkenntnistheorie*).[4] As Christian Krijnen explains these:

> The noetics of validity investigates the act from the outset in terms of its performance for the objectivity; in so doing, it interprets the act as being (psychically) real and with regard to something that is not contained in its own mere reality. (Krijnen 2001, 314; leaving out emphases from the original)

What is assumed in the noetics of validity is the noematics of validity:

> In fact, the specific role of the noematics of validity lies for Rickert in the separation of the cognitive act from the content, from the theoretical meaning pattern: the noematics of validity completely ignores the relation of the object to the reality of cognition. (Krijnen 2001, 316; leaving out references to Rickert)

This distinction makes it possible to distinguish between the subjective and the objective validity of values:

> The subjective value applies either only for this or that subject and is then called an *individual-subjective* value, or the value applies for a numerical totality of subjects and is then called *general-subjective*; in both cases their validity is based on real, factual evaluations. With generally subjective values, Rickert means those values that indicate the quintessence of what man himself aspires to because of his *natural life concerns* (Kant: 'bliss'). However, general-subjective values *in themselves* only guarantee, as Rickert puts it, 'subjectivity'; they do not have, speaking with Kant, 'categorical', unconditional validity, but only a 'hypothetical', conditional validity. For him who does not acknowledge subjective value it does not hold: necessary validity for all subjects cannot be established by subjective generality. However, values that are independent of the act of recognising by real subjects are called *objective values*: they are independent of their actual recognition. (Krijnen 2001, 500–1; leaving out references to Rickert)

Rickert holds on to the noematics of validity as an important task for philosophy. While Rickert may have disagreed with James on how philosophy should be done, what results are most worthwhile to achieve and what is considered 'rational' or 'faith', what is shared by both thinkers is the recognition that philosophy goes beyond natural science and psychology. However, James in the end does not believe that one can come very far by rational reflection on noematics, so he shirks away from engaging the topic and makes it a matter of 'faith'. Still, Rickert in the end, after he has theorised quite a bit about objective values and the necessity of assuming their non-real existence when making any value judgement, must acknowledge that objective values lie beyond what we can know. Rickert's theory of the six domains of ultimate values must thus, by the nature of his transcendental empiricism, remain tentative.

Contemporary reflections on authorities and science-and-religion

How authorities are distributed in practices of science and religion is dependent on many factors. The judgements of participants in these practices are pivotal. There is a fundamental plurality in these judgements and hence a fundamental openness in how practices are conceptually extended. Given the continuing link of concepts to lived experience, however, this does not mean that 'anything goes'. So what is the 'yardstick' that participants use to judge whether a particular articulated judgement 'fits' in their practice or not? The authority of values has philosophical meaning in the transcendental way: for participants' actions in a practice to make sense, the authoritative validity of pertinent values functions as a pre-condition. Given the open-endedness of practices, uncertainty arises in various cultural practices when value-laden judgements are made in context. In addition, as has been seen in Part I, the philosophy of value cannot provide certainty about the values that underpin various practices.

Still, the facts that values can only be realised in fallible ways in practice, and that certainty cannot be obtained about these values, do not negate the separate ontological status of values from sense experience, nor the fact that they hold authority. On top of this complexity in reading values into separate practices – be they of science, religion or other domains – Latour especially highlights the uncertainties associated with crossings of practices from different domains (e.g. 'facts' from science versus 'values' from religion or politics):

> Instead of a *difference* in principle between the world of facts and the world of values, a gulf that must never be crossed if one is to remain rational, we see that we have to become accustomed to a *continuous linkage* of actions that *begin* with facts that *are extended* into a warning and that *point* toward decisions – a process that goes in both directions. (Latour [2015] 2017, 49)

Furthermore, in addressing such crossings a transcendental naturalistic approach maintains assumptions of validity for the different values involved. In this section I analyse how two contemporary authors, Alister McGrath and Joseph Rouse, philosophically assess the ontological status of values, especially that of theoretical truth.

Alister McGrath, in his *The Territories of Human Reason* (2019), sets out systematically to examine where the authorities, or rationalities, of science and religion derive from. He observes that the way we conceive of their respective authorities very strongly determines whether science and religion are to be seen as being in fundamental conflict (McGrath 2019, 8). Contrary to what various forms of scientism may hold, that is, that only scientific people are rational, McGrath poses that 'it is clear that most religious people act according to what they regard as rational principles, which they consider to be justified and reasonable' (McGrath 2019, 15). But how clear is it really that authority, in both scientific and religious practices, derives from fundamentally the same type of conceptual articulation process that gives rise to different, rationally structured practices in response to accumulated experience? This section aims to shed more light on this question. It starts with McGrath's depiction of the rationality of scientific and religious (particularly Christian) practices and continues by engaging in some depth with Joseph Rouse's philosophy of scientific practice (which it extends it to philosophy of religious practice).

For communities, an important way of performing the required boundary work to define authority and rationality within their respective 'territories' has been the use of hierarchy (cf. McGrath 2019, 33). Like the role of clerical hierarchy in the Catholic church, in the seventeenth century precursors of the present notion of 'expert judgement' assumed shape within the communities of people that would later evolve into 'science'. Social hierarchy started to be used to enforce which persons' 'sound reason' or 'right thinking' set the norm for the study of nature. These 'experts' (again, a relatively recent notion, so an anachronism for the seventeenth century) could act as 'judges' to resolve debates. The limits of modern rationality have become clear over the past few centuries, with reflection on uncertainty coming to play a central role in philosophy (see also Part I). This leads to difficult questions of 'how to live without certainty, and yet without being paralyzed by hesitation' (Bertrand Russell, quoted in McGrath 2019, 36). The next section of this chapter aims to address this question for the appropriate role of expert judgement in science advice, especially on deeply uncertain, value-laden public policy problems such as climate change.

Both for science and religion, this social aspect of authority and rationality raises the question of power. First of all, there is a potential circularity involved in rational justification: pre-existing values and beliefs provide the context within which authority functions (McGrath 2019, 79). Furthermore:

> societal norms of rationality both perpetrate and perpetuate forms of epistemic injustice, in that these often distribute such rational credibility unjustly, assigning it to preferred social groups, such as the privileged or powerful. (McGrath 2019, 78)

This extends to the modern Western nation-state, in which 'a variety of epistemic communities [are] jostling for social, political, and intellectual acceptance, and occasionally hegemony' (McGrath 2019, 78). Such a link between authority and power was also implicit in James's portrayal of the influences leading to the establishment of 'authority' as 'all such factors of belief as fear and hope, prejudice and passion, imitation and partisanship, the circumpressure of our caste and set' (James [1897] 1979, 18).

In interacting with wider publics, for instance by making themselves relevant for public policy decisions, both public science and public theology must refrain from basing themselves on hidden or private sources of authority if their inputs are to be perceived as legitimate. The issue then, of course, becomes whether (and if yes to what extent) practitioners who have become acculturated in different 'epistemic communities' are able and willing to justify themselves to wider publics (McGrath 2019, 55). Using Thomas F. Torrance as a guide, McGrath identifies an important similarity in the rationalities of the process of enquiry in different disciplines (such as science and theology, the latter here also taken as a 'science' in the sense of *Wissenschaft* – and flagging a move from considering the practices of religion to the related practices of theology):

> The object which is to be investigated must be allowed a voice in this process of enquiry. The distinctive characteristic of a 'science' is to give an accurate and objective account of things in a manner that is appropriate to the reality being investigated. Both theology and the natural sciences are thus to be seen as a posteriori activities which respond to 'the given' rather than as a priori speculation based on philosophical first principles. (McGrath 2019, 68)

From a transcendental naturalistic point of view, I would like to add that values can, and should, be reflected on in philosophy of science and philosophy of theology; they are not empirically given to us and to an extent we will always remain uncertain about them. When the different disciplines of science and theology engage in genuine conversation about realities to which they provide different lenses, this can be seen as a rational enquiry in itself that can involve creating an imaginative 'space of reasons' (see below) in which multiple approaches are confirmed. Given the additional complexity of having to cope with multiple disciplines that deal with deep uncertainty, there is no way the approach of such a hybrid practice can be expected to be readily codified or normalised (cf. McGrath 2019, 73).

One location in the practices of science and religion (or in this context again, more precisely, theology) where the process of enquiry crucially gets 'steered' is in the criteria applied in theory or model choice. In Chapters 4 and 5 I addressed the fact that the cognitive values of science are plural and that, more generally, the overarching values of scientific and religious practices are different. In McGrath's words:

> scientific theorizing is primarily concerned with achieving an enhanced understanding of the natural world [cf. Latour's mode of reference]; theological theorizing, while also aiming for a deeper understanding of God and the world, is seen to lead seamlessly into the praxis of adoration and prayer [cf. Latour's mode of religion]. (McGrath 2019, 112)

Does the plurality in values both across and within these practices mean that anything goes? It does not! I would argue that since the practices of both science and theology deploy concepts and explore the 'space of reasons' (see below), the presence of a plurality of values guiding theory and model choice does not invalidate the possibility of discussing meaningfully, at a more generic level, the criteria used in making and justifying theory and model choices across both scientific and theological practices. It should be possible to overcome the dichotomy between some overarching rationality and complete disunity observed by McGrath (2019, 100):

> Are there verifiable criteria, based on empirical research, that should be deployed in this manner? Or are these norms essentially pragmatic matters of judgement, determined by the values and working assumptions of a community of practitioners?

Maybe it is a combination of both, as I shall explore below using Rouse.

Like Rickert, McGrath aims for a philosophical probing of worldviews when he claims that

> Christianity may be seen as a worldview or metaphysical system which attempts to make sense of human experience as a whole, and uses criteria similar to those used to judge other forms of explanation. (McGrath 2019, 105)

However, McGrath, again like Rickert, remains acutely aware of the boundary between philosophy and theology when he writes:

> Theology articulates a vision of God which cannot be adequately accommodated by the human intellect, and thus generates a sense

> of intellectual wonder most appropriately expressed in worship. (McGrath 2019, 112)

Where does McGrath stand philosophically with respect to naturalism? When I discussed various versions of naturalism in the previous chapter, the issue was how religious naturalism could incite us poetically, through a limited kind of wonder, to ecological action. The problem that we are dealing with in the present chapter concerns the authority and rationality of naturalism in using scientific models to advise on any action in the context of a plurality of worldviews. I will return to this problem in the next section.

McGrath's discussion of rationality poses the question of:

> how a purely [scientistic] naturalist or materialist interpretation of our world can account for the appearance, through the operation of the laws of physics and chemistry, of conscious beings such as ourselves, who prove to be capable of discovering those laws and understanding the universe that they govern. (McGrath 2019, 147)

Below I describe how Rouse aims to get as far as he can with a naturalistic answer to this question. Philosophically, in Part I of this study, I explored a transcendental naturalistic philosophy, by engaging with James's radical empiricism, Rickert's transcendental empiricism and Latour's occasionalist empiricism. McGrath develops another philosophical approach, which he expounds using William Whewell's concept of the process of 'colligation' – being 'the mental operation of bringing together a number of empirical facts by "superinducing" upon them a way of thinking which unites the facts' (McGrath 2019, 126). McGrath generalises the process of colligation from the setting in which Whewell used it:

> Where Whewell tended to think of colligation as the connection of *observations*, however, I shall use the term to refer to the epistemic process of constructing a 'big picture' that is capable of accommodating and interconnecting multiple *notions or insights*, drawn from across intellectual disciplines, distinguished by their operative rationalities. (McGrath 2019, 211)

What characterises McGrath's approach to science and religion is his conviction that 'some kind of explanatory capacity is an integral – though not necessarily a fundamental or central – theme of the Christian faith' (McGrath 2019, 129).

An important characteristic of different philosophical approaches is how they speak about 'truth'. McGrath uses Karl Popper's declaration that 'truth is above human authority' to make the point that 'neither reason nor observation are "authorities"; they are tools to help us in the task of interpreting and understanding our world' (McGrath 2019, 156). Without the idea of truth 'there can be no objective standards of inquiry; no criticism of our conjectures; no groping for the unknown; no quest for knowledge' (Popper quoted in McGrath 2019, 156). Harking back to the notion of 'abduction'[5] of the pragmatist Charles Sanders Peirce, McGrath further emphasises that 'an abductive reasoning strategy is called for precisely because the idea of God derives from "immediate experience", and hence cannot adequately be accommodated within alternative models of reasoning' (McGrath 2019, 179). So the value of theoretical truth as more than a subjective value – that is, as an objective value – is a driver of the quests to reach deeper explanations in both science and religion, without limiting the enquiry beforehand to the authority of one privileged practice (i.e. science). Let me now turn to Rouse to assess his argument from a naturalistic perspective against objective values.

In his book *Articulating the World: Conceptual understanding and the scientific image* (2015), Joseph Rouse aims at developing a naturalistic philosophy that helps to understand scientific understanding and that satisfies the following four requirements (Rouse 2015, 345): (1) it is answerable to up-to-date science (which means that it can never be finished, since science keeps developing); (2) it focuses on actual scientific practices (instead of just philosophical assumptions of what those practices should be); (3) it 'explicate[s] scientific understanding in ways that would not undercut its authority as conceptually contentful, empirically accountable, and truthful'; (4) it does not appeal to the supernatural. Most existing naturalistic philosophies fail Rouse's requirements (1) to (3) and, partly as a result of that, do not result in as open a naturalism. Rouse's project is to formulate a naturalistic understanding of scientific practices that fulfils all four requirements, in the context of a more general naturalistic understanding of conceptual articulation across all types of practices within human culture (including religion).

Rouse mentions the American philosopher Wilfrid Sellars (1912–1989) as one of his main sources of philosophical inspiration. Sellars

> is known for his attack on the 'myth of the given' and his development of a coherentist epistemology and functional role/inferentialist semantics, for his distinction between the 'manifest image' and the

> 'scientific image' of the world, for his proposal that psychological concepts are like theoretical concepts and for a tough-minded scientific realism. (deVries [2011] 2016, 1)

He also endorses a pragmatist notion of truth (deVries [2011] 2016, 10). Sellars's famous statement on the aim of philosophy is the following: 'to understand how things in the broadest possible sense of the term hang together in the broadest possible sense of the term' (Sellars quoted in Rouse 2015, 8, 30). Here he identifies the importance of meaning and values in making judgements, specifically focusing on the theoretical domain:

> The essential point is that in characterizing an episode or a state as that of *knowing*, we are not giving an empirical description of that episode or state; we are placing it in the logical space of reasons, of justifying and being able to justify what one says. (Sellars quoted in deVries [2011] 2016, 20)

This 'space of reasons' obviously has a normative dimension:

> In order to operate within 'the logical space of reasons', one must be at home with normative discourse, responsive to reasons as such, sensitive to standards. (deVries [2011] 2016, 20)

Rouse distinguishes two dimensions of normativity, one shared by all organisms (whose life processes articulate the world holistically in response to their environment) and the other shared only by humans and those organisms closest to them (this second dimension being a reflective dimension). Among humans, the second dimension has taken the form of 'discursive niche construction', which can be analysed in naturalistic and evolutionary terms, includes an embodiment of Sellars's logical space of reasons and leads to culture:

> Discursive niche contruction … articulates the world along diverse lines, distinguishing conceptual contents, institutions, occupations, rituals, art, games, equipment and social, legal, moral, sacred, or other statuses, all of which remain almost completely opaque within other organisms' ways of life. (Rouse 2015, 350)

With Sellars, Rouse 'situates conceptual normativity within the manifest image of ourselves as reflective rational agents' (Rouse 2015, 10).

He espouses a 'minimalist naturalism' (that is, a naturalism that adheres to the four requirements mentioned above and that in its application to other practices does not resort to any form of scientism). This means that 'our self-conception as rational agents who answer to norms must be consistent with our self-conception as scientifically explicable natural beings'; there is 'nothing mysterious, ineffable, or metaphysically transcendent about conceptual normativity' (Rouse 2015, 10). The latter thus leaves open the possibility of values that are very different from scientific values and that guide other cultural domains, such as religion. However, this analysis of the genesis and functioning of those values needs to remain consistent with the naturalistic approach (no appeal to the supernatural, for instance).

Rouse's whole approach to culture finds resonance in Latour's modes of existence work, although Rouse does not explicitly espouse an occasionalist metaphysics; he more explicitly stresses the evolutionary aspect of the modes of existence, including the emergence of the guiding values themselves.[6] While 'any discursive practice, including scientific practices, can only articulate the world from within' (Rouse 2015, 375), '[j]ust what one is doing in undertaking any ... activities [in different types of practices] depends upon the larger pattern of performances and circumstances to which each [of the activities] belongs' (Rouse 2015, 351).

It is all, according to Latour, about jumping over different gaps, in the context of an evolutionary frame (cf. Chapter 4):

> What is *at issue* for an organism is whatever threatens to end its continuation as an identifiable, goal-directed pattern, and what is *at stake* in its response to those issues is whether it succeeds in maintaining its continuity over time. (Rouse 2015, 353)

The capacity for language use emerged in the evolution of humans, and our ontogenetic reconstructions in each generation

> rely on the same close coupling with our discursively articulated environment that characterizes other organisms' capacities for perceptual and practical responsiveness to their selective environments. (Rouse 2015, 20)

Language is an instrument for humans intentionally to direct themselves, where 'intentional directedness must introduce a possible gap between what is meant and what is actually encountered, such that there is *possibility* of error, even when no errors actually occur' (Rouse 2015, 65). Uncertainty and openness are deeply built into Rouse's naturalistic philosophy:

> The partial openness of who we are to become, and thus of how different possible trajectories of social practice matter, accounts for the element of freedom in social life long recognized as essential to conceptual normativity. (Rouse 2015, 83)

Here is how Rouse captures the dynamics within and between different practices:

> The performances that constitute conceptually articulated practices are both socially differentiated and dynamically responsive to that differentiation through ongoing efforts to sustain the coherence of a common discursive practice. Conceptual understanding is then not the grasp of a static holistic structure but an active capacity to track, adjudicate and respond appropriately to the more or less divergent performances within social practices (of which expressive speech is a paradigmatic example). This tracking and adjudication takes place in two registers simultaneously: for a performance's appropriateness and significance within a practice as a partially autonomous context and for the broader practical and perceptual significance of both the performance and the *only* partially autonomous practices to which it belongs. The results of such adjudication in both registers are also continually reintegrated into ongoing practice in ways that reverberate through the practice as a whole. Conceptually articulated practices sustain a shifting, uneasy equilibrium between these competing pulls toward unity and divergence. (Rouse 2015, 83)

In Latour's terms, what Rouse describes in this passage are the veridiction within modes of existence and the diplomacy across different modes of existence.

What makes Rouse's version of naturalistic philosophy stand out among others is his practice orientation. His approach amounts to an original 'fusion of the manifest and scientific images' (Rouse 2015, 16). The image of science that emerges from scientific practices is itself oriented within the 'manifest image of ourselves as persons responsive and accountable to norms' (Rouse 2015, 16). His philosophy assigns a central role to the deep uncertainty that is associated with the open-endedness of all practices, including scientific ones. This is how all cultural practices emerge and evolve (and how they are also all potentially at risk of extinction). The sciences still have a special role to play within larger culture:

> [T]he sciences initially open new, law-governed conceptual domains, which can nevertheless be already authoritative over scientific and other discursive practices, by developing 'fictional' experimental or other practical contexts that come to exemplify conceptual norms. ... Scientific significance expresses a future-directed accountability to what is at issue and at stake in scientific practices and in the larger patterns of cultural niche construction to which they belong. Scientific significance accrues to both the 'homonomic' conceptual development internal to a law-governed scientific domain and its 'heteronomic' conceptual relations to other practices and concerns that indicate what is at stake in understanding that domain. (Rouse 2015, 34)

These homonomic and heteronomic conceptual relations are all situated within the 'common discursive practice' that Rouse places front and centre of his naturalistic philosophy.

Given the focus of this chapter on authority and rationality, I conclude my discussion of Rouse with an assessment from a transcendental naturalistic perspective. Rouse holds even more strongly than James that rational reflection on noematics (with its focus on objective norms) will not get us very far. All we can rationally reason about is noetics (with its focus on subjective norms). For Rouse, 'epistemic assessment remains important but subordinate to conceptual normativity' (Rouse 2015, 82). He realises that in this he goes against the mainstream in philosophy:

> Most philosophical conceptions of normativity ... presume that determinate norms must already govern the performance accountable to them and thereby already determine what is at stake in the practices they 'govern'. Such conceptions can allow for the practitioners' epistemic uncertainty about these norms, but not any metaphysical indeterminacy in the norms themselves. ... On a normative conception of practices, however, what is at issue and at stake in practices is not just subject to epistemic uncertainty but is also open textured and partially indeterminate in a perspectivally determined way. (Rouse 2015, 165)

However, I maintain that Rickert's discussion of subjective and objective norms is more subtle than what Rouse here portrays as being what 'most philosophical conceptions' of normativity hold. Rickert highlights the philosophical need for separate ontological warrant for transcendental norms, both subjective and objective, whose non-real existence we assume in every value judgement. For instance, Rouse's account, like the naturalistic philosophies of James or Latour, misses the notion of objective theoretical truth that Rickert argues for in his transcendental empiricism and is taken seriously in transcendental naturalism.

Modern rationality and science advice

In the final section of this chapter I delve more deeply into an important case that illustrates very well the issue of different authorities guiding practices that cross each other.[7] The case that I am referring to considers the crossing between the practices of natural science (mode of reference) and climate policy (mode of politics). Using the results of this chapter, I analyse the way in which the IPCC deals with scientific and political values and authorities.[8] I explore the consequence of the fact that scientists acting in their practices are not absolute subjects who are free to evaluate and choose their hypotheses according to an innate, infallible, modern rationality, which then provides for authority. When scientists become 'experts' and provide 'expert judgements' on policy issues with large uncertainty, such as climate change, it is important that we use appropriate ways to assess what their expertise consists in. For this we have to take into account analyses such as that offered by Rouse on how the scientific image emerges from scientific practices and is itself oriented within the 'manifest image of ourselves as persons responsive and accountable to norms', where the norms derive from various cultural practices, including scientific, religious and political practices, that impinge on each other – but which have to be held together in our 'common discursive practice'.

While I have criticised the naturalistic philosophy of both Latour and Rouse for the lack of an explicitly transcendental notion of value, Latour's analysis of the problematique of the relationship between science and politics (each driven by their underlying values) in the case of climate change is spot on – not least because of its emphasis on the different types of uncertainty that characterise these domains. He criticises modern notions of 'political ecology':

> What makes the ecological mutation incomprehensible to those who have been modernized is that there is no possible turning back, since the Moderns believe that they are in a post-apocalyptic epoch. ... In the most profound sense of the term, history for them is always over. (Latour [2015] 2017, 212)

The task that is in front of science advisers briefing governments and intergovernmental organisations on climate change, and that if performed well can add to the 'soft power' of the nation-states and intergovernmental organisations that they are linked to, is to reflect on 'the very visibility of their network' (highlighting the attendant strengths and weaknesses, the uncertainties), which can 'make scientists more credible' (Latour [2015] 2017, 215). Assimilating science into the general culture is hard and many scientists have become 'as morally naïve as they are politically impotent' (Latour [2015] 2017, 215). However, according to Latour, they now have to step up and not be overawed by the co-existence of two conceptions of science – science-in-the-making and ready-made science. Especially in dealing with climate sceptics, there is a risk of joining them in keeping up the old idea of Science. Meanwhile it would be better if climate scientists:

> keep foregrounding the scientific institutions on which they depend, and ... consider themselves as a people endowed with specific interests trapped in a conflict with another people over the production of a series of pertinent data. (Latour [2015] 2017, 215)

Science's appeal to 'nature' had a large power of depoliticisation, carrying out 'a plan that does not depend on the vagaries of the time that is passing' (Latour [2015] 2017, 225) – no risk from politics. This era should now be over.

In the example here I focus on the issue of expertise and expert judgement on the causes of climate change ('attribution'). I invoke the argument from post-normal science that if one wants to assess expertise, one has to engage with an 'extended' peer community (e.g. Petersen et al. 2011). Reflection on assumptions should lead experts to give an account of the epistemic underpinnings of their expertise. I argue that IPCC reports do not do this enough (cf. Meyer and Petersen 2010). In pushing scientists to give such accounts, one must realise that experts often do not like to receive this advice. In getting scientists to do what is required, their expertise should better be considered to be 'on tap', instead of allowing experts to be 'on top' in terms of being free to decide how transparent they will be.

In the first lecture of *Facing Gaia*, Latour emphasises the 'certainties' of climate science:

> it is now clear that the network of instruments, the Vast Machine that the climatologists have built, ends up producing knowledge that is robust enough to withstand the *objections*. In any case, on this Earth, the adjective *objective* has no other meaning. There is no other source that can surpass the type of certainties that you have been capable of accumulating. (Latour [2015] 2017, 33)

Obviously, there is a risk to such emphasis: experts should not feel emboldened themselves to disbelieve different perspectives. The 'tissue of proofs' that Latour refers to, after all, is not so easily distinguishable from a 'tissue of lies' (Latour [2015] 2017, 31). He is aware of this, but, as noted above, at some points he de-emphasises scientific uncertainty and the role of expert judgement. He refers to '*the* climatologists', for instance, in the quote above. Latour makes the important point that having disputes out in the open makes the institution of science visible; he also acknowledges that although there is a high degree of certainty on 'attribution', there is also so much of importance to know about climate change that is still deeply uncertain. A stronger dose of Latourian analysis should be added here. Actually, Latour himself adds that dose in his second lecture, for instance when he warns against using a

> tactic … that bypasses the hard work of politics by attributing to science an incontrovertible certainty that it is far from having. (Latour [2015] 2017, 46)

In this section, I will analyse the uncertainties in a part of climate science that has become much more strongly underpinned over the past decades – that of 'attributing' observed mean surface temperature increases to human causes, highlighting the risk of being insufficiently reflexive of different perspectives.

In the 2001 report of the IPCC, a figure was included that has become iconic at the science–policy interface for attributing climate change to human influences (reproduced here as Figure 7.1). The figure contains three panels. Each shows, on the one hand, the same line with measurements of the global mean surface temperature since 1850 (going up in the beginning of the twentieth century and going up at the end of

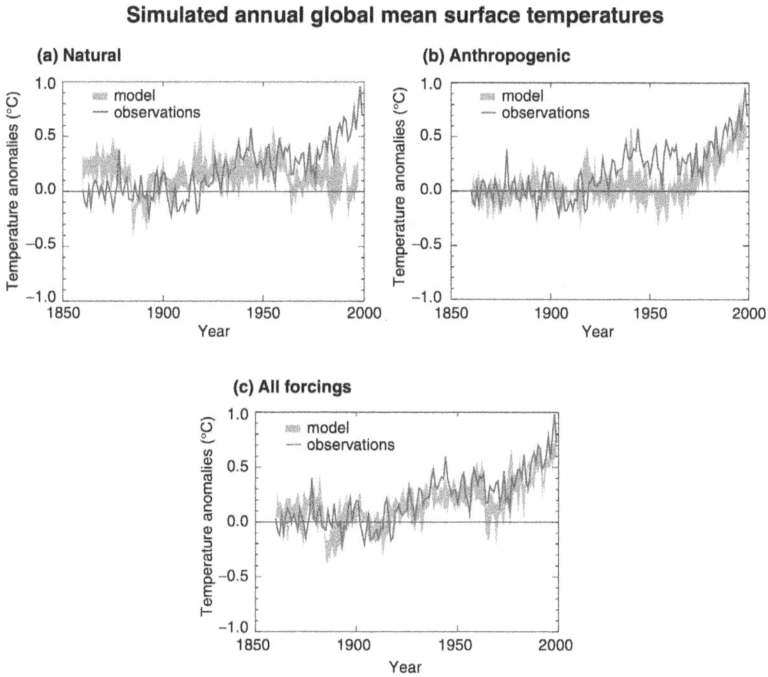

Figure 7.1 Climate-change attribution figure in the 'Summary for Policymakers' of the Third Assessment Report of the IPCC, in which model simulations (bands) are compared with measured changes (line).

Source: IPCC (2001, 14, Figure 4).

the twentieth century). On the other hand, each presents a different band of model results (the bands representing the 'internal' variability of the climate system, that is, the sensitivity to initial conditions). One band portrays only natural external influences on the climate (e.g. volcanoes, sun), another portrays only human ('anthropogenic') external influences on the climate (e.g. greenhouse gases, particles), and a third combines natural and human factors. The latter panel depicts a beautiful match of measurement and model, giving rise to the suggestion that we know everything; there is no room left for any doubt that humans are causing the recent climate change. In fact, the Chair of the IPCC suggested exactly this at a press conference in 2001 (see Petersen [2006] 2012, 145).

Of course, philosophers of science understand that the number of degrees of freedom in climate models is high. Nor will they be surprised to hear that, indeed, virtually all climate-modelling groups in the world are able to present the same final panel with a match. This is not to say that the results are wrong. But how should one communicate that the bands are 'just' model results, whose match with the measurements cannot establish their reliability? The pertinent questions are: how do we know how reliable the models are? In which senses can we say that they are reliable?

The IPCC has developed a methodology, through three subsequent sets of guidance, for assessing and communicating the uncertainties in the findings of its assessments. This methodology includes calibrated terms for communicating probabilities. For the example of climate-change attribution to human influences, the IPCC did not communicate in 2001 that it was 100 per cent certain that humans are causing climate change, even though the picture is beautiful and the line and band match. It said, rather, that it was 'likely' that most of the warming of the last 50 years has been caused by human greenhouse gases. 'Likely' here means a 2/3 (66 per cent) chance, according to the experts, that the finding is true.

I was sitting at the table at the time (in Shanghai, on 20 January 2001) as an IPCC contact group negotiated what I think became one of the most important statements ever from the IPCC: that most of the warming is likely due to human influences (for a transcript of what transpired at that contact group meeting, see Petersen [2006] 2012: 191–7). But I could not understand why they said 'likely'. If you believed the models, the likelihood was already estimated to be way higher than 90 per cent (that is, 'very likely', the next likelihood category). I had to dig deep (through interviews, reviewing internal e-mails, etc.) to determine how the lead authors had reached their judgement. The reason they did not choose 'very likely' was that they did not trust the models enough. So they picked the next lower likelihood category. Nowhere could this reasoning be found in the IPCC report; there was no traceable account of how they had arrived at this crucial judgement.

Six years later, the IPCC panel assessed the same question. The 2007 report features a similar figure as the 2001 report, but now the graphs are shown for every continent and the authors are willing to say 'very likely' (90 per cent). Again I could ask the question: Why not the next likelihood category of 99 per cent or 'virtually certain'?[9] The narrative could have been, 'Even though we still do not fully trust the models, there have been more warm years, there have been more model runs, there have been different types of model experiments, and there is a belief that the models have become more reliable'. I do think that the latter belief is problematic. Again the IPCC featured, in my view, a weak practice of assessing the reliability and the quality of models.

So what I argue has been missing from the Third and Fourth Assessment Reports of the IPCC (2001 and 2007, respectively) – and, I contend, also from subsequent assessment rounds – is sufficient attention being paid to 'methodological reliability' rather than simply 'statistical reliability' (Petersen [2006] 2012; Smith and Petersen 2014). Assessment of methodological reliability requires a qualitative discussion and a corresponding qualitative assessment of the underpinning of results. Additionally, after 'Climategate', the realisation has come that 'public reliability' needs attention too; how to gain back trust and be publicly relied upon is a difficult question for climate scientists. I do not have simple answers here. In this section I am really focused on the importance of the second type of reliability, methodological reliability, as an example of how important transparent assessment of qualitative dimensions in deeply uncertain practices in science is for science advice.

Let me give one example from the negotiations on representing methodological reliability in the Summary for Policymakers in Paris (2007). This is the sentence that was under negotiation:

> Most of the observed increase in globally averaged temperatures since the mid-twentieth century is very likely due to the observed increase in anthropogenic greenhouse gas concentrations.

We have to get a bit into the politics now. Because these IPCC sentences are transferred from the sphere of knowledge assessment to the sphere of political negotiations (in the climate framework convention), there will always be a country that does not want a stronger statement than the last time. A stronger statement would highlight that there is more scientific certainty, which would increase the likelihood of international agreements to curb climate change.

The IPCC meeting in Paris in January 2007 was less than three years from what turned out to be the failure of the Copenhagen Summit at the end of 2009. In this instance, one country used all kinds of ways to prevent this sentence from being included. There is, however, an order of speech within the IPCC, which is: the chapters have been written – hands off, governments cannot touch those chapters! – but government delegates can comment, making use of a set of criteria (such as clarity and representativeness), on sentences in the Summary for Policymakers. Governments obviously will have different views. And the authors have a right of veto on any change made to their summaries. One can imagine how hard it sometimes becomes to negotiate the summary line by line, as is the case in the IPCC. But it works.

Still, I argue that it can be done in a more productive way if both parties, authors and governments, would behave more diplomatically towards each other, understand better where they are both coming from and what their respective rationalities are. One group of actors in these meetings is there on authority of their social, ethical, political and economic values (their role is to represent their publics) and another group of actors is there on authority of their scientific values (their role is to represent, to the best of their ability, the papers they have assessed), for which they must provide good 'reference' (Kouw and Petersen 2018). Now there is much disbelief from the side of the government delegates: they do not believe that the authors' results have been produced according to the norms of science (while allowing for the presence of uncertainty in the mode of reference). There is also much disbelief from the side of the authors: they do not believe that the delegates' interventions have been made according to the norms of political representation (while allowing for the presence of uncertainty in the mode of politics).

Back now to the sentence that was under discussion in the final hours of the Paris meeting. After days of negotiations and having entered very deep into the night, finally we were in agreement – all the countries of the world could agree on this sentence by inserting the following footnote: 'Consideration of remaining uncertainty is based on current methodologies'. Of course, we were all tired. But it is interesting: why would the opposing country agree with this sentence? What is the spin they could give? They might say: 'The methodologies used are based on models. It is just models. It is not reality'. Indeed models are used, but that does not imply that there is no reference to reality; still, that is typical of the argument they would make. How would another country that tends to dramatise climate change and typically wants to downplay uncertainty spin this sentence? They might say: 'Next time the likelihood will go up further, from the original "likely" (66 per cent) it went up to "very likely" (90 per cent), and it will go up again'. And yes indeed, in Stockholm, nearly seven years later in September 2013, it became 'extremely likely' (95 per cent).

One issue with the IPCC methodology of likelihood statements has already been addressed: the methodological unreliability of models has been used to 'downgrade' likelihood statements without saying so. Another issue, related to insufficient transparency of expert judgement in the IPCC, is that there is hardly any reflection on the nature of expert judgement. 'Very likely' means more than 90 per cent chance that a particular statement is true. But what does it really mean? What do these probabilities mean? How reflexive is the IPCC about what is actually happening and what lies behind these statements? The '90 per cent' only means that the few authors who have been selected to do the assessment in a particular chapter have somehow reached this collective expert judgement. Nothing more and nothing less. It carries a lot of weight because these authors have had the scientific training, acquired the relevant skills and have a lot of experience in their scientific practices – they bring all these things to the table. These lead authors are the experts, selected by the IPCC for their expertise. Other experts are then asked to review their statements thoroughly. In the end, however, the lead authors, when they write down their conclusions, get rid of any reference to 'expert judgement'. Suddenly their conclusions are made to flow directly from the underlying science. 'It is not us'. I find it incredible!

Twice we have had to intervene as the Dutch government delegation; we asked to make the Summary for Policymakers more explicit about expert judgement. In Paris in 2007, for example, the authors, when defining their uncertainty terminology, referred in the final draft to the 'assessed likelihood of an outcome or a result'. We added 'using expert judgement' to that phrase. And in Stockholm in 2013, the same problem arose with the definition of 'probabilities':

> Probabilistic estimates of quantified measures of uncertainty in a finding are based on statistical analysis of observations or model results, or expert judgment.

We looked at it and saw that it was going in the wrong direction. We thus changed '*or* expert judgment' into '*and* expert judgment'. I think this amend is important. It is worrisome that scientists who act as science advisers are often unable to say reflexively what they are doing.

Questions on how expert judgement can be reflected in the IPCC are intertwined with questions of how science and politics relate in the IPCC. I would like to frame IPCC assessments as social constructs with elements from both science and politics. Thus different types of values are at play: values both intrinsic and extrinsic to science. How successful is the IPCC? Well, critics would say that they are too successful in terms of connecting with policy and unsuccessful in connecting with science. That issue is what I studied for the Third Assessment Report (published in 2001), to address criticism in the US Senate testimony by Dick Lindzen that the IPCC would not be sufficiently open to sceptics.

In addition to too little reflexivity in the IPCC, I found that the criticism of the lack of openness to sceptics was incorrect. For the report that I studied (I took the chapter on attribution of climate change to human influences), I looked at all the comments which were submitted for that chapter in all the review rounds. I looked at all the responses to those comments, and all the review-editor comments to the responses. In doing so I discovered that there were a lot of critical comments, many of which had led to improvements in the text in terms of more inclusion of uncertainties and better language (Petersen [2006] 2012). So I do think that sceptics (taken in a broad sense, that is, including not only the 'typical' climate sceptics, but also people who for good reasons are critical of climate modelling) play a constructive role in the IPCC process. The final outcome of this process is a policy-relevant assessment. It is not, however, *the* scientific consensus with full certainty and thus it should not be framed in this way. Of course, the IPCC can still further improve its communication of uncertainty, be more transparent and explain where the expert judgements come from. And I think the IPCC could be more reflexive about what is actually happening in these plenaries. They are all closed. Why? Include a webcast, for instance. There is no reason not to do that.

I conclude this section with four lessons that I took from my first 13 years of being a science adviser (Petersen 2014b).

Explicit reflection on uncertainty and values

> Take 'normal science' seriously, but also organise reflection on its uncertainties and value-ladenness.

I have bought into the discourse of post-normal science. Here 'post-' should perhaps read 'extra-': 'extra-normal science'. With 'normal science' I really mean those proceedings where it is the scientific community that is doing whatever they are doing: modelling, publishing, peer reviewing, etc. So when I say that we need to open up and look at ways to bring out the different epistemic and non-epistemic values in this discussion, I mean that we need to organise reflection on uncertainty and value-ladenness also within normal science, without throwing it away. So do not throw away the baby (normal science) with the bathwater (a form of scientism that does not sufficiently reflect the presence of uncertainty in science)! Consequently I do not buy into very simplistic readings of post-normal science.

Addressing methodological and public reliability

> Alongside the *statistical reliability* of results (expressed in terms of probability), devote due attention to their *methodological reliability*

> (expressed in terms of strengths and weaknesses) and their *public reliability* (expressed as the degree of public confidence in the scientists who produce them).

As I have already observed in this section: do not focus only on statistics; also focus on qualitative dimensions of reliability.

Extended peer review

> Involve a larger group of specialists and non-specialists who hold different values in monitoring the quality of scientific assessments.

'Extended peer review', which also comes out of this literature of post-normal science, concerns the ways in which one can engage as wide a group of people as possible who can provide comments that are sensible enough so that they can be processed and responded to, for instance, in the IPCC. Everybody – on the basis of a very minimal claim to expertise – can sign up to be an expert reviewer of the IPCC and can submit comments. It is very important that not only is a very small group of climate modellers, for instance, providing comments on the climate-modelling chapter, but so too are experts in neighbouring disciplines and people who work for NGOs such as Greenpeace. They all have a stake, as well as very valuable contributions to bring, because they can highlight particular risks to the climate that may not have yet become mainstream knowledge in the scientific community.

Acknowledging social complexity

> Be wary of accepting the conclusions of actors and practitioners at face value; try to delve deeper through the layers of complexity by means of narrative methods.

The final point – looking at deeper dimensions and different things that are happening at the same time – is related to the notion of 'social complexity'. Scientists often have a self-image (overly rationalised) of what they are doing, and the country delegates have a self-image (again overly rationalised) of what they are doing. These self-images are too simplistic in what they hold; they do not reflect the complexity of the way different types of values (epistemic and non-epistemic) and rationalities are interwoven in cultural practices.

Conclusion

In this chapter I have shown how uncertainty leads to both a plurality of cognitive authorities among and within different types of practices, including that of science, and put this in the context of Latour's *Facing Gaia*. I started with a discussion of the state-of-play on authorities and science-and-religion around the end of the nineteenth century (James and Rickert holding different views on the feasibility of a rational analysis of objective norms). Subsequently I discussed both McGrath's analysis of the plurality of rationalities and Rouse's analysis of the deep basis of rationalities in practices, then compared their approaches with transcendental naturalism. I ended with a recent example of the problematic role of a notion of expert judgement that is based on modern rationality in the crossing of the practices of science and politics within a particular science-advice organisation, the IPCC. This led to the lesson that arriving at expert judgement under uncertainty is a value-laden exercise. In Chapter 8 we address the issue of opening up the future: how can a plurality of worldviews be used to inform climate-policy decisions under uncertainty?

Notes

1 It is of course Latour in particular who has emphasised the heterogeneity of scientific practice.

2 The way Latour ([2012] 2013b) writes about the mode of preposition (see Chapter 4) as aiming to avoid 'category mistakes', ensuring 'ontological pluralism' and instituting the right 'interpretive keys', suggests some affinity with the sort of theoretical reflection aspired to by transcendental naturalism. However, this remains framed within the metaphysics of his occasionalist empiricism and cannot transcend that.

3 'Noesis' refers to intentional acts or 'act-quality' and 'noema' refers to 'act-matter'. A philosopher who made extensive use of these notions is Edmund Husserl (1859–1938).

4 These two paths were developed by Rickert in his 1909 *Kant-Studien* article and included in subsequent editions of *Der Gegenstand der Erkenntnis*. James was not enthusiastic about this article or Rickert's approach more generally, as becomes clear from a letter he wrote to F. C. S. Schiller on 4 August 1909: 'This country is being eaten up by an innumerable host of caterpillers (unknown here before), they swarm and defoliate all our trees. I am reminded of them by an exquisite specimen of professional philosophy by H. Rickert in Kantstudien, XIV, Heft 2, Zwei Wege der Erkenntnistheorie. Ignoring all phenomenal intermediaries between mind knowing & thing known he swarms over the subject with innumerable scholastic distinctions etc. etc. in the most diseased way. I wish you would review him. He has a couple of most insulting pp. about pragmatism wh[ich], if it have no other advantage, has at least that of decaterpillarizing epistemology from such work as Rickert's' (Skrupskelis and Berkeley 2004, 301). My position on the mutual negative assessment of these two philosophers is: grant each philosopher their own style and keep what one analyses to be crucial for developing a consistent and comprehensive philosophical position, which is what I have aimed for in my synthesis proposal for transcendental naturalism.

5 Abduction is a kind of creative 'search strategy' which leads to the identification or creation of some 'promising explanatory conjecture which is then subject to further test' (Peirce quoted by McGrath 2019, 175). McGrath adds that '[a]bduction is, at least in part, about an imaginative questing for the best explanation of otherwise puzzling observations' (McGrath 2019, 179).

6 Rouse only sparingly refers to Latour's work and not at all to Latour's modes of existence work (published as a book in [2012] 2013, but with much earlier origins).
7 A large part of this section was published earlier as Petersen (2021).
8 I have been a Dutch government delegate to the IPCC from 2001–2014. For a critical assessment of the IPCC from a social science perspective, see the edited volume by De Pryck and Hulme (2023). In Petersen (2023) I critically assess the presence of positive feedback loops between the IPCC and scientific disciplines.
9 This was the next category in that fourth assessment round; in the most recent assessment rounds 95 per cent or 'extremely likely' has been included in the methodology.

8
Futures and climate: modern planning and disregard

Introduction

Now that the issue of the plurality of cognitive authorities has been dealt with in Chapter 7, I will address the third problem caused by scientistic naturalism that I identified, with Latour – the disregard of non-modern worldviews in politics. In *Facing Gaia* Latour confronts moderns with hard questions about how they should engage with non-moderns in making policies to tackle climate change. He portrays the decision-making epoch that we have now entered, the 'new climatic regime', as succeeding a period of scientistic naturalism. New actors have to be regarded, including those that were previously (that is, in the supposedly 'modern' period) disregarded. Latour concludes that 'we have entered irreversibly into an epoch that is at once post-natural, post-human, and post-epistemological' (Latour [2015] 2017, 144).

The meanings that Latour attributes to the terms 'nature', 'human' and 'epistemology' here are largely restricted to how they are used in scientistic naturalism. In contrast, the position of transcendental naturalism argued for in the present book, which assigns different meanings to the same terms of 'nature' (cf. Latour's 'world', Latour [2015] 2017, 35), 'human' (cf. Latour's 'Anthropos', Latour [2015] 2017, 117) and 'epistemology' (cf. Latour's 'anthropology of the Moderns', Latour [2015] 2017, 3), is very apt for the new epoch that Latour describes, with the added understanding that philosophically speaking the new epoch turns out to not be fundamentally – that is, ontologically – new after all. It *does* make us realise, with Latour, that we have never really been modern.

What is original in Latour's analysis is his portrayal of the pressing cultural interconnections between science, religion and politics that become visible in the challenge of climate change. The picture that emerges is unsettling:

> the human as a unified agent, as a simple virtual political entity, as a universal concept, ... has to be decomposed into several distinct peoples, endowed with contradictory interests, competing territories, and brought together by the warring agents – not to say warring divinities. (Latour [2015] 2017, 122)

What is particularly different as compared with some versions of scientistic naturalism is indicated by Latour in his use of the figure of Gaia. This signifies that intentionality resides with each of the actors in the world and *not with the whole* (taken as a system that is regulated in a top-down manner): there are 'as many Providences as there are organisms on Earth' (Latour [2015] 2017, 100). He thus positions himself against determinism:

> The simple result of such a distribution of final causes is not the emergence of a supreme Final Cause, but a fine muddle. (Latour [2015] 2017, 100)

Latour elaborates that this demands an altered stance towards the 'future' and the 'apocalypse', that is, towards 'time'. In short: the end of the world is not to be predicted (or assumed realised, as in utopias). Instead it needs to be preached or prayed for, with 'end' first of all meaning achievement in and with time, while at the same time bringing forth this future through a 'new diplomacy'; 'we cannot continue to believe in the old future if we want to have a future at all' (Latour [2015] 2017, 171).[1] Concretely, this means that for politics in the future this diplomacy does not only involve nation-states. According to Latour:

> After four centuries, after imperial expansions, colonization, decolonization, globalization, there is no longer anything realistic in an assembly of one hundred ninety-five nation-states. (Latour [2015] 2017, 259)

This chapter deals with the role of the 'future' or 'futures' in the practices of science, religion and politics, particularly as these play out in the context of climate change. How open or closed are futures conceived in these practices? How is the space of future possibilities conceived, given uncertainty? How do different worldviews and planning styles provide guidance for humans, individually and collectively, to deal with the future – what gets attention and what gets disregarded? For instance, how does modern planning in climate-change policy deal with non-modern worldviews? The overarching question here is: how do futures relate to uncertainty?

In his 1884 lecture 'The dilemma of determinism',[2] William James characterises the worldview of 'determinism', which he opposes, as follows:

> The future has no ambiguous possibilities hidden in its womb: the part we call the present is compatible with only one totality. Any other future complement than the one fixed from eternity is impossible. The whole is in each and every part, and welds it with the rest into an absolute unity, an iron block, in which there can be no equivocation or shadow of turning. (James [1897] 1979, 117–18)

Even though nowadays – as in James's liberal Protestant religious environment in 1884 – 'the number of purely mechanical or hard determinists ... is small' (James [1897] 1979, 129), there was and still is the lure of a 'soft determinism' that comes in the form of a scientistic naturalism, as I will argue below.

In this chapter I first engage with the perspectives of William James and Heinrich Rickert on futures in connection with science-and-religion, in dialogue with Latour. This informs my subsequent analysis of futures in the context of contemporary science-and-religion and discussions on non-modern worldviews in a public policy context.

James, Latour and Rickert on futures and science-and-religion

In his lecture 'The dilemma of determinism', James argues for a worldview of 'indeterminism' versus a worldview of 'determinism'. He is fully aware that modern rationality cannot provide authority for either one of these options. He aptly links this point to the substance of one of the options: 'our first act of freedom, if we are free, ought in all inward propriety to be to affirm that we are free' (James [1897] 1979, 115). Freedom must be performed, not reasoned for – and he argues the same for the use of uniform laws in science to predict the future (these laws can be 'performed' in the practices of science without having epistemological warrant for their absolute truth). Below we see how James describes the development of both future uniformity in science and future freedom in morality and religion as being in essential tension:

> all the magnificent achievements of mathematical and physical science – our doctrines of evolution, of uniformity of law, and the rest – proceed from our indomitable desire to cast the world into a more rational shape in our minds than the shape into which it is thrown there by the crude order of our experience. The world has shown itself, to a great extent, plastic to this demand of ours for rationality. How much farther it will show itself plastic no one can say. Our only means of finding out is to try; and I, for one, feel as free to try conceptions of moral as of mechanical or of logical rationality. If a certain formula for expressing the nature of the world violates my moral demand, I shall feel as free to throw it overboard, or at least to doubt it, as if it disappointed my demand for uniformity of sequence, for example; the one demand being, so far as I can see, quite as subjective and emotional as the other is. (James [1897] 1979, 115–16)

According to James, '[a]ll our scientific and philosophic ideals are altars to unknown gods. Uniformity is as much so as is free-will' (James [1897] 1979, 116).

In contrast to determinism, 'indeterminism' holds that the parts of the whole 'have a certain amount of loose play on one another', so that deciding on one of them does not necessarily determine all others (James [1897] 1979, 118). Furthermore, indeterminism

> admits that possibilities may be in excess of actualities, and that things not yet revealed to our knowledge may really in themselves be ambiguous. Of two alternative futures which we conceive, both may now be really possible; and the one becomes impossible only at the very moment when the other excludes it by becoming real itself. (James [1897] 1979, 118)

To the view of indeterminism, which assumes ultimate pluralism in the world, 'actualities seem to float in a wider sea of possibilities from out of which they are chosen; and, *somewhere*, indeterminism says, such possibilities exist, and form a part of truth' (James [1897] 1979, 118). James's expression of ultimate pluralism in this address to Harvard Divinity students in 1884 is remarkably continuous with the most elaborated form it reached 24 years later in his lectures to Manchester College, Oxford in 1908 (published as *A Pluralistic Universe* in 1909).

Latour's first epigraph in *Facing Gaia* are seven words from James's *A Pluralistic Universe*: 'Nature is but a name for excess' (Latour [2015] 2017, viii). It is worthwhile to quote the whole sentence here:

> Only concepts are self-identical; only 'reason' deals with closed equations; nature is but a name for excess; every point in her opens out and runs into the more; and the only question, with reference to any point we may be considering, is how far into the rest of nature we may have to go in order to get entirely beyond its overflow. (James [1909a] 1977, 148)

In the same paragraph, James explains that a little future and a little past are in the 'pulse of inner life' (James [1909a] 1977, 148). Latour interprets James's notion of 'pluriverse' as an opening to otherness, observing that 'we have to agree to remain open to the dizzying otherness of existents' and certainly should not regroup them in 'some set, whatever it might be – and certainly not in "nature"' (Latour [2015] 2017, 36). The latter remark by Latour does not refer to James's use of the term 'nature' in the above quotation (where the sense of 'nature' refers, at least in part, to what Latour calls 'world'). Both authors use the term 'nature' (or 'Nature') in their discussions of 'naturalism' (that is, scientistic naturalism), in the sense of what you see of the world if you look through the eyes of generalising (natural) science (cf. Rickert). James's criticism of determinism, further developed in process thought, is mirrored in Latour's criticism of providence and 'Nature':

> 'Nature' ... has inherited ... all the functions of the all-seeing and all-encompassing God of the old days, and who is just as incapable of bringing its Providence to have any effect whatsoever on the Earth! (Latour [2015] 2017, 46)

One could say that in this worldview nothing happens; there is no 'adventure' (Latour [2015] 2017, 54).

According to James, the contrasting worldviews of determinism and indeterminism, since they are a-theoretical worldviews, are not based on 'evidence'; rather they derive from different conceptions of rationality, that is, from different 'faiths'. At issue is not whether people make decisions, obviously with a role to play for the will. What is at stake is the existence or non-existence of possibilities, defined by James as 'things that may, but need not, be'; this possibility-question will forever remain a 'mystery' (James [1897] 1979, 118–19). The possibility-question cannot be answered by facts:

> how can any amount of assurance that something actually happened give us the least grain of information as to whether another thing might or might not have happened in its place? (James [1897] 1979, 119)

Here we see that questions about how open the future may be are bound up with conceptions of rationality:

> To this man the world seems more rational with possibilities in it – to that man more rational with possibilities excluded; and talk as we will about having to yield to evidence, what makes us monists or pluralists, determinists or indeterminists, is at bottom always some sentiment like this. (James [1897] 1979, 119)

Again, whichever conception of rationality one has, after a decision has been made and the universe has taken one particular path, that universe, to our means of observation and understanding, appears just as rational as another path would have appeared. Even assuming that one could stand outside of the universes of determinism and chance and then compare them:

> There would be absolutely no criterion by which we might judge one necessary and the other matter of chance. (James [1897] 1979, 121–2)

The key lies with the 'affordances' that present themselves to experience: they are the possibilities presented to existence that invite, demand and assert an attraction on the experiencing subject, and they are *adjacent* possibilities (cf. Letiche et al. 2011, 39). That the possibilities are 'adjacent' means that 'all of them [are] *kinds* of things already here and based in the existing frame of nature' (James [1897] 1979, 122). James consequently asks:

> Do not all the motives that assail us, all the futures that offer themselves to our choice, spring equally from the soil of the past; and would not either one of them, whether realized through chance or through necessity, the moment it was realized, seem to us to fit that

> past, and in the completest and most continuous manner to interdigitate with the phenomena already there? (James [1897] 1979, 122)

It is interesting to see how James the psychologist rules out the relevance of psychological evidence on decision-making for supporting either determinism or indeterminism: 'The quarrel which determinism has with chance fortunately has nothing to do with this or that psychological detail' (James [1897] 1979, 123). The only thing that psychology can analyse is the psychic fact of decision-making, which involves a process that is fully part of psychic nature: in psychology there is no appeal to an outside moment, related to freedom, to put a stamp on decisions. Decisions 'seem to make nature continuous', transforming an 'equivocal and double future into an inalterable and simple past' by 'granting consent to one possibility and withholding it from another' (James [1897] 1979, 123). The quarrel about the openness of the future is clearly metaphysical.

With the space of future possibilities being indeterminate, for those who oppose determinism, there is an objective role that 'chance' must play in the realisation of the future. James notes that

> the idea of chance is, at bottom, exactly the same thing as the idea of gift – the one simply being a disparaging, and the other a eulogistic, name for anything on which we have no effective *claim*. (James [1897] 1979, 123)

The crucial moments here are that (1) there is something left to choose, but (2) not anything goes! Whether the future will be 'better' (according to any yardstick) for having these chances or gifts in the universe 'will depend altogether on *what* these uncertain and unclaimable things turn out to be' (James [1897] 1979, 124).

After James has made his pitch for indeterminism, acknowledging the limitations of arguments for believing in it, he elaborates what he takes to be the most captivating version of determinism, the right horn of the dilemma of determinism, that of the optimistic determinism which he labels 'subjectivism' (the left horn being 'pessimism'):

> The necessary acts we erroneously regret may be good, and yet our error in so regretting them may be also good, on one simple condition; and that condition is this: The world must not be regarded as a machine whose final purpose is the making real of any outward good, but rather as a contrivance for deepening the

> theoretic consciousness of what goodness and evil in their intrinsic natures are. Not the doing either of good or of evil is what nature cares for, but the knowing of them. (James [1897] 1979, 128)

This subjectivism may take the form of the sort of scientism that James calls 'scientificism', which he had referred to earlier in his 1881 lecture 'Theism and reflex action'. In this lecture he described 'the religion of exclusive scientificism': using '[t]he scientific conception of the world as an army of molecules' as 'exclusive law of the mind' in order to satisfy

> [t]he appetite for immediate consistency at any cost ... – which is nothing but the passion for conceiving the universe in the most labor-saving way. (James [1897] 1979, 104–5)

It does not become entirely clear from James's text whether the next distinction that he introduces, that between hard and soft determinism, also applies to this 'scientificism'. However, I would argue that scientism indeed can come in both hard and soft deterministic forms. Hard determinism means purely mechanical determinism – a version that need not be taken seriously, according to James. Soft determinism does need to be taken seriously, however, and is described by James as:

> the determinism which allows considerations of good and bad to mingle with those of cause and effect in deciding what sort of a universe this may rationally be held to be. ... [I]f determinism is to escape pessimism, it must leave off looking at the goods and ills of life in a simple objective way, and regard them as materials, indifferent in themselves, for the production of consciousness, scientific and ethical, in us. (James [1897] 1979, 129)

There is no need to take a position on James's notion of 'scientificism' here. Below I address what a present-day scientistic naturalism of the soft deterministic kind may look like in the context of disregarding non-modern worldviews in modern planning.

James concludes his lecture by expressing the moral and religious reasons he has for holding on to indeterminism. As summarised by Jeremy Carrette, who also emphasises for this James text the influence of Charles Renouvier (cf. Chapter 6):

> It is the dogmatic nature of determinism that James resists, the sense that we are 'foredoomed and settled long ago'. ... There

> is a moral edge to James's resistance, a sense that determinism creates a 'laziness' and undermines 'effort', such is the voice of a true Calvinist. ... For James, the question of determinism was 'refreshed' by writers such as Renouvier, and, following Renouvier, James maintained the importance of liberty and the choice of individualism while at the same time recognizing and taking account of the social order. ... Both thinkers remain committed to the relations and individuals. (Carrette 2013, 148–9)

James does not want to leave it at what he acknowledges as 'a deep truth' in the pessimistic philosophy of Schopenhauer: 'the illusoriness of the notion of moral progress' (James [1897] 1979, 131). Within determinism he takes subjectivism to be 'the more rational scheme' (James [1897] 1979, 131). Still, he considers subjectivism's optimism to turn into 'an ethical indifference' (James [1897] 1979, 132) and to harbour fatalists and romanticists, the latter of whom 'think the facts of human sensibility to be of all facts the most worthy of attention' (James [1897] 1979, 133). And so as a true Calvinist James decides:

> The only escape is by the practical way. ... [C]onduct, and not sensibility, is the ultimate fact for our recognition. With the vision of certain works to be done, of certain outward changes to be wrought or resisted, it says our intellectual horizon terminates. No matter how we succeed in doing these outward duties, whether gladly and spontaneously, or heavily and unwillingly, do them we somehow must; for the leaving of them undone is perdition. No matter how we feel; if we are only faithful in the outward act and refuse to do wrong, the world will in so far be safe, and we quit of our debt toward it. (James [1897] 1979, 134)

For James, 'chance' means 'that in moral respects the future may be other and better than the past has been' (James [1897] 1979, 137). He further specifies this, providing a glimpse of his thesis of pluralistic panpsychism (assuming no need for an all-knowing mind or infinite God), a foreboding of process thought, by responding to the risk of leaving the notions of an all-knowing mind or infinite God (Providence) behind:

> Does not the admission of such an unguaranteed chance or freedom preclude utterly the notion of a Providence governing the world? Does it not leave the fate of the universe at the mercy of the

chance-possibilities, and so far insecure? Does it not, in short, deny the craving of our nature for an ultimate peace behind all tempests, for a blue zenith above all clouds?

> To this my answer must be very brief. The belief in free-will is not in the least incompatible with the belief in Providence, provided you do not restrict the Providence to fulminating nothing but *fatal* decrees. If you allow him to provide possibilities as well as actualities to the universe, and to carry on his own thinking in those two categories just as we do ours, chances may be there, uncontrolled even by him, and the course of the universe be really ambiguous; and yet the end of all things may be just what he intended it to be from all eternity. (James [1897] 1979, 138)

As I concluded in Chapter 2, a religious person can read in this pluralistic universe possibilities to co-create the world in partnership with God. Obviously process philosophy and theology take a strong cue from the approach outlined by James (without here claiming that James would have followed that step towards a notion of co-creation; my hunch is that he would have found it too theoretical).

It is important to realise that in his conclusion of the lecture, in which we are finally assured that our 'world was safe, and that no matter how much it might zigzag he [God] could surely bring it home at last' (James [1897] 1979, 140), James deviates from his Promethean pragmatist philosophy and shifts to his anti-Promethean mystic self. There is an absolute certainty included in James's metaphysical thought that sits at odds with the fallibilism of his pragmatism. According to James, we can arrive at this certainty from mystical religious experience. In 'The will to believe', discussed in Chapter 7, he describes how one can 'I–Thou' the entire universe:

> The Universe is no longer a mere *It* to us, but a *Thou*, if we are religious; and any relation that may be possible from person to person might be possible here. (James [1897] 1979, 31)

Our mystical self craves unity and abides in the present, while our Promethean self runs ahead of itself into the future. For this conundrum, caused by making metaphysical assumptions, there is no philosophical resolution to be found. As Richard Gale concludes:

> To be human is to accept the unresolvable tension between wanting to be both at the same time. The best we can hope for is

> a taking-turns solution of the first-I'm-this-and-then-I'm-that sort. (Gale 1999, 331–2)

Latour takes his cue from the Jamesian approach to indeterminism, without paying attention to James's mysticism, and offers a non-theistic reading of 'Providence'. Latour refers to 'Gaia' as 'Providences' and specifies those 'Providences' as follows:

> we have to consider Gaia as the name of the process by which variable and contingent occurrences have made *later* events more probable. In this sense, Gaia is a creature no more of chance than of necessity. Which means that it closely resembles what we have come to regard *as history itself*. (Latour [2015] 2017, 107)

Human action is thus situated by Latour in geohistory, which he claims does not amount to 'naturalizing' humans (Latour [2015] 2017, 107). Instead he argues that his position ends what Latour identifies as the 'mononaturalism'/ 'multiculturalism' division (Latour [2015] 2017, 108).

Reinterpreted in terms of transcendental naturalism, the positions of both James and Latour can be taken to imply that freedom is found not in a supposed 'culture' that is without nature – outside of nature, opposed to nature – but instead in a *proper* naturalisation (or 'worlding') of culture. Latour is highly critical of much critical social science:

> Can you recall how much energy the social sciences have expended to fight the dangers of biological reductionism and naturalization? Today it seems difficult to tell whether we gain more freedom of movement if we turn toward nature or toward culture. (Latour [2015] 2017, 108)

Overcoming the opposition between 'nature' and 'culture' constitutes a major plank of Latour's philosophical programme. Also transcendental naturalism – in assuming a notion of 'nature' (taken as 'world') that acknowledges that multiplicity is everywhere, with different peoples making different choices in metaphysics, cosmology and values, that is, in worldviews – holds that there is not one Nature versus a diversity of (non-natural) cultures. Rather, the new naturalistic regime (my term) is 'compositionist', as Latour calls it (Latour [2015] 2017, 238). According to Latour, it is only once this is realised that '[p]olitics' – which is how peoples collectively give shape to their freedom – 'can begin again' (Latour [2015] 2017, 143).

In the discussion of James's work in earlier chapters, we have encountered different notions of truth used by him – both a pragmatist notion, where truth of an idea consists of the fulfilment of the conditionalised predictions attached to the pragmatic (operational empiricist) meaning of the idea, and a notion of truth that actually refers to contents, including theoretical contents. What does James have to say about the truth of the existence of future possibilities, that is, the truth of the existence of a pluralistic universe?

In his 1884 lecture 'The dilemma of determinism', James only touched once upon the philosophical question of the truth about the existence of future possibilities (claiming that 'such possibilities exist, and *form a part of truth*', James [1897] 1979, 118, emphasis added). We saw in Chapter 7 that in his lecture 'The will to believe', in which he discussed the 'belief in truth itself', James argued that philosophical styles (including philosophical approaches to theoretical truth) are taken up by our willing nature on authority of our passions. This exemplifies an approach that later led Rickert to judge that pragmatist philosophy erred in its theoretical interpretation of the value of pragmatist truth, even though it considered theoretical truth in its essence as valuable and understood the knowing human being as a valuing subject. Furthermore, as I showed in Chapter 4, Rickert supported James's intention to outline a pluralistic ontology and to move beyond the notion of '*uni*verse' to that of '*multi*verse', even though he disagreed with the details of James's execution. As far as Rickert is concerned, James's philosophy, by letting truth be a belief that can be willed or not, is philosophically not strong enough for the fight with scientistic naturalism. Therefore, let us here explore a little further how Rickert uses his transcendental notion of theoretical truth to continue that fight and underpin it with his open philosophical system. In a sense, one could say that Rickert has embedded pluralism one step deeper into the apparatus of philosophy itself than has James – and, I will add, Latour.

On the notion of pragmatic truth, Rickert writes:

> 'Pragmatism' has tried to explain just the world built in the service of practical needs as the 'true' one. However, since this thought cancels out the concept of a theoretical truth at all, it cannot itself claim to be theoretically true, and we therefore need not go into it here. (Rickert 1921, 8)

Rickert disagrees with James on the characterisation of philosophy as a choice of worldview (which cannot be grounded theoretically):

> Only if one places the scientific *Weltanschauungslehre* and the purely theoretical worldview that results from it next to or against the a-theoretical worldviews and interacts with them can one hope to achieve the ultimate theoretical clarity about the world and life that is granted to man. So we have to understand that philosophy as science of the world (*Welt-Wissenschaft*) necessarily becomes a *Weltanschauungslehre*. (Rickert 1921, 33)

Rickert does not disagree with James that there are fundamental limits to what can be known philosophically. He adds that this is already the case for problems that do not involve the other side (*das Jenseits*), with which metaphysics is concerned:

> Thinking validity means as much as conceptually separating it [the valid] from the real. We are indeed able to understand the valuing act as a bond between the two areas [of the valid and the real], and with this much has been achieved for an understanding of the meaning of our life. But we cannot take the value that is valid as a cause and thus as having power over the real. Then the one and the other [the heterological alternatives of the valid and the real] would merge into an indiscriminate unity of identity, that is, the concepts of the real and the valid would be lost in one another, and that would again destroy what concepts of the universe we have so far succeeded in working out. So we see *why* all scientific understanding comes to an end here, and that is then also a 'solution' to the problem. (Rickert 1921, 308)

While acknowledging its limits, Rickert keeps the notion of theoretical truth alive. He indicates for metaphysics that it is not the domain of knowledge (*Wissen*) but rather of belief (*Glauben*). However, philosophy, such as transcendental naturalism, aims to avoid making metaphysical statements too early. There are already some quite strong arguments that can be made philosophically against scientistic naturalism without resorting to James's will to believe, for instance. Another example of metaphysics that is not needed (and may be potentially a hindrance) in transcendental naturalism is Latour's 'occasionalism'. Latour claimed that he was 'secularising' philosophy, but then introduces his occasionalist metaphysical assumption:

> For all agents, to act signifies bringing one's existence, one's subsistence, *from the future toward the present*: they act as long as

> they take the risk of filling the breach of existence – or else they purely and simply disappear. (Latour [2015] 2017, 69–70)

However, transcendental naturalism has already found a way to get beyond the subject/object split and is already secular in that sense. One can allow for metaphysics, but one cannot demonstrate it philosophically.

In his *Philosophy of Life* (1920) Rickert argues against 'biologism' (a particular form of scientistic naturalism based on biology), suggesting that it is not able to build up a philosophy in the sense of a theory of the 'world as a *whole*' (*Welt*all) or of worldviews. He states this conclusion early in his book (Rickert 1920, 36) and uses the bulk of the book to make his case. Biologism cannot therefore be used to guide people's lives (as this would constitute a form of moral scientism). Here is how Rickert characterises its 'older' (mechanical) version (mechanical or 'older' biologism):

> We realise that the eternal laws that eradicate the imperfect in the struggle for existence necessarily lead the world towards its true goal and make it more and more perfect. The law of nature is at the same time the law of progress. Natural development means development for the better. If only we let selection go undisturbed, then there will always be created what should be. Therefore we no longer need the old values to which the non-naturalist (*der naturfremde Mensch*) clung in order to give meaning to his life. (Rickert 1920, 89)

The philosophy of life that can be built on the basis of biologism is based on the realisation that

> we are not strangers in the world, but she is our home, and the meaning of our lives can be nothing more than that we seek to obey her laws. From the amoeba to the man of culture, she has everywhere destroyed the imperfect and preserved the perfect. (Rickert 1920, 103)

The 'newer' biologism keeps formally the same philosophical goal, but instead of having

> mechanism [as] the most general framework in which it sets the world … [i]t starts from what mocks any mechanical conception. Life can only be conceived in an anti-mechanistic way, as power

> development, as growth, as a constant increase, as élan vital. Then, in order to arrive at a unity of worldview, life is not arranged in matter, but conversely matter is arranged in life, that is, to understand the seeming death as a form of sinking and exhausting life. The concept of being of the world is thus again 'monistic'. However, it places the emphasis on the opposite side of the dualism to be overcome. (Rickert 1920, 103–4)

Again, a similar philosophy of life accompanies the newer form of biologism: it is the destiny of the human being to participate in the world's processes of growth and decay in a way 'which represents the general world principle' (Rickert 1920, 104).

For philosophising about the future, the possibilities contained in it and the values to be realised, Rickert concludes that any philosophy that stays close to the 'special sciences' (e.g. biology) is unable to deal with values systematically:

> Yes, it misjudges the peculiarity and the intrinsic value of cultural values in particular, by dissolving them all into life values. For the most part, it cannot think of even posing the problem of the relationship between time and eternity, let alone solving it. There is no problem for it here. It is inherently attached to finite, temporal being, and this is incompatible with universal thinking. Thus, this supposedly philosophical movement in every respect exposes an unphilosophical character. (Rickert 1920, 143)

This means that 'worldviews' based on a scientistic naturalism are severely truncated. They will have particular difficulty in dealing genuinely with different dimensions of culture and with other worldviews when they aim to contribute to human decision-making. Many possibilities for the future will not be recognised and will be disregarded.

In his work on philosophy of science, Rickert liberates the historical sciences (or cultural sciences) from scientistic naturalism, and separates philosophy from both types of science:

> In light of its character, history must confine itself to the historical, and thus to what is temporally conditioned. Philosophy always has the task of proceeding beyond the historical to what is timeless or eternal. So if, for the foregoing reasons, we also advance the struggle against the one-sided quality of methodological naturalism, it is precisely the investigation into the character of

historical science that should lead us to understand the following point: Philosophy will progress, on the one hand, only if it takes into consideration not *merely* the natural sciences but the historical sciences *as well* and, on the other hand, only if it also attempts to establish a standpoint beyond *both*. (Rickert [1929] 1986, 18–19)

It is important to realise that Rickert does not make an ontological distinction between the materials of the natural and historical (cultural) sciences. Rather he uses just a methodological distinction regarding whether one looks at empirical material through a generalising or an individualising lens. Given the limited empirical research that had gone into indigenous lifeways, Rickert makes rather unknowledgeable claims about 'natural peoples', for instance:

> We speak of 'natural peoples' [*Naturvölker*] and juxtapose them to 'historical' peoples as well as to 'civilized' or 'cultural peoples' [*Kulturvölker*]. ... [W]e can leave undecided the question of whether there are absolutely unhistorical beings who have no culture at all. But if a people really exhibits no historically essential changes in the entire course of its known development, then in fact we could subsume it only under general concepts of recurrence. In this respect, therefore, we could conceive it only as 'nature', in the logical sense. (Rickert [1929] 1986, 136–7)

The culture of non-modern peoples is further addressed below, given the accumulation of knowledge and differences in approach over the past century.

I conclude this section with what Rickert has to say about mysticism. Firstly, it is important to realise that mysticism, according to Rickert, cannot contribute knowledge:

> We separate the real from the valid. The reality of experience is not the *world* of experience in its entirety. Despite this we can still speak of it as a unity on the basis of our understanding. If, on the other hand, we attempt to bring *everything*, both the real and the valid, into the one thought of the *world* of experience, we have either returned to something empty of content, the theoretical object in general, or we have to follow consistent mysticism in declaring the unity of the universe, which we believe we have found, to be completely incomprehensible and ineffable. But that would not bring us any further in our *knowledge*. What is still missing is the

> concept of world unity, which we seek where we philosophise, and thus every unity in the theoretical sense. (Rickert 1921, 248)

And secondly:

> Mysticism, especially Asiatic, but less consequently Christian too, only wants to perceive God. Man seeks to be absorbed in contemplation. In this he sees the only way to get rid of human imperfection with God's help. So he turns away from everything social, personal and active; indeed he finally becomes so one with God in perception that his own person disappears in the deity. (Rickert 1921, 341–2)

So mysticism receives its own pride of place in Rickert's system of values and his analysis of religion (see Chapter 4). However, further reflection is needed on how moderns can relate to non-modern mystical traditions, for example Buddhism, when there is an incommensurability of worldviews and decisions need to be made about the future.

Contemporary reflections on futures and science-and-religion

How the space of future possibilities is conceived within the practices of science and religion varies considerably across the wide heterogeneity of such practices; it is also influenced by their larger cultural settings. In this chapter, our interest lies with what gets attention and what gets disregarded in these practices, and in particular with how modern and non-modern worldviews can be 'diplomatically' related to one another despite their incommensurability. In order to accomplish such diplomacy, we need to position the Western scientistic naturalistic tradition within its larger context by reflecting on its notions of 'nature' and 'progress'.

Transcendental naturalism, in which nature is taken as 'world', features an openness to a variety of views about the future and what constitutes 'progress'. Latour warns that

> [o]nly if we place ourselves inside this world will we be able to recognize as one particular arrangement the choice of existents and their ways of connecting that we call Nature/Culture and that has served for a long time to format our collective understanding (at least in the Western tradition). (Latour [2015] 2017, 36)

He adds that 'the Nature/Culture pairing is not a universal – a matter that has been well explored by anthropology' (36) and refers the reader to the book *Beyond Nature and Culture* by the French anthropologist Philippe Descola ([2005] 2013), with whom he had interacted over the years.

In this section, I first engage with Descola's empirically informed philosophical anthropology to contextualise scientistic naturalism. I then move on to evaluate (1) how philosopher Richard Jones describes the clash between worldviews connected with mystical experiences and scientistic naturalism; (2) how religious worldviews and their openness to the future in general are characterised philosophically by religious studies scholar Kevin Schilbrack; and (3) how philosopher Koo van der Wal finds similarities between 'spirited' non-modern worldviews and what he labels 'idealistic naturalism'.

Let me begin with Philippe Descola's opening salvo in his book, after he has initially surveyed a wide variety of peoples:

> the modern West's way of representing nature is by no means widely shared. In many regions of the planet, humans and nonhumans are not conceived as developing in incommunicable worlds or according to quite separate principles. The environment is not regarded objectively as an autonomous sphere. Plants and animals, rivers and rocks, meteors and the seasons do not exist all together in an ontological niche defined by the absence of human beings. And this seems to hold true whatever may be the local ecological characteristics, political regimes and economic systems, and the accessible resources and the techniques employed to exploit them. (Descola [2005] 2013, 30–1)

Non-modern cultures are indifferent to – or, one can say, disregard – the distinctions maintained by moderns, and vice versa. Often, as Descola analyses, non-modern cultures treat elements in the environment as persons endowed with cognitive, moral and social qualities similar to those of humans. They also feature fluid modes of communication and possibilities for metamorphosis between humans and non-humans that reflect a focus on relations rather than scientistic naturalistic notions of essences such as 'human' versus 'animal' or other sorts of species. For Latour, the impacts of climate change that peoples have begun to experience and that feature a scale and unpredictability that Latour denotes with the term 'Gaia' force moderns to reconsider their worldviews and their modern notions of 'nature':

> If it is the world that interests us – and no longer 'nature' – then we must learn to inhabit what could be called a *metamorphic zone*. (Latour [2015] 2017, 58)

We have to become open to the fundamentally different ways in which the future may unfold once we learn to leave scientistic naturalism.

In Descola's analysis of modernity, from the seventeenth century, nature and culture (at first still denoted by 'human nature') developed into separate autonomous spheres:

> Thanks to the wide generality of their meanings, Nature and human nature allow one neatly to synthesize the new possibility of effecting a readjustment between the ceaseless pullulation of the analogical multiplicity of beings and the mechanism of induction, with its whole parade of images and reminiscences. Understanding and controlling nonhumans are assigned to a subject who knows or one who acts, the scientist in his heated room or the engineer draining marshland, the physicist manipulating his air pump or the steward of Colbert's forests. (Descola [2005] 2013, 70)

Descola identifies Rickert as the great codifier of the 'natural' versus the 'cultural' sciences, and he approvingly dedicates two pages to explain Rickert's conception of culture. He highlights that:

> [a]s a good Kantian, Rickert held that we live and perceive reality as a disparate continuum whose segmentation into different domains comes about only as a result of the mode of knowledge that we apply to it and the characteristics that we select. (Descola [2005] 2013, 76)

He also puts his finger on Rickert's use of the concept of 'nature' (versus 'history' or 'culture'), where for Rickert '[t]he world becomes nature when we envisage it in its universal aspect; it becomes history when we examine it in its particular and individual aspect' (Descola [2005] 2013, 76). It is in the relationship to values that cultural processes are distinguished from natural processes. Descola applauds Rickert with the result of his philosophy of science project:

> By distinguishing between, on the one hand, objects without meaning whose existence is determined by general laws and, on the other, objects that we apprehend in all their individuality by

virtue of the contingent value that is attached to them, Rickert dealt a blow to the foundations of ontological dualism. More or less all reality can be apprehended through one or another of its aspects, according to whether it is considered in its brute and stubborn factuality or from the point of view of the desires and uses invested in it by those who have deliberately produced or preserved it. (Descola [2005] 2013, 77)

Descola also forgives Rickert that he was inclined (at the turn of the twentieth century when he first published his philosophy of science) to classify the study of *Naturvölker* (primitive peoples) among the natural sciences, given the sparsity of empirical origins inquiries at the time. Effectively what Rickert had accomplished 'was to carve out the space in which twentieth-century anthropology would be able to operate. It would be a study of cultural realities, as opposed to the study of natural realities' (Descola [2005] 2013, 78).

Still, Descola classes Rickert as a contributor to the 'great divide' between nature and culture, despite the fact that Rickert *does not ontologically* separate out nature; while Rickert *does* identify the 'perceptual world' as an ontological domain, this is not the same as separating out nature. Similarly, he notes that also Latour's ethnographic work on the proliferation of hybrids hinges on the modern dualistic scheme of nature and culture: 'in no way does it call into question the absolutely exceptional nature of modern cosmology' (Descola [2005] 2013, 87). He adds:

The fact that dualism masks a practice that contradicts it does not eliminate its directive role in the organization of the sciences, nor does it efface the fact that ethnology derives constant inspiration from an opposition that most of the peoples it describes and interprets do perfectly well without. What primarily interests me are the deforming effects of this perspective on ethnology, for it is here that its creation of illusions is the most pernicious. (Descola [2005] 2013, 87)

Transcendental naturalism emphasises that the term 'nature' (in the sense of the whole world that can be experienced, understood and thought of) should be opposed not to 'culture' (which relates to human value-laden practices and products occurring in nature) but to the 'supernatural' (which can only be described metaphorically through metaphysics). It is my contention that the efforts by Descola and Latour closely to study modes of existence, either across the whole variety of worlds (Descola) or focused more in particular on the Moderns (Latour), all contribute to a next phase of the Rickertian project of explicating what are the values that drive the various cultures, without resorting to the multi-cultural/mono-natural schematism that both Descola and Latour criticise.

It should come as no surprise that where Latour's 'system of values' (Rickert's term) can to some extent still be mapped onto Rickert's system of values (albeit with important differences, as discussed in Chapter 4), Descola's system of values differs dramatically from Rickert's Germanic speculations (which focused largely on the 'higher' cultural elements that he identified in his German culture). In Part Two of his book, titled 'The structures of experience', Descola identifies seven modes of experience (Descola [2005] 2013, 112–15), which I claim can be linked with broad domains of 'values' and function in a transcendental manner. In doing so I do not claim that knowledge can be reached about the objectivity of the specific values giving rise to a particular culture – as we should also be careful to avoid doing for the moderns' values, except possibly theoretical truth. The two primary modes of experience are:

- 'Identification': different values pertaining to establishing 'differences and resemblances between myself and other existing entities by inferring analogies and contrasts between the appearance, behaviour, and properties that I ascribe to myself and those that I ascribe to them'.
- 'Relation': different values pertaining to maintaining 'the external links between beings and things that are detectable in typical behaviour patterns and may be partially translatable into concrete social norms'.

The five subsidiary modes of experience are:

- 'Temporality': different values pertaining to objectifying duration.
- 'Spatiality': different values pertaining to organising and dividing up space.
- 'Figuration': different values pertaining to materially representing beings or things in two or three dimensions.
- 'Mediation': different values pertaining to interposing of 'a conventional device that functions as a substitute, a form, a sign or a symbol, such as sacrifice, money or writing'.

- 'Categorisation': different values pertaining to classifying entities and properties of the world.

Descola uses the first primary mode of experience, that of identification, to propose a typology of four ontologies, based on the culturally universal duality of interiority[3] and physicality:

> Faced with some other entity, human or nonhuman, I can assume either that it possesses elements of physicality and interiority identical to my own, that both its interiority and its physicality are distinct from mine, that we have similar interiorities and different physicalities, or, finally, that our interiorities are different and our physicalities are analogous. I shall call the first combination 'totemism', the second 'analogism', the third 'animism', and the fourth 'naturalism'. (Descola [2005] 2013, 121)

In summary:

- Animism: similar interiorities, dissimilar physicalities
- Totemism: similar interiorities, similar physicalities
- Analogism: dissimilar interiorities, dissimilar physicalities
- Naturalism: dissimilar interiorities, similar physicalities

The modern ontology (labelled 'naturalism' by Descola) is thus shown to be one of four basic cultural options available (all of which are empirically 'occupied' by different cultures).

In terms of diplomacy with other types of cultures, for instance in determining future options for collective decisions that need to be taken, according to Descola the moderns can do little else than frame their differences with other types of cultures in terms of dissimilar interiorities:

> I am different from someone who, speaking another language, believing in other values, thinking according to other categories, and seeing things according to another 'worldview', is no longer just like me because the 'collective representations' to which he adheres and that condition his actions are so very different from mine. A bizarre custom or an enigmatic or repugnant practice can thus be explained by the fact that those who adopt them cannot do otherwise than believe (think, represent to themselves, imagine, judge, suppose ...) that this is the way to proceed if one wishes to achieve such or such an end. It is all a matter of 'mentalities' – a

> fertile domain for history – and if these are reputed to be understandable up to a certain point from the traces that they leave in public expressions of them, it is nevertheless not possible to penetrate their ultimate sources, for I cannot quite slip into the mind of someone else, even someone very close. For naturalist subjects, there is unfortunately no mental equivalent to metamorphosis; all we have at our disposal are the unsuccessful attempts made by poetry, psychoanalysis, or mysticism. In these circumstances, it is understandable that radical otherness seems to lie on the side of those either devoid of minds or who do not know how to use them: savages (in the past), the mentally ill (today), and, above all, the immense multitude of nonhumans, animals, objects, plants, stones, clouds, all this material chaos that exists in a mechanical fashion and with laws of composition and functioning that humans, in their wisdom, work busily to discover. (Descola [2005] 2013, 291)

This should serve as a warning to any Latourian programme of diplomacy that if one undertakes it using methodology based on transcendental naturalism – as I suggest makes most sense for moderns who want to step beyond scientistic naturalism – that there will always remain a fundamental limit to understanding and communicating with, let alone making decisions together with, non-modern cultures. In terms of the weak metamorphosis options available to the moderns, I already discussed poetry in Chapter 6; in the present chapter I address mysticism.

There are some other types of cultures to which moderns can relatively easily relate. Descola observes, for instance, that the analogism of Buddhism can offer a 'spiritual' universalism – that is, a universalism of myriads of diffused subjectivities that animate all things with a will yet to be discovered, a meaning yet to be interpreted, a connection yet to be revealed' (Descola [2005] 2013, 300). 'Eastern wisdoms' can relatively easily be successful in a disenchanted West:

> Zen, Buddhism, and Daoism offer a universalist alternative that is more complete than the truncated universalism of the Moderns. Human nature is not shredded into bits as a result of the force of customs and the weight of habits, since every human being, thanks to meditation, is reputed to be able to draw from within himself or herself the capacity to experience the plenitude of the world without preestablished foundations – that is to say, liberated from the particular foundations that a local tradition might assign to it. (Descola [2005] 2013, 300)

However, mysticism comes with a focus on the present, and mystical experience will not *by itself* aid decision-making on the future, as is discussed below. Interestingly, modernity finds it much harder to relate to the analogism of its own direct precursor, premodern Christianity:

> analogical ontologies have managed to systematize … straggling chains of meaning into ordered and interdependent sets that for the most part are designed to be effective practically: ways to cope with misfortune, the orientation of buildings, calendars, predestination, eschatology, divinatory systems, the compatibility of marriage partners, good government – everything is interconnected in a web so dense and so charged with consequence that it becomes impossible to tell whether it is man who reflects the universe or the universe that takes man as its model. Chains of transitive causality so long and so luxuriant are seldom to be found in animist or totemic ontologies, and in present-day naturalism they appear only as incomplete fragments, nostalgic survivals from an enchanted epoch on which horoscope watchers, adepts of alternative medicines and the followers of New Age sects all tend to draw. (Descola [2005] 2013, 217–18)

Modernity comes with notions of progress in both scientific and religious practices, peaking in the nineteenth century with liberal Protestantism, where ultimately an analogical notion of eschatology came to be replaced by the notion of the human being as co-creator who helps the future along towards its positive end (cf. James in the previous section).[4] Obviously there are alternative interpretations of eschatology, which question whether salvation really has to do with progressing towards the future or whether, instead, that the mode of religion's goal is, on the one hand, for the present to get connected with the end times and, on the other not to assume too great a role for humans in bringing about the coming or the return of the Messiah (Walls 2008).

A fuller understanding of the role of mysticism in thinking about the future can be obtained from Richard Jones's *Philosophy of Mysticism: Raids on the ineffable* (2016). This American philosopher has written the first systematic philosophy book on mysticism in half a century, the topic clearly having been out of fashion. Right at the start of his book, Jones makes clear that the terms 'mystic' and 'mysticism' were only invented in the seventeenth century and warns against present-day bias to focus on mysticism as only a matter of personal experiences, 'solidified' by William James in his *The Varieties of Religious Experience* (Jones 2016, 2):

> mysticism is traditionally more encompassing than simply isolated mystical experiences: it is about living one's whole life aligned with reality as it truly is (as defined by a tradition's beliefs). (Jones 2016, 2)

This already makes it clear that how mystical traditions view the future depends not so much on the mystical experiences *per se*, but rather on their cultural settings.

For the purpose of his book, Jones defines 'mysticism' as 'emptying the mind of conceptualizations, dispositions, emotions, and other differentiated content that distinguishes' (Jones 2016, 4). Two classes of mystical experience are distinguished by Jones: extrovertive and introvertive mystical experiences. Extrovertive mystical experiences include mindfulness states of consciousness, nature mysticism and cosmic consciousness; introvertive mystical experiences include differentiated non-theistic and theistic mystical experiences and the empty so-called 'depth-mystical experience'.

For all types of mystical experience

> mystics do claim that they realize a reality present when all the conceptual, dispositional, and emotional content of the mind is removed. Mystical experiences and states of consciousness are allegedly cognitive. (Jones 2016, 12)

For philosophy, of course, the question remains of how to evaluate this knowledge pertaining to an awareness of the bare being-in-itself or of a direct contact with a transcendent reality. On this point, Jones concludes that any judgement on what mystical experiences reveal 'will depend on factors other than mystical experiences themselves' (Jones 2016, 36). He also emphasises the cultural variety of mysticism:

> classical mysticism was part of different religious traditions and must be understood in that context. Mystics think of themselves as Christians or Shaivaites or whatever, not as 'mystics'. They practice Christianity or whatever, not 'mysticism'. In Buddhism, the goal of the way of life is to end our suffering by escaping the cycle of rebirth – something Abrahamic mystics do not even consider. (Jones 2016, 49)

He also adds that

> all religions have mystical traditions: any religious tradition can accommodate mystics to one degree or another. The influence of mystical experiences on religious doctrines is especially great in many Asian religions. But even with a mainstream view of the absolute otherness of God, the Abrahamic traditions all have had vibrant mystical traditions. (Jones 2016, 50)

In terms of mysticism's contribution to metaphysics, Jones states that

> the basic mystery of the nature of *beingness* is not dispelled by having any type of mystical experience. Beingness may be apprehended in a mindful state or its simplicity directly apprehended in the depth-mystical experience void of any differentiated content, but no new information about its nature is provided in either experience. No answer is given to the question of the relation of an underlying 'being' and the realm of 'becoming' – the problem of 'the one' and 'the many' remains as profound for mystics after even depth-mystical experiences. Extrovertive and introvertive mystical experiences may increase a sense of awe and wonder at the that-ness of things, but they may not – one may serenely or joyfully accept the mundaneness of all of the phenomenal world. And introvertive mystical experiences may lead to a sense that the natural world is not ultimately real. If anything, the mystery of beingness is increased, not diminished, by such experiences. (Jones 2016, 184–5)

Again, this leads one to conclude that each religious tradition's ideas of the purpose of life and the role of mystical experience within that come from considerations outside of these experiences.

It thus depends on the wider cultural setting whether the sense of timelessness that is embedded in mystical experiences also translates into a particular future orientation within the wider cultural worldview. There is obviously a tendency for mysticism to disregard time and change:

> Theologians … have the problem that if what is experienced is timeless (i.e., existing outside of the realm of time), how could it know temporal matters or act in time at all? Mystics also have the sense that the transcendent reality is immutable and thus cannot be affected by anything temporal such as the act of prayer.

> Nonmystical theologians may prefer a god with more personality and the ability to act in the world. (Jones 2016, 91)

To mystics, events in time may be irrelevant to the timeless reality that they orient themselves towards. But that does not mean that mystic worldviews entail that time does not exist:

> [I]s time real or merely a phenomenal illusion? That is, is time merely part of the fabric of the 'dream' realm and not applicable to what is finally real? Mystical experiences appear timeless in the sense that temporal categories are not part of the experience, but extrovertive mystics could accept that time is part of the fundamental structure of the phenomenal world – beingness is outside of time, but structured phenomena are not. Introvertive mystics treat time the way they treat any this-worldly phenomenon. Mystics also can follow the Buddha in leaving questions about the origin and extent of the universe unanswered as simply irrelevant to their basic soteriological concerns. (Jones 2016, 178)

While it may be hard for scientistic naturalists to treat the unfolding world of time as no more than the 'dream' realm of some other reality, it may be attractive for those who want (partially) to step out of the modern tradition to turn to mysticism, an appropriation at which Descola already hinted.

From the above observations on a variety of 'religions' around the world, we can conclude that there are different 'religious' ways to relate to the openness, or not, of the future. I now complement the argument that I made in Chapter 7 for a philosophy of science conception of scientific experience and understanding that positively appreciates uncertainty (while reflecting on the objectivity of values in a transcendental approach), with a similar argument directly focused on religious experience and understanding. For that purpose I turn to Kevin Schilbrack, a philosopher of religion who shows a real sensitivity to practices.

In his book *Philosophy and the Study of Religions: A manifesto* (2014), Schilbrack states that

> religion is *largely* a set of practices in which people engage in order to make their lives better: participating in the three kinds of religious practices provides the participants with rituals that heal, with disciplines that train their children in morality and

> with structures for their communal lives that reflect a higher law. (Schilbrack 2014, 19)

This description refers to a very direct future orientation of participants in all religious practices: making their lives better (cf. James in the previous section), in both the short and the long term, individually and collectively. The practices that religion consists of can be seen as cognitive and involving beliefs. Yet besides this they are also (in many cases even primarily) 'ways to communicate, teach, or inculcate the claims that a religious community wants to make' (Schilbrack 2014, 32):

> Religious practices promise a wide variety of benefits to those who participate in them. In some cases, the benefits of the practice are concrete – like recovery from an illness, finding love, or being successful in an endeavour. In other cases, the benefits are less concrete – the community may hold that participating in their practices is the way for one to learn propriety or to become an adult. And even less concretely, some religious practices are said to lead to liberation or salvation. It may be that, like work, such religious practices pursue an end outside themselves or it may be that, like play, they are done as an end in themselves. But on either interpretation they can be seen as opportunities for cognition about health, love, duty, maturity, sovereignty, purpose, or – at the most abstract – the nature of human existence. (Schilbrack 2014, 44)

On Schilbrack's account of religion, religious practices can 'serve as opportunities for inquiry about the superempirical resources that make the practice successful' (Schilbrack 2014, 45). It is this last element, the superempirical resources that religious practices are about, which distinguishes religious practices from non-religious practices. Their inquiries are open-ended and the religious practices can provide 'physically, linguistically, and socially extended cognition that enables participants to ask and answer questions about the features of and the conditions for their normative paths' (Schilbrack 2014, 45).

Schilbrack argues that James was right when he defined religion as belief in an unseen order (even though he claims that the emphasis of James, like that of many other philosophers, was too much on beliefs). This is because 'it is precisely the beliefs of the participants that give the religious performances, practices, experiences, artefacts, and lives their sense' (Schilbrack 2014, 56). Worldviews, including those fed by religions, do have a cognitive component:

> Do religious people commit themselves to a certain view of things by engaging in their religious lives? Here I think that the answer is Yes. All human behaviour – and therefore all religious behaviour – involves attitudes of taking some propositions as true. ... Beliefs in the taking true sense are universal in that they are a contemporary philosophical account of what it means to feel, calculate, act, or speak with an understanding of one's environment. (Schilbrack 2014, 71)

Thus every religion, according to Schilbrack, necessarily has to assume the value of truth, even if it is not made explicit:

> The very idea of belief implies that what one believes may not be the case. That is, to have the concept of belief is to have the concept of truth and falsity independent of one's attitudes. (Schilbrack 2014, 75)

Below I consider the question of the way in which truth here functions as an (objective) value, and what are the limits for philosophy to speak about objective (truth) values pertaining to religion.

What distinguishes religious practices from non-religious ones is not their normative orientation *per se*. Schilbrack notes that the criterion of normativity:

> cannot suffice because all of culture is composed of normative practices. A culture simply is a normative order. To define religion as teaching beneficial ways to act is not yet to distinguish religion from other aspects of culture like medicine or sports or politics or art. Though it is valuable to frame religion as functional or pragmatic and not as, say, simply a product of theoretical speculation, it is not enough: one still must specify which normative practices are the religious ones. (Schilbrack 2014, 126)

Religious practices, then, are 'those normative practices that also refer to a religious reality' (Schilbrack 2014, 126). Like Rickert, Schilbrack assumes the need for practices to assume the validity of religious values (implying metaphysical commitments), making an interesting connection with religious practices' orientation towards the future in terms of wanting 'promises' to come true:

> If we see religions as making promises, then the desire among religious communities to 'go ontological' is not the product of metaphysical wonder or disconnected fantasy but rather a discursively expected implication of making a promise. Religions make ontological claims because such claims answer the question: what makes the promise true? (Schilbrack 2014, 128)

However, unlike Rickert, Schilbrack attributes objectivity (independent validity from individual or group judgements) to only religious values:

> All forms of culture involve nonempirical judgments. All forms of culture are evaluative and will seek to speak through symbols and metaphors to describe invisible orders of significance and value. As a consequence, one cannot say that the difference between what is and is not religion is that religions speak of nonempirical realities. The difference, rather, is this: if we ask whether the existence of those nonempirical realities – the norms of goodness, beauty, and justice and so on – depends on the human and other beings of the empirical world, religious communities are those that answer: no. (Schilbrack 2014, 134)

Here is where I differ with Schilbrack and choose to take Rickert's side in a transcendental naturalistic approach. What distinguishes religious from non-religious practices is exactly the non-empirical beings that religious practices speak of, and not any difference in the fundamental nature of their normativity. Still, there is one element in Rickert's view of religious values that does hint at a difference from other values. I flagged in Chapter 4 that religious values must lead by their nature to a far-reaching intolerance in religious people: according to Rickert, religious practitioners cannot put their religious values at the same level as the other values, but they must put them at a higher level: you can only be a truly religious person if you subsume all other cultural goods to your religion. However, in this potential subordination of non-religious values to religious values, no distinction is made between the non-religious values supposedly being subjective and the religious values being objective – the distinction between subjective and objective applies to all kinds of values (with only the objectivity of theoretical truth being known).

Here is how Schilbrack describes the issue of uncertainty in the context of fallible realisations of the religious values:

> religious practices informed by metaphysical claims may presumably turn out to be ungrounded projections of human fantasy, out of touch with reality. In fact, all religious practices may be. I am not arguing that the metaphysical claims that religious communities make are true. In fact, I think that they often contradict each other and most of them – and perhaps even all of them – are false. … If religious accounts of the character of reality are false, it is because those accounts of the world get things wrong. It is not because they are not in touch with reality. (Schilbrack 2014, 170)

The future in religious practices is shaped as an openness towards that non-empirical reading of reality.

The way in which that non-empirical religious reading of reality can be seen as folded into a wide view of 'nature' is the subject of a book by Dutch philosopher Koo van der Wal. In *New Perspective on Reality: For another philosophy of nature* (van der Wal [2012] 2017), German title *Die Wirklichkeit aus neuer Sicht: Für eine andere Naturphilosophie*, van der Wal argues in favour of considering 'spirit' as a natural phenomenon. Based on his reading of scientific developments in the sciences of life, consciousness and ecology, he describes the possibility of moving towards a new philosophy of nature, a new perspective on reality, which leaves the classical mechanical view behind:

> It is … the image of a dynamic, creative, open and diverse nature that continually produces emergent new types of phenomena with new properties and behaviours. In this way it forms the great antithesis to the classical-modern ('Newtonian' or 'mechanised') worldview, according to which reality is monotonous, 'flat' and passive. Last but not least, this image of nature was so problematic because it had no place for humans ('gypsies at the edge of the universe'), as well as for all those 'immaterial' phenomena such as life, consciousness, sociality, culture, normativity and the whole sphere of products of science, art, spirituality – and, not to forget, philosophy itself. In this sense, the classical-modern perspective on reality was characterised by a radical decoupling of reality and ideality; it was in other words completely disenchanted. (van der Wal [2012] 2017, 321–2)

In addition, van der Wal observes that 'interestingly enough, the postclassical perspective on nature shows some convergence with the premodern perspective'. He adds that 'in that sense one can speak of a rehabilitation of aspects of the premodern vision of reality that had been eliminated from the modern image of nature' (van der Wal [2012] 2017, 321).

van der Wal labels his approach 'idealistic naturalism', to flag how ideal phenomena are embedded in nature and have evolved. For a proper philosophical analysis of the ideal dimension, van der Wal leans towards a transcendental approach:

> [I]nwardness, subjectivity, consciousness, self-confidence, meanings, they all belong to the 'fabric of reality' and show themselves in favourable circumstances. A philosophy of nature such as the one presented here thus creates room in a general sense for these spheres of reality, positions them, but then leaves the conceptions of inwardness to the arts, sciences and philosophies of the various realms, to bring to light the riches that can be found therein. (van der Wal [2012] 2017, 324)

For van der Wal, a philosophy such as that of Rickert[5] can definitely be used to analyse culture under the assumption of a separate ontological status of values, as long as one understands that the 'spheres of reality' those values pertain to are actualised in developments full of uncertainty and embedded within 'nature', taken again in its widest possible meaning.

For the question that I wish to address in this chapter – that is, how open or closed are the futures conceived in scientific and religious (and, to add to that, political and other cultural) practices, and how different worldviews, including different views of openness, may disregard each other – van der Wal offers a relevant insight on the difference between premodern and postclassical perspectives:

> The postclassical perspective on nature considers life with its inwardness, consciousness with its meaning dimension, and sociality, culture and morality, and products of art and science all as manifestations of a nature-based order. However, this order is not a simple fact – that is probably one of the great differences with the premodern perspective on reality. It is an order that is always in progress ('in the making') and is both actively accomplished from within (the theme of self-organisation) and contextual. In other words: we are always dealing with 'the same' nature, which is continually organising itself in a different way, thus manifesting

> itself in a multiplicity of different forms of being, which bring to light more and more new dispositions lying in that nature. (van der Wal [2012] 2017, 328–9)

Some contemporary non-modern worldviews hold a premodern perspective on reality; they can therefore be expected to disregard the modern and postclassical notion of the future bringing some kind of larger 'progress'. A proper postclassical philosophy, such as the transcendental naturalistic position developed in this book, critically reflects on modernity's notion of progress and keeps open a much wider set of possibilities for the future – but the modern worldview disregards ways of life that do not share its notion of progress. The consequences of this fundamental difference in the context of how modern planning in public policy deals with non-modern worldviews is discussed in the next section.

Modern planning and non-modern worldviews

In this section I illustrate the issues addressed in this chapter using two examples where modern and non-modern worldviews have clashed in modern planning and public policy (featuring three-way crossings between science, religion and politics). These two examples concern the following acute and intractable questions for public policy on climate change:

1. How should one evaluate the risk that ecosystems, species and indigenous ways of life are threatened by disregard in modern plans for large-scale carbon-dioxide removal, for instance in Bolivia?
2. How should one evaluate the risk that Buddhist ways to combat floods are threatened by disregard in modern large-scale delta plans, for instance in Thailand?

Both are examples that show how a present-day scientistic naturalism of the soft deterministic kind (cf. James) impacts the science–policy interface in modern planning in the context of climate change through disregarding non-modern worldviews. In Latour's terms, one can also say that both examples stand under the shadow of Gaia. The examples may seem specific and contained, but I would argue that they are indicative of the new situation that the Moderns find themselves in. If seriously taken to heart, they could induce uncertainty among Moderns 'about what they are, as well as about the epoch in which they live and the ground on which they stand' (Latour [2015] 2017, 219). 'Naturalists' (new style) take the real possibility of hostilities seriously; they are aware that they can deny existence of other beings (disregard), while their own existence can in the present situation of Gaia also be denied. Peace has to be invented 'through the establishment of a specific diplomacy' (Latour [2015] 2017, 238). The first glimpses of such (failed) diplomacy may be gleaned from these examples.

Let me start with the first example. A few years ago I witnessed a discussion between country representatives and climate scientists taking place within the IPCC (the Intergovernmental Panel on Climate Change, see also Chapter 7).[6] Bolivia requested the term 'Mother Earth' – whose rights have been legally guaranteed in Bolivia since 2010[7] – to appear in the Summary for Policymakers of the large IPCC report of 2014. The request did not succeed. As the chapters had already been written without any reference to this concept, and the scientists involved had difficulty in using 'Mother Earth' as a scientific term, the IPCC volume dealing with 'Impacts, Adaptation and Vulnerability' (about the consequences of and adaptation to climate change and the vulnerability of human and natural systems), after negotiations between delegates and authors, could only offer the following formulation in response to Bolivia's concerns:

> Indigenous, local, and traditional knowledge systems and practices, including indigenous peoples' holistic view of community and environment, are a major resource for adapting to climate change, but these have not been used consistently in existing adaptation efforts. (IPCC 2014, 26)

However, the term 'Mother Earth' returned with full force in the subsequent Plenary Session, on the IPCC volume dealing with 'Mitigation' (about reducing greenhouse gases). The scientists advising on climate change had assumed in their models that limiting global warming to two degrees above pre-industrial level would involve large-scale bioenergy with carbon capture and storage (CCS; combined 'BECCS'). Bolivia called in 'Mother Earth' to argue that this implied a new colonialist 'invasion' of developing countries with all the attendant risks, including moral and legal injustices, for ecosystems and the local population: BECCS is associated with the large-scale planting of crops, which can cause destruction of natural habitats and repression of food production. I was tasked, on behalf of the Netherlands, with solving this problem as co-chair of a contact group, together with Brazil. The solution was found in the more comprehensive and clear explanation in the summary of the risks and uncertainties surrounding the large-scale use of carbon-dioxide removal (of which BECCS is a form).

What becomes clear from this example is that the scientists involved in the IPCC found it incredibly difficult to do justice to what 'Mother Earth' stands for. A serious engagement with the indigenous communities and a holistic approach conversant with animism are what is called for. In a sense a 'religious' approach would be needed, which in Latour's analysis means being careful not to neglect issues that you or members of other collectives 'consider extremely important and that they need to care for constantly'; in such an approach a scientific adviser would 'learn to behave as a diplomat' (Latour [2015] 2017, 152). However, according to Latour, Science inherited from 'counter-religions' (that is, the Mosaic religions) a form of 'fundamentalism': they are risking not being able to execute diplomacy because 'no cult but its own' can 'be tolerated' (Latour [2015] 2017, 156). What needs to happen is that scientific advisers must learn to understand the origin of the rupture between their scientistic naturalistic image of 'Nature' and a transcendental naturalistic view of the world. In Latour's terms, one must try

> to pacify the relation of the people of Nature to the Earth and, incidentally, to offer scientists a version that does not oblige them to believe in the portrait the epistemologists have drawn of them. (Latour [2015] 2017, 167)

Now for the second example. A recent study I led (Hogendoorn et al. 2018) was concerned with differences in how Bangladesh, Myanmar, Vietnam and Thailand cope with their deltas. The study has shown that Bangladesh, Myanmar and Vietnam have internationally committed to creating a Dutch-style 'delta plan' (which is no coincidence, since Dutch diplomacy has led to an export of this 'product'), but Thailand has not. All these deltas are confronted with economic growth and climate change. The Dutch way of delta planning is often marketed as being of help in dealing with uncertainties (for instance, by Petersen and Bloemen 2015). Even then, however, such delta plans rely heavily on the use of scientific forecasts and model scenarios, so that policy (often for large-scale infrastructural projects) can be formulated for alternative economic growth paths and different speeds of climate change (in particular changes in precipitation patterns and rising sea levels).

Our study concluded that despite the spread of the delta-plan approach in neighbouring countries, Thailand is not following such an approach – a situation due, we tentatively argue, to a difference in worldview between (in particular) the Netherlands and Thailand. Delta plans fit better in a progressive Protestant culture than in a Buddhist one (ingrained in the national institutions in Thailand, which has no colonial past). The latter places greater value on inner experience and available resources and less importance on hypothetical visions of the future (along with attendant modern notions of 'progress'). In Thailand, the 'structural adjustment' policy of the World Bank had raised much resistance early on in the process of implementing this policy; the required liberalisation was seen not to fit with their own worldview.

In response, King Rama IX formulated an alternative development ideology called 'Sufficiency Economy'. This Sufficiency Economy is a mixture of Buddhism, development economics and water management. The first Royal Sufficiency Economy project took place in 1951. When Rama IX died in 2016, a total of 4,596 such projects had been developed.

What is important to realise in this second example is that Dutch delta planning has an element of utopianism, fed by Protestantism that followed 'prior politicization of the religious mind' (cf. Latour [2015] 2017, 199). What went wrong, in a sense, is that 'Modernization retain[ed] all the apocalyptic features but deprive[d] itself of the uncertainty that was required to keep science, politics, and religion from getting mixed together' (Latour [2015] 2017, 199). Specifically, in the Dutch context:

> Protestants ... believed fate was predestined. A select few would make Heaven in a distant future of resurrection. The Protestant could study to find clues in the world on their own fate, and clues were made probable for those who performed public deeds in line with reason. ... The Dutch governmental institutions in which the original delta plans were developed arose in formerly Protestant regions. ... The delta of the Rhine and Meuse and around the 'Zuiderzee' were also firmly Protestant. Not surprisingly, delta plans fit well with the Protestant [worldview]. Delta planning, we propose, favors the following order: seek clues for future possible states of the world (a gaze outward), then help select for actions expected to bring about a subset of publically desired states. (Hogendoorn et al. 2018, 382)

The Dutch scientistic naturalistic frame in trying to 'sell' delta planning to the Thai authorities did not allow for sufficient openness to elements from the Buddhist worldview that still influences Thai public administration.

In both examples we can witness a clash between a modern worldview (in both examples model-based) and a non-modern worldview (in the first example regarding knowledge based on indigenous ways of life included in a national law and in the second example regarding Buddhist notions included in national institutions), or between 'disenchanted' and 'enchanted' worldviews. As what we see in both examples are attempts at deriving action perspectives (having to grow energy crops and having to implement delta plans respectively) from a scientific way of thinking, these can be classified as two examples of (attempted) scientistic naturalism. The type of scientism involved here is a 'moral scientism' (deriving norms for action from a scientific worldview).

There are many possible choices here for the future, which is really open with options. We could reason from the models and perform cost–benefit analyses of the benefits and risks of large-scale carbon-dioxide removal (a disenchanted, modern worldview) or allow for more holistic approaches, such as those of 'Mother Earth' in Bolivia (an enchanted, non-modern worldview), to contribute seriously to the policy planning discourse on carbon dioxide removal. Similarly, we could reason from the models and plan how optimally to manage an entire delta (a disenchanted, modern worldview); or let more holistic notions, such as those of the Buddhist Sufficiency Economy in Thailand (an enchanted, non-modern worldview), play a role in planning discussions on water management.

Conclusion

In this chapter I have dealt with the question of how the future's openness can be conceived philosophically, in the context of Latour's *Facing Gaia*. After discussing James's early views on determinism versus indeterminism and his religious reading of a pluralistic universe that gives possibilities to co-create the world in partnership with God, I reviewed Rickert's arguments against scientistic naturalism. Subsequently I reviewed views on the future from different non-modern traditions, making use of Descola's work, then went on to discuss both Schilbrack's practice-oriented and van der Wal's nature-oriented approaches towards science-and-religion. I concluded with two recent examples of mutual disregard by, on the one hand, modern planning and science, and, on the other hand, by non-modern worldviews; these again were explored in context of the crossing of the practices of science and politics.

In terms of lessons for diplomacy, the confrontation of the moderns with non-moderns in the context of climate change provides an interesting angle on 'soft power': dealing with climate change requires nation-states for as long as they still play a central role to discover new ways of allowing other worldviews and actors to join the world stage. This will facilitate the tackling of problems that

> are intertwined in the most inextricable way, to the point where all these problems have become, as it were, *transversal*. (Latour [2015] 2017, 259)

Nation-states can gain in soft power if they do this well, if they successfully lead the way in bringing in new actors, new diplomats. This will become the new Realpolitik. Nation-states find themselves thus affected by other delegations who claim to be exercising their authority over (portions of) the same ground – they will modify the definition of what they value most of all. As Latour concludes:

> You enter into the negotiation with one idea of your interests; you come away with a different idea. ([2015] 2017, 270)

In emerging with what is in effect a form of regard, we can see how, in essence, 'the "brilliant art of diplomacy" is learned' (270).

This concludes Part II of this study. The next and final chapter will review the overall findings and implications of this book's argument.

Notes

1 I opened my inaugural address as Adjunct (or 'Special', *bijzonder*) Professor of Science and Environmental Public Policy at the VU University Amsterdam on 29 September 2011 with a similar claim: 'Prophecies are rarely fulfilled, although this does not deter the prophets and their followers. Throughout history, many cults have told us that the end of the world is nigh, and they look forward to the ensuing "ecstasy". In their view, the world is a bad place and must be put out of its misery. They believe that they will be spared, and in preparation they live their earthly lives in accordance with their particular interpretation of the Kingdom of God. Even when their latest prediction of the end of the world fails to materialize, they continue to insist that they are right and that they are indeed "the chosen ones". Prophets who unconditionally predict the end of the world are false prophets. A theologian might tell us that a true prophet is someone who tries to awaken mankind, to alert us to certain risks. A true prophecy is thus not the same as a prediction' (Petersen 2012, 19).

2 The lecture was originally published in the same year and was republished 13 years later as one of the essays in *The Will to Believe* (1897).

3 Descola describes 'interiority' as follows: 'The vague term "interiority" refers to a range of properties recognized by all human beings and partially covers what we generally call the mind, the soul, or consciousness: intentionality, subjectivity, reflexivity, feelings, and the ability to express oneself and to dream. It may also include immaterial principles that are assumed to cause things to be animate, such as breath and vital energy, and, at the same time, notions even more abstract, such as the idea that I share with others the same essence, the same principle of

action, or the same origin: all these ideas may be objectivized in a name or an epithet common to us all. In short, interiority consists in the universal belief that a being possesses characteristics that are internal to it or that take it as their source' (Descola [2005] 2013, 116). Descola claims that the distinction between interiority and physicality is universal across cultures. One piece of evidence that he mobilises for this claim is that 'all languages distinguish between a level of interiority and a level of physicality within a certain class of organisms, whatever may be the extension given to such a class and whatever the words used to convey the two' (Descola [2005] 2013, 119).

4 Precursors to such a kind of liberal religious thinking have also developed into a full-fledged religious naturalism, as captured by Willem Drees: 'One characteristic is the *openness* to research and the readiness to challenge authority focused on persons or ancient books; its concept of piety is not submissive. … Another feature is a positive *appreciation of this world*, not necessarily naive, sometimes even renouncing materialism *qua* lifestyle, but in contrast with investing hope in a different world to come. … A third, related feature is an *activist* attitude, as redemption is not expected to happen to us; improvement is to be brought about by human activity. … Furthermore, even though some religious naturalists build upon a particular religious tradition, there seems to be a *universalist* intention, in that the religious naturalist expects his approach to be open in principle to persons from all walks of life, of all cultures, and of all faiths. With this universalism, the religious naturalists are *moralists*, who are not just interested in understanding nature, but who seek to articulate humanist values in relation to their understanding of reality' (Drees 2006, 120–1).

5 Although van der Wal does not mention Rickert in his book, he is familiar with Rickert's work and acted as one of the advisers for Zijderveld's (2006) doctoral thesis on Rickert.

6 For a public report of this discussion (for which I myself, as a Dutch delegate, acted as the informant), see Paul Luttikhuis, 'Mother Earth does not exist', blog nrc.nl, 31 March 2014, www.nrc.nl/nieuws/2014/03/31/moeder-aarde-bestaat-niet (in Dutch).

7 While these laws providing for the rights of Mother Earth are still quite unique, they should not yet be interpreted as a success in terms of the (non-)regulation of extractive industries in Bolivia (Villavicencio Calzadilla and Kotzé 2018).

9

Conclusion: A transcendental naturalistic approach beyond Bruno Latour

In this final chapter I aim to bring together the different components of this book. I seek to do so by assessing what we have gained from developing a transcendental naturalistic approach in order to develop an appropriate philosophy in response to climate change, inspired by Latour's *Facing Gaia*, while tackling questions about (1) uncertainty and values, (2) humans and nature in the new climatic regime and (3) God or the Transcendent.

In this book I have assessed Latour's work through the lens of the philosophical framework of transcendental naturalism. As I have emphasised throughout the text, transcendental naturalism is based on combining an expansive concept of 'nature' with an emphasis on the separate ontological status of transcendental values (that also belong to the world 'on this side' – that is, nature), its metaphilosophical position being that philosophy should limit itself to theorising only about the world that is 'on this side' and not try to specify any other world 'beyond'. Even though in Chapter 4 I characterised Latour's *Inquiry*, from the standpoint of transcendental naturalism, as being unreflexive of the transcendental role of values and their realisation in practices, I think that Latour's entire oeuvre deserves to be read as a philosophy of value (thus, as I recommend, stripping off its metaphysical load).[1] I also believe that it holds some important lessons in store for science, religion and politics, in the context of climate change.

This chapter aims to show what the heightened attention to uncertainty shown by the transcendental naturalism proposed in this book can bring to philosophy under climate change, to thinking with and beyond Latour and, more generally, to the science-and-religion debate on theistic, atheistic and agnostic forms of naturalism. In conclusion, I give a final assessment of the book's argument.

Uncertainty and values

Uncertainty is an epistemological notion that relates to a 'lack of knowledge' residing in the concepts that we have (negative qualification) even as it underpins human creativity (positive qualification). In this book I have argued that there is a fundamental plurality in how concepts capture underlying experiences, and that collective sharing of wonder pertaining to uncertainty proceeds via concepts that feature a fundamental openness to how practices are conceptually extended (Chapters 2 and 7). In addition, experience itself remains fundamentally open; there is consequently open theoretical space for real, factual novelty happening in the world (Chapters 2 and 8). No certainty can be reached about the values that underpin actual cultural practices; nevertheless their validity stems from the *a priori*, the unreal sphere of values (Chapters 4 and 7). There always remains a gap between models and reality; their reliability is thus established tentatively in practices that are open, depending on the values that govern the types of practices in which the models are used (Chapters 5 and 7).

In *Facing Gaia* Latour characterises the new climatic regime as 'a profound mutation in our relation to the world' (Latour [2015] 2017, 8). Something new and unexpected has happened: the new climatic regime arose. Latour thanks the climate sceptics (discussed from his perspective in Chapters 5 and 7) for allowing him to make his point on the instability of nature – and with him the discipline of science studies as a whole:

> without the immense undermining work undertaken by the climate skeptics against the sciences of the Earth System, we would never have grasped the extent to which the invocation of the 'natural world' had ceased to be stable. Thanks to this false quarrel, an argument that had remained the discovery of a small number of historians of science is now becoming visible in broad daylight. (Latour [2015] 2017, 24)

He observes that 'sceptics' have been successful in:

> convincing a large part of the public that climate science remains completely uncertain, and that climatologists are just one lobby among others, the Intergovernmental Panel on Climate Change (IPCC) is just an attempt on the part of mad scientists to dominate the planet, the chemistry of the upper atmosphere is just a plot 'against the American way of life', and ecology is just an attack on

> humanity's inviolable right to modernize itself. (Latour [2015] 2017, 26)

However, they have not been able to manage 'to shake the consensus of the experts, a consensus whose validity has become more solid every year' (Latour [2015] 2017, 26). As I showed in Chapter 7, there is definitely significant remaining uncertainty concerning the causes and – I should add particularly – the consequences of climate change. However, especially the expert judgement on the likelihood of humans causing most of the observed warming, the strength of the underpinning evidence and the consensus about all this within the relevant scientific communities combine to confirm Latour's claim about 'consensus'. Still, one should not conflate this near-universal consensus with 100 per cent certainty (which Latour does not, but many activists do).

With respect to uncertainty in climate science and politics, Latour observes that climate scientists have said too often in public settings that they are sticking with the 'facts' only. This has led to a policy outcome that they had not expected, since they were hoping for 'automatic' authority in the policy domain on the basis of their expertise in climate science. Latour remarks:

> This is why for some twenty years now we have been watching the astonishing spectacle of a pitched battle between one party that has perfectly grasped the normative function that invocations of the natural world perform – and for this reason denies the existence of that world – and another party that does not dare unleash the prescriptive force of the facts it has discovered and must limit itself, as if it had its hands tied behind its back, to speaking only of 'science'. ... In a superb reversal of the situation, the earth science experts are the ones today who look like over-excited militants of a cause; fanatics, catastrophists, and climate skeptics are the ones assuming the role of stern scientists who at least do not confuse the way the world is going with the way it ought to go! They have even succeeded in appropriating – while reversing its meaning – the fine word 'skeptic'. (Latour [2015] 2017, 28)

Is the alternative that Latour sketches – that is, for scientists to become activists and declare that they 'are on the warpath!' (Latour [2015] 2017, 30), a move that was featured in Chapter 2 – really a solution? Latour acknowledges that scientists do not in fact follow a warpath, but he concludes that all of us will have to choose sides politically on climate change. Is a solution then to implement a 'Parliament of Things'?[2] Here is a relevant capturing of what such a Parliament of Things could do, stated in the form of Latour's advice to an imaginary climate scientist:

> Why aren't you proud of having invented this extraordinary equipment that allows you to give voice to mute things as if they were in a position to speak? If your adversaries tell you that you are engaged in politics by taking yourselves as representatives of numerous neglected voices, for heaven's sake answer 'Yes, of course!' If politics consists in representing the voices of the oppressed and the unknown, then we would all be in a much better situation, instead of pretending that the others are the ones engaged in politics and that you are engaged 'only in science', you recognized that you were also in fact trying to assemble another political body and to live in a coherent cosmos composed in a different way. If it is entirely correct that you are not speaking in the name of an institution limited by the borders of nation-states and that the basis for your authority rests on a very strange system of election and proofs, this is precisely what makes your *political power to represent* so many new agents so important. That power of representation will be of capital importance in the coming conflicts over the form of the world and the new geopolitics. Don't sell it for a mess of pottage. (Latour [2015] 2017, 32–3)

The important thing to note here is that Latour is not asking the climate scientists to become politicians instead of scientists. He is rather requesting that they should work out how best to do diplomacy at the crossing between science and politics. In Chapters 7 and 8 I discussed the challenges of such diplomacy in the context of scientistic expert judgement pitted against governments and non-modern worldviews respectively.

On a more philosophical note in *Facing Gaia*, after alluding to his 'modes of existence' work, Latour warns against armchair philosophy and proposes to do what he did in his earlier anthropology of the Moderns: 'to remain open to the dizzying otherness of existents' (Latour [2015] 2017, 36); I cited the full passage in Chapter 2. Latour ultimately aligns his philosophy with that of William James and advocates a very open approach towards determining what actually are the different values that give meaning to different cultural domains (though he does not often use the term 'culture' in its widest meaning). The transcendental naturalism that I have laid out in this book is consistent with taking an empirical approach to inform the philosophical reflection on what are the values guiding different cultural practices: armchair philosophy does not provide the required richness of material that must be considered to understand a particular practice as one that can be distinguished and valued as such.

By not denying the existence of the sphere of the *a priori* (an unreal versus real part of the world) – which in this book has not been taken as synonymous to 'logical' or 'certain' (as Kant has often been seen to have done), but rather as denoting that which is independent of sense experience – I argue that empirical philosophy such as that of Latour can be enriched through reflexively incorporating a non-metaphysical transcendental procedure. This in turn allows for more fundamental philosophical reflection on uncertainty, making one more aware of where philosophy proper becomes metaphysics. Transcendental naturalism is also reflexively open to the a-theoretical – which is, in the end, more important for finding meaning in life than the theoretical. Latour's metaphysics should thus be recognised for what it is: an occasionalist empiricism that can be taken (or rejected) on faith. Let me add here that it has become clear in my investigation that Latour's emphasis on activity (versus contemplation) caused him to leave out a mode of 'mystics' from his scheme of values, which I think is a serious omission.

Humans and nature in the new climatic regime

With Latour, I have taken humans, and the values that drive their cultures, to be part of nature.[3] The relationship between humans and the rest of nature is necessarily conceptualised in ways that involve uncertainty, with the new climatic regime fundamentally altering that relationship. In this book I have argued that the emotion of wonder about human nature, non-human nature and nature as a whole can receive poetic expression (Chapters 2 and 6). The cultural products in different value domains remain uncertain; in moving towards the future, such products are continually tested for their robustness (Chapters 3 and 8). Since values can be realised in practice only in fallible ways, poetry that expresses the value of nature can be regarded as a means for fallible expressions of a-theoretical truths (Chapters 4 and 6). Models for the relationship between humans and the rest of nature that solely rely on science and do not connect with peoples' individual experiences will find difficulty in providing meaning and motivating action (Chapters 5 and 6).

Latour states that 'nature' and 'culture' should not be seen as two separate 'domains'; they are rather 'one and the same *concept* divided into two parts' (Latour [2015] 2017, 15). In this book I have instead argued for using 'nature' in the sense of 'world' or Latour's 'nature two' (see Chapter 6) – which then avoided this division of nature/culture and underpinned my plea for a 'naturalism' that is not scientistic. I have argued that in addition to a culture's real part (a fallible realisation of values in the world) it has an unreal part (its values, both subjective and objective), giving rise to the term '*transcendental* naturalism'.

Arguing against scientistic naturalism, Latour identifies a polemical dimension in the invocation of nature to define a moral law, to 'recall to order';[4] he understands why 'critics' feel obliged to 'spring into action' whenever they see '"naturalizing" a simple set of facts into a legal imperative' going on (Latour [2015] 2017, 24). In the context of climate change Latour emphasises that the circumstances have now fundamentally changed: humans are changing nature (the climate) and the changing climate is deeply impacting humans. I argue that this is a form of 'naturalisation', but in the sense of taking (natural) science seriously and not allowing supernatural causes into one's philosophy. I have also defended 'critics' who adhere to transcendental naturalism and use transcendental philosophy as a methodological basis for the science–religion discussion, both in the context of climate change and more widely.

Transcendental naturalism does not rely on a distinction between humans and the rest of nature in its transcendental procedure. Values, and thus 'culture', are seen as part of nature – being understood as 'the world as a whole' (on this side). I argue that the transcendental procedure contributes to philosophy a means to detect where metaphysical proposals are made in the interpretation of 'nature', as, for instance, in 'religious naturalism' (now taken in its non-scientistic form, thus different from the 'religion of nature' identified by Latour). This gives one the possibility of reflecting critically on the possibilities and uncertainties associated with a form of climate action that builds on poetic inspiration, expert authority and futures methods in policy-making. I will now turn to reflections on God or the Transcendent and on the religious outlooks of naturalism, from the perspective of transcendental naturalism.

God or the Transcendent

God or the Transcendent is a topic that goes beyond philosophy proper (that is, according to the metaphilosophy of transcendental naturalism). In this book I have argued that poetry (including poetry in science) can enchant the world and judgements can be arrived at that correspond to a fullness of thought to which no linguistic expression on its own is fully adequate; this in turn can lead to intimations of God or the Transcendent (Chapters 3 and 6). The power of reflective judgement has the ability to open up particular aspects of the world that cannot be fully captured in theories, with part of judgement residing in the aesthetic (Chapters 3 and 7). There is deep uncertainty about, and openness towards, the future; however, the metaphysical question about the wider influence of our free will in the totality of being cannot be answered within philosophy (Chapters 4 and 8). It is an unanswerable question whether in future there will be a 'consonance' or 'colligation' between the respective series of models in science and in religion (Chapters 5 and 7).

In *Facing Gaia* Latour addresses the issue of (counter-)religion,[5] after having made clear that his reference to 'Gaia' is to a secular figure for nature:

> The paradox is rather amusing: Gaia is accused of being 'a religion taken for a science', when it is the emergence of Gaia, on the contrary, that obliges us to redistribute the features of the preceding epoch, including the strange idea that construed the Nature known to Science as something that had to *oppose* Religion (I am keeping the capital letters here not as a sign of solemnity but as a reminder that we are dealing with figures of speech, not with domains of the world). If we were to try to separate Science and Religion today, from the vantage point of the Anthropocene, it would be a real massacre, given how much Science there is in Religion and how much Religion there is in Science. By trying to separate them, such as they are, before rethinking them both, we would lose any chance of bringing them both back to Earth, *separately at last*. (Latour [2015] 2017, 150)

Subsequently Latour compares scientistic naturalists ('People of Nature') with non-naturalistic theists of a dogmatic type ('People of Creation'). He concludes that in many respects they differ very little except on the question of animation, where the scientistic naturalists take nature as deanimated and the dogmatic theists take nature as overanimated (because of their supernatural assumptions).

Latour sketches a contrasting image of religion that he considers more appropriate:

One may call it 'God', but it is also the *end* of all the gods and divinities, and even in a sense *the end of God*, in the well-known sense of the death of God. … In this sense, the counter-religion is indeed 'counter' – against – itself, engaged in a continual struggle over the figure that it is to give its supreme authority. When one begins with iconoclasm, one never ends. In any case, the reassuring figure of an ordering God who protected the earlier people makes no sense, since order precisely does not pre-exist in relation to its own history. No Providence precedes it – not any more than a world made of deanimated matter, indisputable, universal, and external laws would make sense.

But the counter-religion has no use, either, for an overanimated matter that would shift attention toward another world while imposing neglect of the radical alterity that it is a question, on the contrary, of sensing. … Unlike the other two, this counter-religion is profoundly embodied, since it constantly renews its participation in a present world, definitively judged, achieved, saved, celebrated, and situated, but from which it is not a matter of extracting oneself for another world, since everything goes on as before. No world detached from the ground, no ultra-world, and thus no lower world either.

It is especially in the conception of time that the originality of this other counter-religion stands out: there is indeed the feeling of a radical break, but with the crucial nuance that the break must constantly be *taken up again*. One cannot escape from this fundamental instability, from this indecision: 'The end time has come', yes, but it goes on. And this prolongation gives decision the same lacunary, incomplete, fragile, mortal character it had before the end time came. This contradiction must not be overcome. (Latour [2015] 2017, 176)

We can here see how Latour's empirical philosophy approach can help us to register different types of values, in this case the value of (Christian) religion. In Chapter 4 I showed how Latour's approach to religion constitutes one pole (the activity-oriented one) of Rickert's approach to religion, which also includes another (contemplation-oriented) pole, that of mystics.

Thus transcendental naturalism, I argue, keeps an even more open view on religion than Latour – although I take it that Latour would in principle agree that his tentative empirical philosophy could be extended to encompass other types of religion than those featured in activity-oriented Christianity, such as a mode of 'mystics' that can be found in, for instance, Buddhism (but also Christianity), provided that the necessary empirical work is done to substantiate that as a separate mode of existence. In Chapter 8 I discussed some possible ingredients for such a mode of mystics using Richard Jones's *Philosophy of Mysticism*.

What the transcendental procedure adds is a reflection on deep uncertainty associated with the power of reflective judgement and its ability to open up a-theoretical aspects of the world. Transcendental naturalism makes one realise reflexively that God or the Transcendent will go beyond philosophy proper. Still, despite emphasising that religious values are deeply uncertain and will remain out of reach for theoretical underpinning, transcendental naturalism does make one aware of the overwhelming importance of religious values, which also influence social values relevant for addressing climate change.[6]

Transcendental naturalism and the religious outlooks of naturalism

Now to which religious position *vis-à-vis* naturalism does the transcendental naturalism laid out in this book bring us? In brief, my answer is to any and none, meaning that either theistic, atheistic or agnostic positions can be adopted, but none can be demonstrated philosophically. Let me illustrate this with reference to works related by Willem Drees (2006; 2010), Karl Peters (2002) and Michael Ruse (2019). Willem Drees (2006) argues against interpreting 'naturalism' as only including existing atheistic forms. He offers 'agnostic naturalism' as an 'epistemically more appropriate' version of naturalism (Drees 2006, 117), and he also adds the option of theistic naturalism. In a later publication Drees writes:

> Any science-inspired naturalism has an open end which allows for a theistic, a religious naturalistic or an agnostic view. (Drees 2010, 10)

In Chapter 1 I gave the examples of work by Donald Crosby and Ursula Goodenough as belonging to 'religious naturalism'. Karl Peters offers an example of theistic naturalism (or 'naturalistic theism' as he calls it) and Michael Ruse offers an example of agnostic naturalism.

In 2002 Karl Peters published his book *Dancing with the Sacred: Evolution, ecology, and God*, which expounds a 'naturalistic theism'.

Peters's approach aims 'not so much [at] a shift in religious thinking as in philosophical thinking regarding the general categories we use to conceptualize all existence'. He labels the model of God that he develops as 'process thought' but then based on *non*-personal metaphors and models, in contrast to the personal metaphors and models typically used in process theology (Peters 2002, vii).[7] Peters explains his approach as follows:

> As a naturalistic theist I do not deny that God is more than the world, but I do want to focus continually on how we can know and be related to God in our natural world. This to me is crucial for religious living. (Peters 2002, vii)

Now this approach can also be interpreted in a transcendental naturalistic vein: a metaphysical assumption can be made that God exists not as a 'thing' outside of the world, but rather as a being omnipresent to all things in nature; God can thus be experienced in nature as when we judge and transcendentally assume *a priori* values, but with an awareness that God is radically other than nature. Such an assumption can be understood as providing a religious outlook on the emergence of new possibilities in nature, including in human life. It should be clear, however, that the specific metaphysical assumption made by Peters, who bases his model of God on science, cannot be demonstrated. Being able to make the latter observation without destroying the possibility for this version of a naturalist's religious outlook is one of the benefits of the transcendental naturalistic position.

Michael Ruse, in his book *A Meaning to Life* (2019), shares the emphasis given in this book on uncertainty. With respect to religion, when comparing the different religions of Christianity and Buddhism, he argues:

> Buddhism is like Christianity in having at its core a sense of being that transcends human understanding and description. ... Different religions do at their cores speak of the ineffable – truly good if not truly understood. [But there is a] difference ... between Christianity and Buddhism. Christianity is God-centered, and Buddhism is soul-centered, whatever that might mean precisely. Their ineffables seem not to be of the same thing, although I suppose one could say that is precisely what happens with ineffables. Who is to say that they are not the same in some fundamental sense? (Ruse 2019, 92)

Ruse observes that some who find that regular religions do make unwarranted supernatural assumptions that go against a scientific worldview, such as E. O. Wilson (and others, who propose an 'epic of evolution' or 'new cosmology', as discussed in Chapter 6), have made Darwinism into their religion (with the assumption that values of progress can be derived from Darwinism). However, as Ruse concludes, Darwinism interpreted correctly leads to different conclusions pertaining to religion:

> Regular religion cannot do the job [of credibly providing meaning], so make up a naturalistic religion of your own. Neither approach takes the Darwinian Revolution quite as seriously as it should. ... Darwinian thinking takes meaning out of the world. (Ruse 2019, 131)

Ruse pleads for a 'Darwinian existentialism':

> There you have my formula for the meaningful life in the Darwinian world – family, friends and others, works of the creative imagination – and I mean science here as much as the arts. (Ruse 2019, 161)

On the theism–atheism spectrum, Ruse puts himself in the middle as an 'agnostic':

> In the end ... I am an agnostic. I just don't know whether life has any – time for those capitals – Ultimate Meaning. (Ruse 2019, 169)

I argue that transcendental naturalistic philosophy theorises the cultural values that Ruse identifies as providing meaning to life and is compatible with Ruse's agnostic version of naturalism.

Final assessment of the transcendental naturalistic approach

This brings me finally to rehearsing the extent to which this book has reached its overall aim, as was posed in Chapter 1:

> to formulate – in the context of dealing with climate change – a transcendental naturalistic philosophy of culture that enables adequate reflection on uncertainty in science and religion.

The seven main chapters of this book have provided in-depth answers to the questions formulated in Chapter 1 on how wonder, judgement, values, models, poetics, authorities and futures are respectively related to uncertainty, in particular in the practices of science and religion. To summarise, my transcendental naturalistic position has been developed in the following seven steps (the first four of which have set out the framework and the last three of which have added corollaries relevant to politics in the context of climate change – all developed in discussion with Latour and going beyond him):

1. The emotion of wonder facilitates a positive reading of uncertainty and intimations of metaphysical transcendence.
2. Humans retain aesthetically felt freedom in arriving at judgement; uncertainty is attached to determining the *a priori* contribution to judgement.
3. Values are part of nature and are assumed in judgements; uncertainty arises in various cultural practices when value-laden judgements are made under freedom and in context.
4. Models should not be interpreted realistically other than in a weak form of referential realism: experience features percepts that are referred to by concepts, but uncertainty remains attached to the concepts.
5. Poetics are available to read meaning, including religious meaning, in the world via judgement under uncertainty.
6. A plurality of cognitive authorities should be recognised in any practice, including that of science, so that arriving at expert judgement under uncertainty is acknowledged to be a value-laden exercise.
7. Futures must be kept really open in politics under uncertainty by breaking through the mutual disregard by, on the one hand, modern planning and science, and, on the other hand, non-modern worldviews.

The cross-cutting results from this study, and how they relate to philosophy under climate change, have been brought together in the sections above. The book's overall argument is effectively embedded in the combination of the seven chapters, as highlighted in this concluding chapter, and the seven points listed above.

The transcendental naturalistic philosophy of culture that has been developed in this book makes a methodological contribution to the field of science and religion. It enables societally relevant reflection on 'crossings' between the practices of science, religion and politics in the context of climate change. It also provides a corrective against scientistic and many other formulations of naturalism and offers an openness towards a variety of religious options, including theistic, agnostic and atheistic forms of naturalism. Transcendental naturalism also allows for a philosophical understanding of possible 'solutions' to some of modernity's problems rendered acute by climate change – for instance the religious disenchantment of nature, the scientific disbelief in a plurality of value-laden perspectives and the disregard for non-modern worldviews in politics. Last but not least, it offers philosophical insight into the works of Bruno Latour that pertain to these topics and are shown to be very relevant.

Further research is warranted into both transcendental naturalism itself (for example, by exploring further the positionings of Latour, James and Rickert *vis-à-vis* various naturalisms) and the linkages with other philosophers and/or philosophical schools, particularly in modern European thought. As is recognised by William Desmond, in early modernity both rationalism and empiricism (between which transcendental naturalism is trying to find a middle ground) 'contributed to the voiding of being and the undoing of metaphysics', with rationalism's focus on scientific and mathematical exactitudes and empiricism's focus on 'aesthetic univocity' (Desmond 2013, 549). The challenge remains to keep ontology open towards metaphysics in a way that appropriately relates to a pluriverse of meaning, without giving up the tools of *Wissenschaft* in the light of uncertainty.

Notes

1 Note that I am not claiming that his metaphysics is wrong; in fact, demonstrating whether it is true or false is impossible philosophically.

2 This term has been used in Latour ([1991] 1993), but not in his recent work, which speaks more of 'diplomacy'.

3 'Nature' is here understood in the sense of Latour's 'nature two' or 'world' (discussed in Chapters 6 and 8).

4 Latour explains this further: 'to *order* (in the sense of ordering the world) is to *order* (in the sense of giving orders)' (Latour [2015] 2017, 34).

5 As I indicated in Chapter 6, Latour uses the word 'counter-religion' to refer to monotheism, leaving the word 'religion' for traditional religion.

6 Christopher Ives and Jeremy Kidwell argue that 'religion is [a] key process that can enable the emergence and dissemination of values across multiple social scales' (Ives and Kidwell 2019, 1360). However, they warn against instrumentalisation of religion and plead for the cultural sciences (my term) to study empirically why certain social values emerge in different contexts – given that, as anthropologists show, 'individual communities birth and express values in unique

ways, precluding meaningful conclusions about value universality' (Ives and Kidwell 2019, 1355) and 'the mediating effect of political ideology and economic status is a far stronger predictor than religiosity *per se*, and this varies enormously across cultures' (Ives and Kidwell 2019, 1357).

7 Without here assessing the merits of process thought, a first observation that I would make from a transcendental naturalistic perspective is that one can be a naturalist while also using personal models of God.

References

Allen, Paul L. 2006. *Ernan McMullin and Critical Realism in the Science–Theology Dialogue*. Aldershot, UK: Ashgate.

Baldwin, Jennifer, ed. 2018. *Navigating Post-Truth and Alternative Facts: Religion and science as political theology*. Lanham, MD: Lexington Books.

Barbalet, Jack. 2004. 'Consciousness, emotions, and science'. In *Theory and Research on Human Emotions – Advances in Group Processes*, vol. 21, edited by Jonathan H. Turner, 245–72. Bingley, UK: Emerald.

Barbour, Ian G. 1974. *Myths, Models and Paradigms: The nature of scientific and religious language*. London: SCM Press.

Barnes, L. Philip. 2013. 'Values and the phenomenology of religion'. In *The Routledge International Handbook of Education, Religion and Values*, edited by James Arthur and Terence Lovat, 16–27. London: Routledge.

Barth, Karl. [1947] 2001. 'Kant'. In *Protestant Theology in the Nineteenth Century* [Original title: *Die protestantische Theologie im 19. Jahrhundert: Ihre Geschichte und ihre Vorgeschichte*], 252–98. London: SCM Press.

Burhoe, Ralph W. and Robert B. Tapp. 1966a. 'Editorial', *Zygon: Journal of Religion and Science* 1 (1): 1–10.

Burhoe, Ralph W. and Robert B. Tapp. 1966b. 'Theological resources from the science: Editorial', *Zygon: Journal of Religion and Science* 1 (1): 11–13.

Campbell, Norman Robert. [1920] 1957. *Foundations of Science: The philosophy of theory and experiment*. [Original title: *Physics: The elements*.] New York: Dover Publications.

Carr, David. 2013. 'Religious meaning, practical reason and values'. In *The Routledge International Handbook of Education, Religion and Values*, edited by James Arthur and Terence Lovat, 5–15. London: Routledge.

Carrette, Jeremy. 2008. 'William James'. In *The Oxford Handbook of Religion and Emotion*, edited by John Corrigan, 419–37. New York: Oxford University Press.

Carrette, Jeremy. 2013. *William James's Hidden Religious Imagination: A universe of relations*. New York: Routledge.

Cartwright, Nancy. 1983. *How the Laws of Physics Lie*. Oxford: Clarendon Press.

Chandrasekhar, S. 1987. *Truth and Beauty: Aesthetics and motivations in science*. Chicago: University of Chicago Press.

Clayton, Philip, ed. 2006. *The Oxford Handbook of Religion and Science*. Oxford: Oxford University Press.

Copernicus, Nicholas. [1543] 1978. *On the Revolutions*. Baltimore, MD: Johns Hopkins University Press.

Crosby, Donald A. 2002. *A Religion of Nature*. Albany, NY: State University of New York Press.

Crosby, Donald A. 2015. *Nature as Sacred Ground: A metaphysics for religious naturalism*. Albany, NY: State University of New York Press.

Crowe, Benjamin. 2010. 'Faith and value: Heinrich Rickert's theory of religion', *Journal of the History of Ideas* 71 (4): 617–36.

Daston, Lorraine and Katherine Park. 2001. *Wonders and the Order of Nature, 1150–1750*. New York: Zone Books.

De Pryck, Kari and Mike Hulme, eds. 2023. *A Critical Assessment of the Intergovernmental Panel on Climate Change*. Cambridge: Cambridge University Press.

de Regt, Henk W. 2015. 'Scientific understanding: Truth or dare?', *Synthese* 192 (12): 3781–97.

de Regt, Henk W. 2017. *Understanding Scientific Understanding*. New York: Oxford University Press.

de Regt, Henk W., Sabina Leonelli and Kai Eigner, eds. 2009. *Scientific Understanding: Philosophical perspectives*. Pittsburgh: University of Pittsburgh Press.

de Vries, Gerard. 2016. *Bruno Latour*. Cambridge: Polity Press.

Deane-Drummond, Celia. 2006. *Wonder and Wisdom: Conversations in science, spirituality and theology*. London: Darton, Longman and Todd.
Descola, Philippe. [2005] 2013. *Beyond Nature and Culture*. Chicago: University of Chicago Press.
Desmond, William. 2013. 'The metaphysics of modernity'. In *The Oxford Handbook of Theology and Modern European Thought*, edited by Nicholas Adams, George Pattison and Graham Ward, 543–63. Oxford: Oxford University Press.
deVries, Willem. [2011] 2016. 'Wilfrid Sellars'. In *The Stanford Encyclopedia of Philosophy*, edited by Edward N. Zalta. Stanford, CA: Stanford University. https://plato.stanford.edu/archives/win2016/entries/sellars.
Dewey, John. [1927] 2012. *The Public and Its Problems: An essay in political inquiry*. University Park, PA: Pennsylvania State University Press.
Drees, Willem B. 2002. *Creation: From nothing until now*. London: Routledge.
Drees, Willem B. 2006. 'Religious naturalism and science'. In *The Oxford Handbook of Religion and Science*, edited by Philip Clayton, 108–23. Oxford: Oxford University Press.
Drees, Willem B. 2010. *Religion and Science in Context: A guide to the debates*. London: Routledge.
Duhem, Pierre. [1892] 1996a. 'Some reflections on the subject of physical theories'. [Original title: 'Quelques réflexions au sujet des théories physiques'.] In *Essays in the History and Philosophy of Science*, 1–28. Indianapolis, IN: Hackett Publishing Company.
Duhem, Pierre. [1903] 1996b. 'Analysis of Mach's *The Science of Mechanics: A critical and historical account of its development*'. [Original title: 'Analyse de l'ouvrage de Ernst Mach, *La mécanique. Etude historique et critique de son développement*'.] In *Essays in the History and Philosophy of Science*, 112–30. Indianapolis, IN: Hackett Publishing Company.
Duhem, Pierre. [1906, 1914^2] 1954. *The Aim and Structure of Physical Theories*. [Original title: *La théorie physique: Son objet, sa structure*.] Princeton, NJ: Princeton University Press.
Ellis, Fiona. 2014. *God, Value, and Nature*. Oxford: Oxford University Press.
Flanagan, Owen. 2006. 'Varieties of naturalism'. In *The Oxford Handbook of Religion and Science*, edited by Philip Clayton, 430–52. Oxford: Oxford University Press.
Friedman, Michael. 1992. 'Causal laws and the foundations of natural science'. In *The Cambridge Companion to Kant*, edited by Paul Guyer, 161–99. Cambridge: Cambridge University Press.
Funtowicz, Silvio O. and Jerome R. Ravetz. 1990. *Uncertainty and Quality in Science for Policy*. Dordrecht: Kluwer Academic.
Funtowicz, Silvio O. and Jerome R. Ravetz. 1993. 'Science for the post-normal age', *Futures* 25 (7): 739–55.
Gale, Richard M. 1999. *The Divided Self of William James*. New York: Cambridge University Press.
Giere, Ronald N. 1988. *Explaining Science: A cognitive approach*. Chicago: University of Chicago Press.
Goodall, Jane. 2003. 'Education for effective stewardship'. In *Sharing the Planet: Population – consumption – species. Science and ethics for a sustainable and equitable world*, edited by Bob van der Zwaan and Arthur Petersen, 228–33. Delft: Eburon Academic Publishers.
Goodenough, Ursula. 2000. 'Religiopoiesis', *Zygon: Journal of Religion and Science* 35 (3): 561–66.
Goodenough, Ursula. [1998] 2023. *The Sacred Depths of Nature: How life has emerged and evolved*. 2nd edn. New York: Oxford University Press.
Gould, Stephen Jay. [1990] 2000. *Wonderful Life: The Burgess Shale and the nature of history*. London: Vintage.
Hacking, Ian. 1992. 'The self-vindication of the laboratory sciences'. In *Science as Practice and Culture*, edited by Andrew Pickering, 29–64. Chicago: University of Chicago Press.
Hajer, Maarten A. 1995. *The Politics of Environmental Discourse: Ecological modernization and the policy process*. Oxford: Oxford University Press.
Hallyn, Fernand. [1987] 1990. *The Poetic Structure of the World: Copernicus and Kepler*. New York: Zone Books.
Haralambous, Bronwen and Thomas W. Nielsen. 2014. 'Wonder as a gateway experience'. In *Wonder-full Education: The centrality of wonder in teaching and learning across the curriculum*, edited by Kieran Egan, Annabella Cant and Gillian Judson, 219–38. London: Routledge.
Harman, Graham. 2016. 'A new occasionalism?' In *Reset Modernity!*, edited by Bruno Latour, 129–38. Cambridge, MA: MIT Press.
Harrington, Donald Szantho. 1966. 'Science and the search for a rational religious faith', *Zygon: Journal of Religion and Science* 1 (1): 97–107.

Harrison, Peter, ed. 2010. *The Cambridge Companion to Science and Religion*. Cambridge: Cambridge University Press.
Harrison, Peter. 2015. *The Territories of Science and Religion*. Chicago: University of Chicago Press.
Hayward, John F. 1966. 'Commentary on theological resources from the physical sciences', *Zygon: Journal of Religion and Science* 1 (1): 31–2.
Hedlund-de Witt, Annick. 2013. 'Worldviews and their significance for the global sustainable development debate', *Environmental Ethics* 35 (2): 133–62.
Hefner, Philip. 1984. 'The Creation'. In *Christian Dogmatics*, vol. 1, edited by Carl E. Braaten and Robert W. Jenson, 323–8. Philadelphia: Fortress.
Hefner, Philip. 1988. 'Theology's truth and scientific formulation', *Zygon: Journal of Science and Religion* 23 (3): 263–79.
Heisenberg, Elisabeth. 1984. *Inner Exile: Recollections of a life with Werner Heisenberg*. Boston: Birkhäuser.
Heisenberg, Werner. 1971. *Physics and Beyond: Encounters and conversations*. New York: Harper & Row.
Hesse, Mary B. 1963. *Models and Analogies in Science*. London: Sheed and Ward.
Hesse, Mary B. 1974. 'In defence of objectivity'. In *1972 – Proceedings of the British Academy*, vol. 58, 275–92. London: British Academy.
Hogendoorn, Daniel, Arjen Zegwaard and Arthur C. Petersen. 2018. 'Difficult travels: Delta plans do not land in the Chao Phraya delta', *Environmental Science and Policy* 89: 378–84.
IPCC. 2001. *Climate Change 2001: The Scientific Basis. Contribution of Working Group I to the Third Assessment Report of the Intergovernmental Panel on Climate Change*. Cambridge: Cambridge University Press.
IPCC. 2014. *Climate Change 2014: Impacts, Adaptation, and Vulnerability. Part A: Global and Sectoral Aspects. Contribution of Working Group II to the Fifth Assessment Report of the Intergovernmental Panel on Climate Change*. Cambridge: Cambridge University Press.
Ives, Christopher and Jeremy Kidwell. 2019. 'Religion and social values for sustainability'. *Sustainability Science* 14 (5): 1355–62.
James, William. [1890] 1981. *The Principles of Psychology*. The Works of William James. Cambridge, MA: Harvard University Press.
James, William. [1897] 1979. *The Will to Believe, and Other Essays in Popular Philosophy*. The Works of William James. Cambridge, MA: Harvard University Press.
James, William. [1902] 1985. *The Varieties of Religious Experience: A study in human nature*. The Works of William James. Cambridge, MA: Harvard University Press.
James, William. [1907] 1975. *Pragmatism*. The Works of William James. Cambridge, MA: Harvard University Press.
James, William. [1909a] 1977. *A Pluralistic Universe*. The Works of William James. Cambridge, MA: Harvard University Press.
James, William. [1909b] 1975. *The Meaning of Truth*. The Works of William James. Cambridge, MA: Harvard University Press.
James, William. [1911] 1979. *Some Problems of Philosophy: A beginning of an introduction to philosophy*. The Works of William James. Cambridge, MA: Harvard University Press.
James, William. [1912] 1976. *Essays in Radical Empiricism*. The Works of William James. Cambridge, MA: Harvard University Press.
Jones, Richard H. 2016. *Philosophy of Mysticism: Raids on the ineffable*. Albany, NY: State University of New York Press.
Kant, Immanuel. [1783] 2004^2. *Prolegomena to Any Future Metaphysics*. Cambridge Texts in the History of Philosophy. Cambridge: Cambridge University Press.
Kant, Immanuel. [1786] 2004. *Metaphysical Foundations of Natural Science*. Cambridge Texts in the History of Philosophy. Cambridge: Cambridge University Press.
Kant, Immanuel. [1790, 1793^2] 2000. *Critique of the Power of Judgment*. The Cambridge Edition of the Works of Immanuel Kant. Cambridge: Cambridge University Press.
Kant, Immanuel. [1793] 1996. *Religion within the Boundaries of Mere Reason*. In *Religion and Rational Theology*, 39–215. The Cambridge Edition of the Works of Immanuel Kant. Cambridge: Cambridge University Press.
Kant, Immanuel. [1798] 1996. *The Conflict of the Faculties*. In *Religion and Rational Theology*, 233–327. The Cambridge Edition of the Works of Immanuel Kant. Cambridge: Cambridge University Press.

Kareem, Sarah Tindal. 2014. *Eighteenth-century Fiction and the Reinvention of Wonder*. Oxford: Oxford University Press.

Kouw, Matthijs and Arthur C. Petersen. 2018. 'Diplomacy in action: Latourian politics and the Intergovernmental Panel on Climate Change', *Science & Technology Studies* 31 (1): 52–68.

Krijnen, Christian. 2001. *Nachmetaphysischer Sinn: Eine problemgeschichtliche und systematische Studie zu den Prinzipien der Wertphilosophie Heinrich Rickerts*. [*Post-metaphysical Meaning: A problem-historical and systematic study on the principles of Heinrich Rickert's philosophy of value*.] Würzburg: Königshausen & Neumann.

Krijnen, Christian. 2015. 'Philosophy as philosophy of culture?' In *New Approaches to Neo-Kantianism*, edited by Nicolas de Warren and Andrea Staiti, 111–26. Cambridge: Cambridge University Press.

Lamberth, David C. 1999. *William James and the Metaphysics of Experience*. Cambridge: Cambridge University Press.

Latour, Bruno. 1987. *Science in Action: How to follow scientist and engineers through society*. Cambridge, MA: Harvard University Press.

Latour, Bruno. [1991] 1993. *We Have Never Been Modern*. Cambridge, MA: Harvard University Press.

Latour, Bruno. [2002] 2013a. *Rejoicing: On the torments of religious speech*. Cambridge: Polity Press.

Latour, Bruno. 2004. 'Why has critique run out of steam? From matters of fact to matters of concern', *Critical Inquiry* 30 (Winter): 225–48.

Latour, Bruno. [2012] 2013b. *An Inquiry into Modes of Existence: An anthropology of the Moderns*. Cambridge, MA: Harvard University Press.

Latour, Bruno. [2015] 2017. *Facing Gaia: Eight lectures on the new climatic regime*. Cambridge: Polity Press.

Latour, Bruno. 2016. 'Procedure 3 – Sharing Responsibility: Farewell to the sublime'. In *Reset Modernity!*, edited by Bruno Latour, 167–83. Cambridge, MA: MIT Press.

Laudan, Larry. 1984. *Science and Values: The aims of science and their role in scientific debate*. Berkeley, CA: University of California Press.

Le Poidevin, Robin. 2010. *Agnosticism: A very short introduction*. Oxford: Oxford University Press.

Leidenhag, Mikael. 2018. 'Religious naturalism: The current debate', *Philosophy Compass* 13 (8): 1–11.

Letiche, Hugo, Michael Lissack and Ron Schultz. 2011. *Coherence in the Midst of Complexity: Advances in social complexity theory*. New York: Palgrave Macmillan.

Lovely, Edward W. 2012. *George Santayana's Philosophy of Religion: His Roman Catholic influences and phenomenology*. Lanham, MD: Lexington Books.

Mach, Ernst. [1883, 1933⁹] 1960. *The Science of Mechanics: A critical and historical account of its development*. [Original title: *Die Mechanik in ihrer Entwicklung, historisch-kritisch dargestellt*.] La Salle, IL: Open Court.

Mach, Ernst. [1896] 1910⁴. 'Die ökonomische Natur der physikalischen Forschung'. ['The economic nature of physical research'.] In *Populär-wissenschaftliche Vorlesungen*, 219–44. Leipzig: Barth.

Martin, R. N. D. 1991. *Pierre Duhem: Philosophy and history in the work of a believing physicist*. Chicago, IL: Open Court.

McFague, Sallie. 1982. *Metaphorical Theology: Models of God in religious language*. Philadelphia: Fortress Press.

McGinn, Colin. 1993. *Problems in Philosophy: The limits of inquiry*. Oxford: Blackwell.

McGrath, Alister. 2002. *The Reenchantment of Nature: The denial of religion and the ecological crisis*. New York: Doubleday.

McGrath, Alister E. 2019. *The Territories of Human Reason: Science and theology in an age of multiple rationalities*. Oxford: Oxford University Press.

McMullin, Ernan. 1984. 'A case for scientific realism'. In *Scientific Realism*, edited by Jarrett Leplin, 8–40. Berkeley, CA: University of California Press.

McMullin, Ernan. 1985. 'Realism in theology and in science: A response to Peacocke', *Religion and Intellectual Life* 2 (4): 39–47.

Meyer, Leo A. and Arthur C. Petersen, eds. 2010. *Assessing an IPCC Assessment: An analysis of statements on projected regional impacts in the 2007 Report*. PBL Report 500216002. The

Hague and Bilthoven: PBL Netherlands Environmental Assessment Agency. www.pbl.nl/en/publications/2010/Assessing-an-IPCC-assessment.-An-analysis-of-statements-on-projected-regional-impacts-in-the-2007-report.

Miedema, Siebren. 2002. 'James's metaphysics of experience and religious education'. In *William James & Education*, edited by Jim Garrison, Ronald Podeschi and Eric Bredo, 74–88. New York: Teachers College Press.

Miller, Jerome A. 1992. *In the Throe of Wonder: Intimations of the sacred in a post-modern world*. Albany, NY: State University of New York Press.

Morrison, Margaret. 1999. 'Models as autonomous agents'. In *Models as Mediators: Perspectives on natural and social science*, edited by Mary S. Morgan and Margaret Morrison, 38–65. Cambridge: Cambridge University Press.

Morrison, Margaret and Mary S. Morgan. 1999. 'Models as mediating instruments'. In *Models as Mediators: Perspectives on natural and social science*, edited by Mary S. Morgan and Margaret Morrison, 10–37. Cambridge: Cambridge University Press.

Newton, Isaac. [1713[2]] 1999. *The Principia: Mathematical principles of natural philosophy*. Berkeley, CA: University of California Press.

Northrop, F. S. C. 1962. *Man, Nature and God: A quest for life's meaning*. New York: Simon & Schuster.

Northrop, F. S. C. 1966. 'Commentary on theological resources from the physical sciences', *Zygon: Journal of Religion and Science* 1 (1): 22–6.

Nubiola, Jaime. 2014. 'The reception of William James in continental Europe'. In *William James and the Transatlantic Conversation: Pragmatism, pluralism, and philosophy of religion*, edited by Martin Halliwell and Joel D. S. Rasmussen, 15–29. Oxford: Oxford University Press.

Nuzzo, Angelica. 2014. 'The place of the emotions in Kant's transcendental philosophy'. In *Kant on Emotion and Value*, edited by Alix Cohen, 88–107. Basingstoke, UK: Palgrave Macmillan.

Otto, Rudolf. [1917] 1923. *The Idea of the Holy*. London: Oxford University Press.

Peels, Rik. 2023. *Ignorance: A philosophical study*. New York: Oxford University Press.

Perry, Ralph Barton. 1935. *The Thought and Character of William James, Volume II: Philosophy and psychology*. Boston: Little, Brown and Company.

Peters, Karl E. 2002. *Dancing with the Sacred: Evolution, ecology, and God*. Harrisburg, PA: Trinity Press International.

Petersen, Arthur C. [2006] 2012. *Simulating Nature: A philosophical study of computer-simulation uncertainties in climate science and policy advice*, 2nd edn. Boca Raton: FL: CRC Press.

Petersen, Arthur C. 2012. 'Good prospects: Uncertainty and the responsible governance of Earth as a system', *Sustainability in Debate* 3 (1): 19–34.

Petersen, Arthur C. 2014a. 'Uncertainty and God: A Jamesian pragmatist approach to uncertainty and ignorance in science and religion', *Zygon: Journal of Religion and Science* 49 (4): 808–28.

Petersen, Arthur C. 2014b. 'The ethos of scientific advice: A pragmatist approach to uncertainty and ignorance in science and public policy'. In *Building Bridges: Connecting science, technology and philosophy – Essays presented to Hans Radder*, edited by Henk de Regt and Chunglin Kwa, 53–62. Amsterdam: VU University Press.

Petersen, Arthur C. 2016. 'Procedures to deal with Modernity without irony', *EASST Review* 35 (2): 21–2.

Petersen, Arthur C. 2021. 'Values and accountability in science advice: The case of the IPCC'. In *Science, Values, and Democracy: The 2016 Descartes Lectures by Heather Douglas*, edited by Ted Richards, 97–108. Tempe, AZ: Consortium for Science, Policy & Outcomes, Arizona State University.

Petersen, Arthur C. 2023. 'Disciplines'. In *A Critical Assessment of the Intergovernmental Panel on Climate Change*, edited by Kari De Pryck and Mike Hulme, 107–15. Cambridge: Cambridge University Press.

Petersen, Arthur C., Albert Cath, Maria Hage, Eva Kunseler and Jeroen P. van der Sluijs. 2011. 'Post-normal science in practice at the Netherlands Environmental Assessment Agency', *Science, Technology, and Human Values* 36 (3): 362–88.

Petersen, Arthur C. and Pieter Bloemen. 2015. 'Planned adaptation in design and testing of critical infrastructure: The case of flood safety in The Netherlands'. In *Proceedings of the International Symposium for Next Generation Infrastructure*, 30 September–1 October

2014, 223–7. Schloss Laxenburg, Vienna: International Institute of Applied Systems Analysis (IIASA).

Picht, Georg. 1989. *Der Begriff der Natur und seine Geschichte.* [*The Concept of Nature and Its History.*] Stuttgart: Klett-Cotta.

Pickering, Andrew. 1992. 'From science as knowledge to science as practice'. In *Science as Practice and Culture*, edited by Andrew Pickering, 1–28. Chicago: University of Chicago Press.

Pihlström, Sami. 2003. *Naturalizing the Transcendental: A pragmatic view.* Amherst, NY: Humanity Books.

Plantinga, Alvin. 2011. *Where the Conflict Really Lies: Science, religion, and naturalism.* New York: Oxford University Press.

Polanyi, Michael. [1958] 1998. *Personal Knowledge: Towards a post-critical philosophy.* London: Routledge.

Porte, Joel. 1990. 'Santayana's *Interpretations of Poetry and Religion*: An introduction'. In *Interpretations of Poetry and Religion*, George Santayana, xiii–xxxi. The Works of George Santayana, vol. 3. Cambridge, MA: MIT Press.

Radder, Hans. [1984] 2012. *The Material Realization of Science: From Habermas to experimentation and referential realism.* Dordrecht: Springer.

Rickert, Heinrich. [1892, 1904^{2}] 2018. *Der Gegenstand der Erkenntnis* [*The Object of Knowledge*], 1st–2nd edn. Heinrich Rickert: Sämtliche Werke, vol. 2/1. Berlin: Walter de Gruyter.

Rickert, Heinrich. [1915^{3}, 1921^{4,5}, 1928^{6}] 2018. *Der Gegenstand der Erkenntnis* [*The Object of Knowledge*], 3rd–6th edn. Heinrich Rickert: Sämtliche Werke, vol. 2/2. Berlin: Walter de Gruyter.

Rickert, Heinrich. [1896–1902, 1913^{2}, 1921^{3,4}] 1929^{5}. *Die Grenzen der Naturwissenschaftlichen Begriffsbildung: Eine logische Einleitung in die historischen Wissenschaften.* Tübingen: Mohr Siebeck.

Rickert, Heinrich. [1929] 1986. *The Limits of Concept Formation in Natural Science: A logical introduction to the historical sciences.* [Original title: *Die Grenzen der Naturwissenschaftlichen Begriffsbildung.*] Abridged edition. Edited and translated by Guy Oakes. Cambridge: Cambridge University Press.

Rickert, Heinrich. [1899] 1926^{7}. *Kulturwissenschaft und Naturwissenschaft.* [*Cultural Sciences and Natural Sciences.*] Tübingen: Mohr Siebeck.

Rickert, Heinrich. [1926] 1962. *Science and History: A critique of positivist epistemology.* [Original title: *Kulturwissenschaft und Naturwissenschaft.*] Princeton, NJ: Van Nostrand.

Rickert, Heinrich. 1909. 'Zwei Wege der Erkenntnistheorie: Transscendentalpsychologie und Transscendentallogik' ['Two paths of epistemology: Transcendental psychology and transcendental logic'], *Kant-Studien* 14 (1–3): 169–228.

Rickert, Heinrich. 1920. *Die Philosophie des Lebens: Darstellung und Kritik der philosophischen Modeströmungen unserer Zeit.* [*The Philosophy of Life: Presentation and criticism of the philosophical trends of our time.*] Tübingen: Mohr Siebeck.

Rickert, Heinrich. 1921. *Allgemeine Grundlegung der Philosophie* [*System der Philosophie*, vol. 1]. [*General Foundation of Philosophy* [*System of Philosophy*, vol. 1]]. Tübingen: Mohr Siebeck.

Rickert, Heinrich. 1924. *Kant als Philosoph der modernen Kultur: Ein geschichtsphilosophischer Versuch.* [*Kant as a Philosopher of Modern Culture: A historical-philosophical attempt.*] Tübingen: Mohr Siebeck.

Rickert, Heinrich. 1934a. *Grundprobleme der Philosophie: Methodologie, Ontologie, Anthropologie.* [*Fundamental Problems of Philosophy: Methodology, ontology, anthropology.*] Tübingen: Mohr Siebeck.

Rickert, Heinrich. [1934b] 1999. 'Die Heidelberger Tradition and Kants Kritizismus (Systematische Selbstdarstellung)'. ['The Heidelberg tradition and Kant's criticism (Systematic self-presentation)'.] In *Philosophische Aufsätze* [*Philosophical Essays*], edited by Rainer A. Bast, 347–411. Tübingen: Mohr Siebeck.

Rorty, Richard. 1997. 'Religious faith, intellectual responsibility, and romance'. In *The Cambridge Companion to William James*, [*Philosophical Essays*] edited by Ruth Anna Putnam, 84–102. Cambridge: Cambridge University Press.

Rouse, Joseph. 1987. *Knowledge and Power: Toward a political philosophy of science.* Ithaca, NY: Cornell University Press.

Rouse, Joseph. 2015. *Articulating the World: Conceptual understanding and the scientific image*. Chicago: University of Chicago Press.
Ruse, Michael. 2019. *A Meaning to Life*. New York: Oxford University Press.
Santayana, George. [1900] 1990. *Interpretations of Poetry and Religion*. The Works of George Santayana, vol. 3. Cambridge, MA: MIT Press.
Schilbrack, Kevin. 2014. *Philosophy and the Study of Religions: A manifesto*. Chichester, UK: Wiley Blackwell.
Schmidgen, Henning. [2011] 2015. *Bruno Latour in Pieces: An intellectual biography*. New York: Fordham University Press.
Scruton, Roger. 2012. *Our Church: A personal history of the Church of England*. London: Atlantic Books.
Sideris, Lisa H. 2017. *Consecrating Science: Wonder, knowledge, and the natural world*. Oakland, CA: University of California Press.
Skrupskelis, Ignas H. and Elizabeth M. Berkeley, eds. 2004. *The Correspondence of William James, Volume 12: August 1908–August 1910*. Charlottesville, VA: University Press of Virginia.
Smith, Leonard A. and Arthur C. Petersen. 2014. 'Variations on reliability: Connecting climate predictions to climate policy'. In *Error and Uncertainty in Scientific Practice*, edited by Marcel Boumans, Giora Hon and Arthur C. Petersen, 137–56. London: Pickering & Chatto.
Soskice, Janet Martin. 1985. *Metaphor and Religious Language*. Oxford: Clarendon Press.
Staiti, Andrea. [2013] 2018. 'Heinrich Rickert'. In *The Stanford Encyclopedia of Philosophy*, edited by Edward N. Zalta. Stanford, CA: Stanford University. http://plato.stanford.edu/archives/win2018/entries/heinrich-rickert.
Stenmark, Lisa and Whitney Bauman. 2018. 'Foreword'. In *Navigating Post-Truth and Alternative Facts: Religion and science as political theology*, edited by Jennifer Baldwin, vii–ix. Lanham, MD: Lexington Books.
Topham, Jonathan R. 2010. 'Natural theology and the sciences'. In *The Cambridge Companion to Science and Religion*, edited by Peter Harrison, 59–79. Cambridge: Cambridge University Press.
van der Wal, Koo. [2012] 2017. *Die Wirklichkeit aus neuer Sicht: Für eine andere Naturphilosophie*. [*New Perspective on Reality: For another philosophy of nature*.] Wiesbaden: Springer.
van der Zwaan, Bob and Arthur Petersen, eds. 2003. *Sharing the Planet: Population – consumption – species. Science and ethics for a sustainable and equitable world*. Delft: Eburon Academic Publishers.
van Fraassen, Bas C. 1980. *The Scientific Image*. Oxford: Clarendon Press.
van Klinken, Johan and Jan van Hooff. 2003. 'Sharing with other species'. In *Sharing the Planet: Population – consumption – species. Science and ethics for a sustainable and equitable world*, edited by Bob van der Zwaan and Arthur Petersen, 98–116. Delft: Eburon Academic Publishers.
Villavicencio Calzadilla, Paola and Louis J. Kotzé. 2018. 'Living in harmony with nature? A critical appraisal of the rights of Mother Earth in Bolivia', *Transnational Environmental Law* 7 (3): 397–424.
Walls, Jerry L. 2008. 'Introduction'. In *The Oxford Handbook of Eschatology*, edited by Jerry L. Walls, 3–18. New York: Oxford University Press.
Ward, J. Neville. 1967. *The Use of Praying*. London: Epworth Press.
Wartenberg, Thomas E. 1992. 'Reason and the practice of science'. In *The Cambridge Companion to Kant*, edited by Paul Guyer, 228–48. Cambridge: Cambridge University Press.
Weinert, Friedel. 1999. 'Theories, models and constraints', *Studies in History and Philosophy of Science Part A* 30 (2): 303–33.
Weisberg, Michael. 2013. *Simulation and Similarity: Using models to understand the world*. New York: Oxford University Press.
Wettstein, Howard. 2012. *The Significance of Religious Experience*. Oxford: Oxford University Press.
Wieland, Wolfgang. 2001. *Urteil und Gefühl: Kants Theorie der Urteilskraft*. [*Judgement and Feeling: Kant's theory of the power of judgement*.] Göttingen: Vandenhoeck & Ruprecht.
Wieman, Henry Nelson. 1966. 'Commentary on theological resources from the social sciences', *Zygon: Journal of Religion and Science* 1 (1): 81–5.
Zijderveld, Anton C. 2006. *Rickert's Relevance: The ontological nature and epistemological functions of values*. Leiden: Brill.

Index